SSAT 실전 모의고사 완결판
한세희의
SSAT®
PRACTICE TESTS

초판 발행 2024년 4월 5일

지은이 한세희
펴낸이 최영민
펴낸곳 헤르몬하우스
출판등록 제406-2015-31호
주소 경기도 파주시 신촌로 16
전화 031-8071-0088
Fax 031-942-8688
이메일 hermonh@naver.com

ⓒ 한세희, 2024. Printed in Korea.

이 책은 저작권법에 의해 보호를 받는 저작물이므로, 저자와 출판사의 허락없이
내용의 일부를 인용하거나 발췌하는 것을 금합니다.

ISBN 979-11-92520-50-6 (13740)

- 헤르몬하우스는 피앤피북의 임프린트입니다.
- 책값은 뒤표지에 있습니다.
- 잘못된 책은 구입하신 곳에서 교환해드립니다.

SSAT 실전 모의고사 완결판

한세희의
SSAT®
PRACTICE TESTS

한세희 (SSATKorea 대표) 지음

Preface

Brewing espresso introduces us to the delicate layer of cream known as 'crema' in Italian. Similarly, among students, there exists a special group that can be likened to this "crema" – individuals who transcend the conventional definition of academic excellence and personal achievement. They embody qualities that make you marvel, "How do they manage to encompass such a spectrum?"

Firstly, they exhibit an extraordinary level of empathy. Their genuine care for others is not only noticeable but also extends to their ability to navigate social dynamics, knowing when to step forward and when to step back, leaving an indelible mark among friends. Whether it's a blend of high IQ and emotional intelligence or a knack for balancing personal and interpersonal aspects, these students not only excel in their individual pursuits but also understand the intricate tapestry of human relationships. They leverage this skill to craft a positive group atmosphere, portraying true leadership. However, a distinctive trait in these individuals is their exceptional resilience.

Resilience, in their case, is not just about bouncing back from failure but embracing it as a form of practice. Understanding that success is a result of persistent effort, they willingly embrace setbacks as part of the journey. Rather than aiming for perfection through meticulous preparation, they believe in trying, learning from failures, improving, and trying again – a continuous process of self-improvement. Even if the world recognizes their failures, their attitude towards them sets them apart, earning the respect of others.

The American education system, like any other, may not be flawless, but the key lies in the quantity and quality of opportunities it presents. Possessing even a modicum of resilience opens doors to multiple chances in prestigious schools worldwide. However, if one succumbs to the fear of failure and refrains from attempting anything, progress remains stagnant. Schools, regardless of their reputation, welcome those who try, experience setbacks, and embark on a journey of self-discovery.

PREFACE

    This philosophy extends to examinations like the SSAT. It may not always be a smooth journey, and success might seem elusive at times, but it has a way of surprising us. Seniors who have navigated this path always emphasize the importance of endurance. If you persist, success becomes inevitable. It might sound like a well-worn cliché, but the essence lies in nurturing and encouraging oneself, bouncing back from setbacks, and persevering until the end. Every year, we witness individuals who embody these qualities, turning dreams into reality. Now, it's your turn to embrace this journey.

    Wishing you the best.

Sehee Han

Boarding School Insights
Testimonials

Deerfield Academy

My journey into boarding school began by chance. Having attended small international schools in Seoul during my elementary and middle school years, I had no knowledge of the "boarding school world" and had no friends or family who had attended such institutions. While planning for my seventh-grade summer, my family and I learned about a junior boarding summer program through an acquaintance. Seeing it as a beneficial and enjoyable experience, I decided to participate in the Eaglebrook summer program. Looking back, the application process for this program served as my introduction and a suitable trial run for the extensive journey that lay ahead.

Following my brief but enjoyable time at Eaglebrook, I decided that I wanted to attend a boarding school. Fortunately, my parents supported my decision. However, despite my determination, I honestly lacked the sense of urgency required during the preparation phase. While I knew I wanted to continue the positive experiences I had during the previous summer, my goals were somewhat vague. As I looked at the extensive application process, which included GPA, extracurricular activities, essays, interviews, and the SSAT, I doubted my ability to create a compelling application that would showcase the best version of myself and more. It had been less than three months since I first heard about boarding schools, so I didn't know where to begin. The lack of a clear picture or a well-defined path added to my apprehension. To make matters worse, the SSAT proved to be extremely challenging, as reflected in my first practice exam scores: 50% in Verbal, 60% in Math, and 40% in Reading.

Despite the positive growth, my final practice test score was 93%, just shy of the safety zone for my desired top boarding schools. The time came for my first official test. Although I thought I did well, my scores were 88%, 93%, and 86%. Not bad, but not good enough. The bad news was that due to my schedule, I had to take my second official exam in the middle of my interview tour. However, with the help of Sehee Han, I gradually improved. She held onto my anxious heart, infusing it with confidence, and continuously offered me valuable guidance enriched with in-depth school information. Three weeks later, when I checked my

email, I couldn't believe what I saw. I received a special email from the SSAT administering organization, EMA congratulating me on my perfect score. I got a perfect score of 2400 by answering all the questions on the test correctly.

With my SSAT scores and continuous efforts in other aspects of the application, I was fortunate enough to be accepted to many of the schools I applied to, including Andover, Deerfield, Choate, St. Paul's, Lawrenceville, and Groton. After careful contemplation, research, and participating in re-visit days and Korean alumni receptions, I made up my mind.

Describing my time at Deerfield is considerably difficult, as I had so much growth and diverse experiences in various facets. However, if I had to, I would say "intense." I excavated and carved the identity of the person I currently am. In academics, I laid a strong foundation and discovered my passion for medical technology. In wrestling, I gained a healthy workout habit, the ability to show up and do things when I don't want to, and a solid understanding of my body. In relationships, I have earned more than eight friends who I believe will last forever, as our unchanged level of communication despite the physical distance and a year of time since graduation proves.

Boarding school is a society in itself. We almost autonomously lead every aspect of our lives inside the campus. The experience in this society becomes a trial run as we move on to college and to the "real" outer society. It lays a strong foundation and prepares us to achieve our aspirations.

In a book called "My Life," Deerfield is one of the most important chapters. I hope the prospective students reading this article find the right boarding school and have an enriching time. Wish the best.

by A. Lim

Groton School

I arrived on Groton with both curiosity and skepticism. Surprisingly, after completing the interview, I was determined to attend this school. Despite its small size, the institution displayed profound academic enthusiasm, and each student appeared as a valuable asset to the school community. The campus layout, with all the school buildings centered around the 'Circle,' evoked a strong sense of a close-knit community. Moreover, I was already studying Latin at the time and was passionate about humanities, so the required Latin classes and liberal arts courses appeared as an added advantage to me.

Like this, I diligently prepared for each step of the application while studying for the SSAT with teacher Sehee Han, and consistently improved my test scores. Her passion and dedication constantly instilled confidence in me, and through rich information and flexible coaching, she transformed me. As a result, I was able to receive rewarding acceptance letters from multiple schools including Groton, St.Paul's, Hotchkiss, Lawrenceville, and Taft. I heard the delightful news from Groton prior to the official notification date, presumably thanks to the genuine enthusiasm translated into my essays. Without any hesitation, therefore, I made up my mind to enroll at Groton.

Despite being accepted into my dream school, I had many concerns. Among my peers at Fay, I was the only one from my grade going to Groton, and unlike many friends who repeated a grade, I was planning to advance to 10th grade. It seemed daunting to settle amongst my grade who would have already been acquainted with each other after spending a year together. I also wondered if I could withstand the 'Groton Grind' that entailed immense academic expectations—a well-known reputation of the school.

Although Groton Grind—the insane level jump of the Latin course, our tough chemistry teacher who taught beyond the AP curriculum, the demanding requirements for English essays, and research papers for World/US history that took half a semester to complete—was indeed a reality, overcoming each obstacle that tested my limits helped me cultivate independent study habits and foster personal growth. The valuable insights I gained at

Groton were not limited to this. By taking advantage of the resources of a small but diverse community environment, I had the opportunity to explore various activities and discover my interest beyond the music, sports, and club activities I have been involved with in the past.

Particularly, during my junior year, I got an offer to join the women's crew team as a coxswain, which I quickly found incredibly enjoyable and soon realized was the right fit for me. Being part of the varsity team allowed me to participate in interscholastic and regional competitions and provided me with rewarding experiences I never could have imagined. Furthermore, through taking electives such as AMT (Advanced Math Topics) and Religion and the Public Sphere which are college-level courses that one can take after completing the course requirement, I could gain a clear idea of the subjects I wish to major in the future. Among the various electives I took, two of them left a lasting impression on me.

One was an English elective called 'Waste Land,' where we read T.S. Eliot's masterpiece, "The Waste Land," and wrote our versions of the poem as a final project. It was the most challenging yet fascinating English class I have ever taken. The second class was a two-semester-long international relations course titled 'America in Vietnam/Iraq," in which two Vietnam War veterans joined us through Zoom for every class, sharing vivid stories of their time in the war. This course was particularly meaningful to me because it sparked my interest in regional studies and allowed me to form a mentorship relationship with my teacher, with whom I have maintained contact to this day.

Looking back on my three years at this school, there were indeed moments when I wanted to give up. However, there were also moments that made me forget about those challenges. Even now, when I talk with my fellow graduates, we would often reminisce about both of the moments. I still recall crying in my empty room after prize day, realizing that I might never see these friends and teachers again. However, I am incredibly grateful to have formed enduring connections with friends and teachers who I still reach out to even after graduation. I hope this can provide some insight to readers who are considering boarding school or studying abroad.

by Y.Lim

Phillips Academy Andover

I was hungry on the morning I walked into Phillips Academy Andover's Admissions Office. Not just hungry— I was at a level of hunger in which you have to wonder if the person next to you could hear your stomach grumbling. That was simply not acceptable, as I was there for an interview. Andover's Admissions Office was quite beautiful, but the most beautiful thing I could see was a tray full of what seemed to me more precious than gold. Slices piled upon slices on lemon pound cake. Even better? A hot chocolate station was right next to the tray.

Taking my cold fingers out of my coat pockets, I hurried through the process of telling the nice admissions officer my name and the grade I was applying to— 9th, as a repeat. I was told to wait for a few minutes before the interviewer came down to greet me and my mom. They did not need to tell me twice. With as much dignity as I could muster, I speed-walked to the snacks station and helped myself to an exquisite-looking slice of lemon pound cake. It tasted better than it looked— and I would have thought it impossible to be so. I was savoring the warm cup of hot chocolate along with my last bite of the cake when a man walked up to me. I swallowed with great effort and followed him up to his office, my stomach finally satiated with the deliciousness of my quick breakfast.

The interview started off pleasant. The interviewer asked me about my time at Fay, the school I was attending at the time. I replied exactly as I did for the nine other schools I had applied to. The standard, people-pleasing answer. He went down the standard line of questioning— favorite projects, subjects I don't like, one time I asked for help, etc. Then, after flipping through my file, he asked in a casual tone: "Why would you repeat ninth grade?"

I had not been prepared for this question at all. What did he mean? Obviously, I wanted to have the full Andover experience! I wanted to build up a nice narrative for college! What was I supposed to say? "I," I started. I cleared my throat. "I wanted to have a full Andover experience." I winced at how unsure I sounded. His reply was terse: "Are you implying that students who enter into 10th grade do not have a full Andover experience?" I hesitated to answer, dropping a few filler words to buy myself some time to prepare an answer for such a sharp question.

My interviewer, apparently, was not a particularly patient person. He leaned forward and dropped the last bomb:

"And moreover, if so, could you say that to their faces?"

My brain, previously roaring with potential replies, froze. Refused to think. I knew precious seconds were passing by, but no amount of impromptu debate exercises or theater improv activities could have prepared me for such bluntness. I said the first thing that came to my mind.

"That's not what I meant," I blurted out. The interviewer leaned back into his chair, a small frown on his face. "I have been a transfer student my whole life. A year here, a year there— even Fay, I entered into 8th grade, not 7th. I just want to enter with my friends at the same time for once, for a change." I knew the excuse wasn't solid. It could easily be broken down with a prod or two.

The interviewer, however, softened his expression. He started gently explaining the benefits of entering into tenth grade instead of repeating ninth. I was of age. I had good grades. I went to Fay, a junior boarding school, so I was extra prepared. I could take a gap year later. I didn't play any varsity sports, so sports wouldn't be an issue for me. He made good points.

I came out of the interview on the verge of tears. My hand was trembling so much that my mom had to carry the brochures to the car. I would not have been able to carry a single feather without dropping it on our way to the parking lot. I bit my lips to stop myself from crying on our way to the next school. I barely remember the rest of that day. I thought I had totally flunked the interview. There was no chance for me to go to Andover. The lemon pound cake must have been a parting present— "It was nice to see you. Hope to never see you again" kind of thing.

Weeks later, I emailed my interviewer, informing him of my decision to change my application from ninth grade to tenth. He said he was glad that I took my time to think over such an important decision.

And even later, my computer screen was full of pixelated confetti, fluttering down to the bottom of the screen. I had been accepted into the tenth-grade class at Andover.

The lemon pound cake turned out to be a hello from Andover, not a farewell.

As I embark on a new journey to be a student at Phillips Academy, I have a few words for the students who dream of attending top boarding schools like Andover. If the story above was not enough to convince you that interviews are not as scary as they seem, please continue reading!

Interviewers are not evil. They do not want to trick you or get you flustered. They want to know that you are an interesting person, so give interesting answers. Be respectful to your interviewers because they have a say in whether or not your name makes it to the final list. At Phillips Exeter Academy, I accidentally "nerded out" about the political response of Ronald Reagan to South Africa's Apartheid policies. It was a response to a question asking me about my favorite project that I did recently. I most likely spent much more than five minutes gushing about how the United States did not have a proper stance on Apartheid because of its economic ties to South Africa. When I was done, I was so embarrassed. I apologized to the interviewer for "nerding out." He laughed and told me that "nerdy was cool at Exeter." After I was accepted into Exeter, I received a card from the interviewer. He described the interview as "fun" and "interesting." I thought I had messed the interview up, and expected a hostile response from the interviewer— but instead got what I wanted. The interviewer enjoyed the interview because I was passionate. I knew what I liked and I could explain it to someone else. Show that you are human! It's alright!

Good luck!

by KOO

Culver Military Academy

The idea of attending a boarding school or even the existence of boarding schools was not in our family's consideration until the summer before my 8th-grade school year. Seeing that it was my chance to go to the States and also dive into the wider world, I almost immediately committed to the goal of attending a boarding school.

Our family started researching the processes of applying to boarding schools. Learning that the SSAT was a crucial requirement and aspect of the application, I immediately got scared. Knowing that I was not a great test-taker, the idea of taking a major nationwide exam at just the age of 13 was daunting. Wanting to fight through the fear and excel at the test, I started to study for the SSAT. Preparing for the SSAT with Teacher Han Se-hee was a prominent experience for me. Thanks to her enthusiasm and positivity, I was able to develop a sense of confidence and also increase my SSAT scores significantly. Not only did she help with the SSAT, but her vast information about boarding schools and advice she often gives on choosing which boarding schools to attend were extremely helpful.

With the advice Teacher Han Se-hee provided and the research my family and I did, I started narrowing down the schools I wanted to apply to. Coming from a family where leadership was a quality that was highly valued, Culver Academies became my dream school.

During my interviews with different schools, I always researched each school before I interviewed with each respective school. Every school I interviewed always started with the question of 'why our school?' This question was no surprise to me because Teacher Han Se-hee would often mention that schools want to see how well students know about their school and want to see how much the students want to become a part of their community.

My first year at Culver was extremely tough. As a new cadet and a new student, balancing academics, military, and athletics was extremely difficult. Every day was terrifying as old men would scream at your face during daily inspections. I was never given any free time due to the nature of the military leadership program. Though it felt like an eternity the stressful military program was also what brought me and my friends together and was also what made time fly by. Having to work together with my peers to get through the tough new cadet year made me and my peers become more like a family.

After passing the new cadet phase and becoming an old man myself, Culver was amazing. Furthermore, it is impossible to experience everything that Culver has to give. Culver has so many programs such as horsemanship, sports, etc. I was able to participate in the horsemanship program at Culver. We would ride horses almost every day and participate in various events. One particularly significant event I participated in was the presidential inauguration. Having a tradition of over 100 years, Culver has ridden in the presidential inauguration. For President Biden's inauguration, I was able to ride in the parade and become part of an important tradition and program.

Culver Academies was more than just a school. It was a place where I could call home. It was a place where I was able to meet lifelong friends. It was a place where I learned to be a student, an athlete, and a leader. While many people will have the thought of transferring schools during their time at Culver due to the difficulty and workload, everyone who graduates from Culver and passes through the Iron Gate will always be thankful for attending and graduating from Culver. They will always remember the Culver song and the ones that made Culver a home.

by J. Lee

Loomis Chaffee

The idea of sending off a fourth-grade boy to Deerfield, Massachusetts, by himself made my parents slightly reluctant about the decision they were about to make, but I was just excited for a new summer, finally away from the same house, the same park, the mundane days that I got accustomed to in Seattle. Despite leaving home with the sole goal of having a more entertaining summer, my love for Eaglebrook quickly outweighed the simple and superficial joy I thought I would have. It was not long until I signed up for the second summer camp the following year, where I decided I had to attend Eaglebrook.

After three years on the hill, it was time for me to apply to secondary school, and I believe how I differed from the other hundreds of Asian male students in a junior boarding school was the attitude I had towards my school. None of my work, none of my extracurriculars, none of my sports were pressured by anyone. I did not strategize anything. I loved singing and performing, so I participated in the theater, musical, and adlibs. My love for wrestling and crew led me into taking part in those teams. However, when I put my heart into those activities, opportunities opened up. I was able to sing the national anthem at America's most beloved ballpark - Fenway. I was able to participate at New Englands and multiple regattas for crew and wrestling. It is a lie to say that I loved every single moment of those competitions and performances, but they were all something I was passionate about, and something that I will never regret doing.

When I got to interviewing schools, I went on for hours. Not being arrogant and listing all my awards and accomplishments, but I just genuinely found enjoyment talking about subjects I loved and how the programs work around in different schools. Blessed with the opportunity to choose between many competitive schools, I was given the chance to tour around an array of schools and campuses that each had their own beauty and charm. Loomis was where I had the gut feeling of "belonging."

My gut feelings turned into a definitive "yes" as the school started to introduce us new students to their programs. The famous writing workshop of Loomis provides a step-by-step guide throughout every student's sophomore year on how to write one of the most high, sophisticated writings a high school student can produce. Loomis's resource does not end here. For students who feel pressure to ask their teacher for feedback, there is a student writing resource center where peer students who are in high English level courses edit and comment on your essay. This process provides students an opportunity to learn comfortably and get a fresh perspective on their essay. Any alumni from Loomis will be able to say that even in college their writing skills are top of their class, through the rock-solid foundation that Loomis provided. My writing was also not top-notch; it was flimsy and couldn't escape the "amateur" level. However, by the end of my senior year, I was awarded with a handful of writing awards from NYT, the local newspaper, and more.

Loomis was more than a school where I learned academic material. It was where I could confidently call home, a place where all my friends stayed, a place where I experienced great success and failure. Loomis was not all about getting the highest grade, or a warm-up stop for college. It was four years of growth, and perhaps in one of my most important years. It was a place where I can still make mistakes and Loomis would always be there to hold me up but also prepare me so that I am aware that this is the last place where second chances could be an option.

Every school out there has their own message, own story, and own value that they give to their alumni and students. Loomis Chaffee will always have the alumni that have one of the most outstanding, analytical writers, the strongest, resilient athletes any college or company will find. They will always have one Latin phrase engraved somewhere inside them. "Ne Cedes Malis". Do not yield to adversities. Godspeed to all reading this.

by A.Choi

St. Mark's School

Hello! I am a student from St. Mark's School, and I am eager to express my gratitude to Teacher Sehee Han. It seems like just yesterday when I was engrossed in reading Teacher Sehee's book, inspired by the acceptance reviews from seniors. Now, I am honored to share my own experiences.

In the beginning, I found myself lacking motivation in the SSAT class, driven only by a curiosity to enhance my English and vocabulary skills. Despite a slow start, the enthusiasm of my classmates, coupled with Teacher Sehee's unwavering dedication, and my improving scores became powerful motivators. A month of intense study played a significant role in boosting my final SSAT score.

Making personal visits to schools is vital for a comprehensive understanding of the institutions you're considering. Adequate preparation is crucial for interviews; instead of relying on memorized responses, categorize your answers based on your personality, interests, and background stories. This approach enhances your ability to improvise during interviews, fostering more genuine and engaging conversations.

When it comes to extracurricular activities, meticulous documentation of your achievements is essential. Keep your teachers informed of your progress by regularly updating them on new accomplishments between January and March, showcasing your ongoing commitment and growth.

Upon receiving an acceptance, focus on refining your skills for discussions and presentations, especially for Harkness Table classes. Additionally, pay attention to building your physical strength, as a well-rounded and resilient approach to your education will contribute to a more enriching and successful high school experience.

Studying for the SSAT is just the beginning of your new chapter. Work hard, and may your efforts lead to countless shining experiences in the future. I'm cheering for you wholeheartedly!

by C.Kim

차례

PREFACE • 4
Boarding School Insights • 6

Practice Test 1

ANSWER SHEET 1	23
Writing Sample	25
SECTION 1	27
SECTION 2	37
SECTION 3	52
SECTION 4	60

Practice Test 2

ANSWER SHEET 2	75
Writing Sample	77
SECTION 1	79
SECTION 2	89
SECTION 3	104
SECTION 4	112

Practice Test 3

ANSWER SHEET 3	127
Writing Sample	129
SECTION 1	131
SECTION 2	141
SECTION 3	158
SECTION 4	166

Practice Test 4

ANSWER SHEET 4	179
Writing Sample	181
SECTION 1	183
SECTION 2	193
SECTION 3	207
SECTION 4	215

Answers & Explanations

Practice Test 1	229
Practice Test 2	254
Practice Test 3	277
Practice Test 4	299

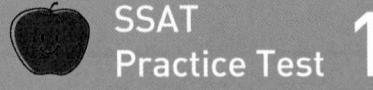

SSAT Practice Test 1

SSAT
Practice Test 1

UPPER LEVEL (Grade 8–11)

Section	Time Allotted (Number of Questions)
Writing Sample	25 minutes (1Q)
Break	10 minutes
Quantitative (Section 1)	30 minutes (25Q)
Reading (Section 2)	40 minutes (40Q)
Break	10 minutes
Verbal (Section 3)	30 minutes (60Q)
Quantitative (Section 4)	30 minutes (25Q)
Experimental (Section 5)	15 minutes (16Q)
Totals	3 hours, 10 minutes

* Of the 167 items including the writing sample, only 150 questions are scored.

ANSWER SHEET 1

Be sure each mark completely fills the answer space.

Start with number 1 for each new section of the test. You may find more answer spaces than you need. If so, please leave them blank.

Section 1

1 Ⓐ Ⓑ Ⓒ Ⓓ Ⓔ	6 Ⓐ Ⓑ Ⓒ Ⓓ Ⓔ	11 Ⓐ Ⓑ Ⓒ Ⓓ Ⓔ	16 Ⓐ Ⓑ Ⓒ Ⓓ Ⓔ	21 Ⓐ Ⓑ Ⓒ Ⓓ Ⓔ
2 Ⓐ Ⓑ Ⓒ Ⓓ Ⓔ	7 Ⓐ Ⓑ Ⓒ Ⓓ Ⓔ	12 Ⓐ Ⓑ Ⓒ Ⓓ Ⓔ	17 Ⓐ Ⓑ Ⓒ Ⓓ Ⓔ	22 Ⓐ Ⓑ Ⓒ Ⓓ Ⓔ
3 Ⓐ Ⓑ Ⓒ Ⓓ Ⓔ	8 Ⓐ Ⓑ Ⓒ Ⓓ Ⓔ	13 Ⓐ Ⓑ Ⓒ Ⓓ Ⓔ	18 Ⓐ Ⓑ Ⓒ Ⓓ Ⓔ	23 Ⓐ Ⓑ Ⓒ Ⓓ Ⓔ
4 Ⓐ Ⓑ Ⓒ Ⓓ Ⓔ	9 Ⓐ Ⓑ Ⓒ Ⓓ Ⓔ	14 Ⓐ Ⓑ Ⓒ Ⓓ Ⓔ	19 Ⓐ Ⓑ Ⓒ Ⓓ Ⓔ	24 Ⓐ Ⓑ Ⓒ Ⓓ Ⓔ
5 Ⓐ Ⓑ Ⓒ Ⓓ Ⓔ	10 Ⓐ Ⓑ Ⓒ Ⓓ Ⓔ	15 Ⓐ Ⓑ Ⓒ Ⓓ Ⓔ	20 Ⓐ Ⓑ Ⓒ Ⓓ Ⓔ	25 Ⓐ Ⓑ Ⓒ Ⓓ Ⓔ

Section 2

1 Ⓐ Ⓑ Ⓒ Ⓓ Ⓔ	9 Ⓐ Ⓑ Ⓒ Ⓓ Ⓔ	17 Ⓐ Ⓑ Ⓒ Ⓓ Ⓔ	25 Ⓐ Ⓑ Ⓒ Ⓓ Ⓔ	33 Ⓐ Ⓑ Ⓒ Ⓓ Ⓔ
2 Ⓐ Ⓑ Ⓒ Ⓓ Ⓔ	10 Ⓐ Ⓑ Ⓒ Ⓓ Ⓔ	18 Ⓐ Ⓑ Ⓒ Ⓓ Ⓔ	26 Ⓐ Ⓑ Ⓒ Ⓓ Ⓔ	34 Ⓐ Ⓑ Ⓒ Ⓓ Ⓔ
3 Ⓐ Ⓑ Ⓒ Ⓓ Ⓔ	11 Ⓐ Ⓑ Ⓒ Ⓓ Ⓔ	19 Ⓐ Ⓑ Ⓒ Ⓓ Ⓔ	27 Ⓐ Ⓑ Ⓒ Ⓓ Ⓔ	35 Ⓐ Ⓑ Ⓒ Ⓓ Ⓔ
4 Ⓐ Ⓑ Ⓒ Ⓓ Ⓔ	12 Ⓐ Ⓑ Ⓒ Ⓓ Ⓔ	20 Ⓐ Ⓑ Ⓒ Ⓓ Ⓔ	28 Ⓐ Ⓑ Ⓒ Ⓓ Ⓔ	36 Ⓐ Ⓑ Ⓒ Ⓓ Ⓔ
5 Ⓐ Ⓑ Ⓒ Ⓓ Ⓔ	13 Ⓐ Ⓑ Ⓒ Ⓓ Ⓔ	21 Ⓐ Ⓑ Ⓒ Ⓓ Ⓔ	29 Ⓐ Ⓑ Ⓒ Ⓓ Ⓔ	37 Ⓐ Ⓑ Ⓒ Ⓓ Ⓔ
6 Ⓐ Ⓑ Ⓒ Ⓓ Ⓔ	14 Ⓐ Ⓑ Ⓒ Ⓓ Ⓔ	22 Ⓐ Ⓑ Ⓒ Ⓓ Ⓔ	30 Ⓐ Ⓑ Ⓒ Ⓓ Ⓔ	38 Ⓐ Ⓑ Ⓒ Ⓓ Ⓔ
7 Ⓐ Ⓑ Ⓒ Ⓓ Ⓔ	15 Ⓐ Ⓑ Ⓒ Ⓓ Ⓔ	23 Ⓐ Ⓑ Ⓒ Ⓓ Ⓔ	31 Ⓐ Ⓑ Ⓒ Ⓓ Ⓔ	39 Ⓐ Ⓑ Ⓒ Ⓓ Ⓔ
8 Ⓐ Ⓑ Ⓒ Ⓓ Ⓔ	16 Ⓐ Ⓑ Ⓒ Ⓓ Ⓔ	24 Ⓐ Ⓑ Ⓒ Ⓓ Ⓔ	32 Ⓐ Ⓑ Ⓒ Ⓓ Ⓔ	40 Ⓐ Ⓑ Ⓒ Ⓓ Ⓔ

Section 3

1 Ⓐ Ⓑ Ⓒ Ⓓ Ⓔ	13 Ⓐ Ⓑ Ⓒ Ⓓ Ⓔ	25 Ⓐ Ⓑ Ⓒ Ⓓ Ⓔ	37 Ⓐ Ⓑ Ⓒ Ⓓ Ⓔ	49 Ⓐ Ⓑ Ⓒ Ⓓ Ⓔ
2 Ⓐ Ⓑ Ⓒ Ⓓ Ⓔ	14 Ⓐ Ⓑ Ⓒ Ⓓ Ⓔ	26 Ⓐ Ⓑ Ⓒ Ⓓ Ⓔ	38 Ⓐ Ⓑ Ⓒ Ⓓ Ⓔ	50 Ⓐ Ⓑ Ⓒ Ⓓ Ⓔ
3 Ⓐ Ⓑ Ⓒ Ⓓ Ⓔ	15 Ⓐ Ⓑ Ⓒ Ⓓ Ⓔ	27 Ⓐ Ⓑ Ⓒ Ⓓ Ⓔ	39 Ⓐ Ⓑ Ⓒ Ⓓ Ⓔ	51 Ⓐ Ⓑ Ⓒ Ⓓ Ⓔ
4 Ⓐ Ⓑ Ⓒ Ⓓ Ⓔ	16 Ⓐ Ⓑ Ⓒ Ⓓ Ⓔ	28 Ⓐ Ⓑ Ⓒ Ⓓ Ⓔ	40 Ⓐ Ⓑ Ⓒ Ⓓ Ⓔ	52 Ⓐ Ⓑ Ⓒ Ⓓ Ⓔ
5 Ⓐ Ⓑ Ⓒ Ⓓ Ⓔ	17 Ⓐ Ⓑ Ⓒ Ⓓ Ⓔ	29 Ⓐ Ⓑ Ⓒ Ⓓ Ⓔ	41 Ⓐ Ⓑ Ⓒ Ⓓ Ⓔ	53 Ⓐ Ⓑ Ⓒ Ⓓ Ⓔ
6 Ⓐ Ⓑ Ⓒ Ⓓ Ⓔ	18 Ⓐ Ⓑ Ⓒ Ⓓ Ⓔ	30 Ⓐ Ⓑ Ⓒ Ⓓ Ⓔ	42 Ⓐ Ⓑ Ⓒ Ⓓ Ⓔ	54 Ⓐ Ⓑ Ⓒ Ⓓ Ⓔ
7 Ⓐ Ⓑ Ⓒ Ⓓ Ⓔ	19 Ⓐ Ⓑ Ⓒ Ⓓ Ⓔ	31 Ⓐ Ⓑ Ⓒ Ⓓ Ⓔ	43 Ⓐ Ⓑ Ⓒ Ⓓ Ⓔ	55 Ⓐ Ⓑ Ⓒ Ⓓ Ⓔ
8 Ⓐ Ⓑ Ⓒ Ⓓ Ⓔ	20 Ⓐ Ⓑ Ⓒ Ⓓ Ⓔ	32 Ⓐ Ⓑ Ⓒ Ⓓ Ⓔ	44 Ⓐ Ⓑ Ⓒ Ⓓ Ⓔ	56 Ⓐ Ⓑ Ⓒ Ⓓ Ⓔ
9 Ⓐ Ⓑ Ⓒ Ⓓ Ⓔ	21 Ⓐ Ⓑ Ⓒ Ⓓ Ⓔ	33 Ⓐ Ⓑ Ⓒ Ⓓ Ⓔ	45 Ⓐ Ⓑ Ⓒ Ⓓ Ⓔ	57 Ⓐ Ⓑ Ⓒ Ⓓ Ⓔ
10 Ⓐ Ⓑ Ⓒ Ⓓ Ⓔ	22 Ⓐ Ⓑ Ⓒ Ⓓ Ⓔ	34 Ⓐ Ⓑ Ⓒ Ⓓ Ⓔ	46 Ⓐ Ⓑ Ⓒ Ⓓ Ⓔ	58 Ⓐ Ⓑ Ⓒ Ⓓ Ⓔ
11 Ⓐ Ⓑ Ⓒ Ⓓ Ⓔ	23 Ⓐ Ⓑ Ⓒ Ⓓ Ⓔ	35 Ⓐ Ⓑ Ⓒ Ⓓ Ⓔ	47 Ⓐ Ⓑ Ⓒ Ⓓ Ⓔ	59 Ⓐ Ⓑ Ⓒ Ⓓ Ⓔ
12 Ⓐ Ⓑ Ⓒ Ⓓ Ⓔ	24 Ⓐ Ⓑ Ⓒ Ⓓ Ⓔ	36 Ⓐ Ⓑ Ⓒ Ⓓ Ⓔ	48 Ⓐ Ⓑ Ⓒ Ⓓ Ⓔ	60 Ⓐ Ⓑ Ⓒ Ⓓ Ⓔ

Section 4

1 Ⓐ Ⓑ Ⓒ Ⓓ Ⓔ	6 Ⓐ Ⓑ Ⓒ Ⓓ Ⓔ	11 Ⓐ Ⓑ Ⓒ Ⓓ Ⓔ	16 Ⓐ Ⓑ Ⓒ Ⓓ Ⓔ	21 Ⓐ Ⓑ Ⓒ Ⓓ Ⓔ
2 Ⓐ Ⓑ Ⓒ Ⓓ Ⓔ	7 Ⓐ Ⓑ Ⓒ Ⓓ Ⓔ	12 Ⓐ Ⓑ Ⓒ Ⓓ Ⓔ	17 Ⓐ Ⓑ Ⓒ Ⓓ Ⓔ	22 Ⓐ Ⓑ Ⓒ Ⓓ Ⓔ
3 Ⓐ Ⓑ Ⓒ Ⓓ Ⓔ	8 Ⓐ Ⓑ Ⓒ Ⓓ Ⓔ	13 Ⓐ Ⓑ Ⓒ Ⓓ Ⓔ	18 Ⓐ Ⓑ Ⓒ Ⓓ Ⓔ	23 Ⓐ Ⓑ Ⓒ Ⓓ Ⓔ
4 Ⓐ Ⓑ Ⓒ Ⓓ Ⓔ	9 Ⓐ Ⓑ Ⓒ Ⓓ Ⓔ	14 Ⓐ Ⓑ Ⓒ Ⓓ Ⓔ	19 Ⓐ Ⓑ Ⓒ Ⓓ Ⓔ	24 Ⓐ Ⓑ Ⓒ Ⓓ Ⓔ
5 Ⓐ Ⓑ Ⓒ Ⓓ Ⓔ	10 Ⓐ Ⓑ Ⓒ Ⓓ Ⓔ	15 Ⓐ Ⓑ Ⓒ Ⓓ Ⓔ	20 Ⓐ Ⓑ Ⓒ Ⓓ Ⓔ	25 Ⓐ Ⓑ Ⓒ Ⓓ Ⓔ

점선을 따라 오려서 사용하세요

Writing Sample

Schools would like to get to know you better through an essay you write. If you choose to write a personal essay, base your essay on the topic presented in A. If you choose to write a general essay, base your essay on the topic presented in B.

> A. Tell me about a moment when you went against the grain and made a choice you typically wouldn't. What led you to take a different path, and what was the outcome?

> B. What can students learn from participating in group projects? What are the pros and cons of group work?

Use this page and the next page to complete your writing sample.

Continue on the next page

SECTION 1

+ Quantitative (Math) (25 Questions / 30 Minutes) +

Following each problem in this section, there are five suggested answers. Work each problem in your head or in the blank space provided at the right of the page. Then look at the five suggested answers and decide which one is best.

Note: Figures that accompany problems in this section are drawn as accurately as possible EXCEPT when it is stated in a specific problem that its figure is not drawn to scale.

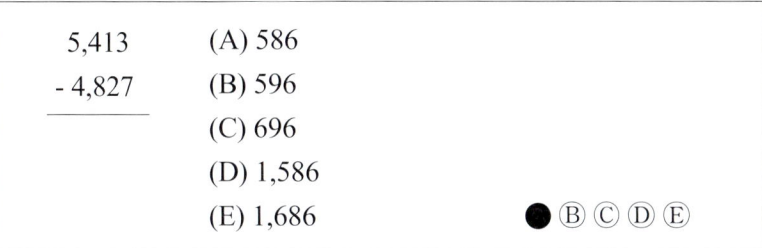

Sample Problem:

USE THIS SPACE FOR FIGURING

1. If $(0.0003)x = 0.0003$, then $x =$
   (A) 1
   (B) 0.1
   (C) 0.01
   (D) 0.001
   (E) 0.0001

2. If n is a positive integer divisible by 3, and if $n < 60$, what is the greatest possible value of n?
   (A) 53
   (B) 54
   (C) 55
   (D) 56
   (E) 57

→ GO ON TO THE NEXT PAGE

Practice Test 1

3. A store has 330 books in stock. If 30 percent of these books are on sale, how many books are not on sale?
   (A) 99
   (B) 230
   (C) 231
   (D) 300
   (E) 320

4. At his last job, Alex was paid $9 an hour for the first 10 hours he worked. For the time he worked beyond 10 hours, he was paid $12 an hour. If he worked 16 hours on this job, how much was Alex paid?
   (A) $144
   (B) $162
   (C) $192
   (D) $210
   (E) $336

5. If $x^2 = n$, where x and n are integers, the following could be the value of n ?
   (A) 2
   (B) 3
   (C) 6
   (D) 9
   (E) 12

USE THIS SPACE FOR FIGURING

6. If 40 percent of *n* is 60, what is 30 percent of *n*?

   (A) 15
   (B) 25
   (C) 35
   (D) 45
   (E) 55

7. If six beds out of ten in the furniture store are bunk beds, what is the probability that a bed selected randomly from the store will be a bunk bed?

   (A) $\dfrac{2}{3}$
   (B) $\dfrac{3}{5}$
   (C) $\dfrac{2}{3}$
   (D) $\dfrac{1}{2}$
   (E) $\dfrac{1}{6}$

8. When a number *x* is subtracted from 24, and the difference is divided by x, the result is 2. What is the value of *x*?

   (A) 4
   (B) 8
   (C) 12
   (D) 18
   (E) 24

➜ GO ON TO THE NEXT PAGE

9. On a piano keyboard, the pitch difference between two consecutive white keys is a whole step, and the pitch difference between a white key and its adjacent black key is a half step.
Let's say a musician plays an A note and wants to move up by three whole steps and one half step. What note will they end up playing?

   (A) A
   (B) B#
   (C) C
   (D) D
   (E) D#

10. If n is any negative number, which of the following must be positive?

    (A) $\dfrac{n}{3}$
    (B) $3n$
    (C) $n+3$
    (D) $n-3$
    (E) $3-n$

11. Ted used four pieces of masking tape, each 6 inches long, to put up each of his posters. Ted had a 200-foot roll of masking tape when he started. If no tape was wasted, which represents the number of feet of masking tape left on the roll after he put up *n* posters?

    (A) $200-6n$
    (B) $200-4n$
    (C) $200-2n$
    (D) $200-\dfrac{1}{2n}$
    (E) $200-\dfrac{1}{4n}$

12. Together, Megan and Josephine bought 173 pieces of chocolate. Megan bought 39 more pieces of chocolate than Josephine did. Of the following, which could be the number of chocolates that Megan bought?

    (A) 39
    (B) 64
    (C) 82
    (D) 106
    (E) 134

13. There are 17 boys and 16 girls in Matthew's class. The names of each of Matthew's classmates are written on individual slips of paper and placed in a box. Leonardo is to select a project partner by drawing the name of one classmate from the box. What are the chances that he will draw a boy's name?

    (A) 1 in 1
    (B) 1 in 16
    (C) 17 in 32
    (D) 16 in 17
    (E) 1 in 2

14. Monica reads 4 pages in 10 minutes. At this rate, how much time will she need to read a 128-page book?

    (A) 1 hour 10 minutes
    (B) 1 hour 36 minutes
    (C) 2 hours 40 minutes
    (D) 4 hours 10 minutes
    (E) 5 hours 20 minutes

15. Figure 1 consists of two circles with the same center. If the shaded area is 32π sq.in. and the smaller circle has a radius of 2 in., what is the radius, in inches, of the larger circle?

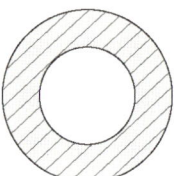

Figure 1

(A) 2
(B) 3
(C) 6
(D) 12
(E) 18

16. The ratio of 1.5 to 1 is equal to which of following ratios?
(A) 1 to 2
(B) 12 to 1
(C) 5 to 6
(D) 3 to 2
(E) 15 to 1

→ GO ON TO THE NEXT PAGE

17. Josh's lock combination consists of 3 two digit numbers. The combination satisfies the three conditions below.

    • One number is even.
    • One number is a multiple of 5.
    • One number is the day in the month of Josh's birthday.

    If each number satisfied exactly one of the conditions, which of the following could be the combination to the lock?

    (A) 33-25-48
    (B) 81-35-27
    (C) 13-18-16
    (D) 20-11-15
    (E) 39-20-22

18. In a certain school, there are n classes with k students in each class. If a total of p erasers are distributed equally among these students, how many erasers are there for each student?

    (A) $\dfrac{p}{kn}$

    (B) $\dfrac{kn}{p}$

    (C) $\dfrac{kn}{n}$

    (D) $\dfrac{np}{k}$

    (E) npk

19. In Figure 2, what is the value of $x + y$?

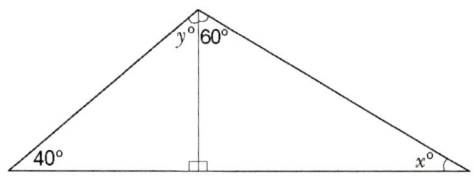

Figure 2

(A) 80
(B) 90
(C) 100
(D) 120
(E) 140

20. By 8:00 P.M., $\frac{1}{4}$ of the class had arrived at the school dance. By 9:00 P.M., 20 more students had arrived, raising attendance to $\frac{1}{2}$ of the class. How many people are in the class?

(A) 30
(B) 80
(C) 120
(D) 180
(E) 240

→ GO ON TO THE NEXT PAGE

21. A circular piece of cardboard is cut in half along a diameter. If the diameter is 6 inches, what is the perimeter, in inches, of one of the semicircular pieces?

    (A) 3π
    (B) $3\pi + 6$
    (C) $6\pi + 6$
    (D) $12\pi + 12$
    (E) 36π

22. If 14 millimeters of a certain liquid has a mass of 16 grams, what is the mass, in grams, of 28 liters of this liquid? (1 liter = 1,000 milliliters)

    (A) 8
    (B) 32
    (C) 3,200
    (D) 8,000
    (E) 32,000

23. While driving on a 300-mile trip, Mr. Emerson averages 60 miles per hour for the first t hours. In terms of t, where $t < 5$, how many miles remain to be traveled?

    (A) $60t - 300$
    (B) $300 - 60t$
    (C) $18,000 - t$
    (D) $300 - \dfrac{60}{t}$
    (E) $\dfrac{300}{60t}$

→ GO ON TO THE NEXT PAGE

24. In a bag of marbles, $\frac{1}{2}$ of the marbles are yellow, $\frac{1}{4}$ of them are green, and $\frac{1}{5}$ of them are blue. If the remaining two marbles are red, what is the number of green marbles in the bag?

(A) 4
(B) 5
(C) 8
(D) 10
(E) 20

25. If the sum of the consecutive integers from -25 to x, inclusive, is 81, what is the value of x?

(A) 23
(B) 24
(C) 28
(D) 50
(E) 75

IF YOU FINISH BEFORE TIME IS CALLED,
YOU MAY CHECK YOUR WORK ON THIS SECTION ONLY.
DO NOT TURN TO ANY OTHER SECTION IN THE TEST.

SECTION 2

+ Reading (40 Questions / 40 Minutes) +

Read each passage carefully and then answer the questions about it. For each question, decide on the basis of the passage which one of the choices best answers the question.

He was a very silent man by custom. All day he hung round the cove or upon the cliffs with a brass telescope; all evening he sat in a corner of the parlor next the fire and drank rum and water very strong. Mostly he would not speak when spoken to, only look up sudden and fierce and blow through his nose like a fog-horn; and we and the people who
5 came about our house soon learned to let him be. Every day when he came back from his stroll he would ask if any seafaring men had gone by along the road. At first we thought it was the want of company of his own kind that made him ask this question, but at last we began to see he was desirous to avoid them. When a seaman did put up at the Admiral Benbow (as now and then some did, making by the coast road for Bristol) he would look
10 in at him through the curtained door before he entered the parlor; and he was always sure to be as silent as a mouse when any such was present. For me, at least, there was no secret about the matter, for I was, in a way, a sharer in his alarms. He had taken me aside one day and promised me a silver fourpenny on the first of every month if I would only keep my "weather-eye open for a seafaring man with one leg" and let him know the
15 moment he appeared. Often enough when the first of the month came round and I applied to him for my wage, he would only blow through his nose at me and stare me down, but before the week was out he was sure to think better of it, bring me my four-penny piece, and repeat his orders to look out for "the seafaring man with one leg."

How that personage haunted my dreams, I need scarcely tell you. I would see him in a
20 thousand forms, and with a thousand diabolical expressions. Now the leg would be cut off at the knee, now at the hip; now he was a monstrous kind of a creature who had never had but the one leg, and that in the middle of his body. To see him leap and run and pursue me over hedge and ditch was the worst of nightmares. And altogether I paid pretty dear for my monthly fourpenny piece, in the shape of these abominable fancies.

1. The man described in the passage asks every day if any seafaring men have passed by because
   (A) he wants to ensure that he can avoid encountering any seafaring men.
   (B) he hopes to make friends who share his seafaring lifestyle.
   (C) he wishes to learn to prevent seasickness before embarking on his significant journey.
   (D) he has a strong desire to pursue a career as a sailor.
   (E) he intends to purchase a new boat.

2. The author's tone in the last paragraph is best described as
   (A) obsessive
   (B) ebullient
   (C) relentless
   (D) sorrowful
   (E) persistence

3. "Fancies" most nearly means
   (A) elegant items
   (B) expensive things
   (C) imaginative thoughts
   (D) evil conundrums
   (E) generous gifts

4. The last sentence infers the watchman paid with
   (A) money
   (B) disquiet
   (C) time
   (D) placidity
   (E) resilience

5. Through the context, "Admiral Benbow" is most likely a
   (A) lodging
   (B) reserve
   (C) acquaintance
   (D) rendezvous
   (E) occasion

→ GO ON TO THE NEXT PAGE

Have you heard the phrase "dreamers often lie"? Sometimes, the meaning of old phrases is **self-evident**, as with "make your hair stand on end." But quite often, we encounter some language that seems to spring **out of the blue** and does not appear to signify anything in particular - *even-steven*, *fit as a fiddle*, or *paint the town red*, for
5   instance. Explanations for the origins of such phrases are frequently suggested but are too often unpersuasive. One popular dictionary, for example, suggests that the word pundit might be connected to a pun, but in fact, they have different origins and meanings. Pun originates from pundigron, which is perhaps a humorous alteration of the Italian *puntiglio*, meaning "equivocation, trivial objection," while the root of *pundit*
10   means "a learned man, scholar," and comes from the Sanskrit *payndita*.

6. Which of the following phrases would the author be most likely to add to the list in line 4?
   (A) take a chance
   (B) jump for joy
   (C) lend an ear
   (D) apple of my eyes
   (E) break the rules

7. The last sentence of the passage primarily serves to
   (A) cite a well-known fact
   (B) invalidate a claim
   (C) make a veiled accusation
   (D) note a puzzling incident
   (E) explain the origins of a phrase

8. The word "self-evident" means
   (A) obvious
   (B) cryptic
   (C) reliable
   (D) confusing
   (E) mysterious

9. Which is the closest meaning of "out of the blue" used in the passage?
   (A) fiercely
   (B) unexpectedly
   (C) positively
   (D) respectively
   (E) recklessly

10. The main idea of this passage relates to
    (A) Phrases have different origins.
    (B) A dawdler in one thing is a dawdler in all.
    (C) Everything will come out in the wash.
    (D) Traditional old sayings and phrases are falling out of use.
    (E) The origins and meanings of some phrases are not self-evident.

→ GO ON TO THE NEXT PAGE

There were long-held beliefs that only humans have evolved nervous systems sophisticated enough to recognize human facial expressions. However, pigeons have called this notion into question. In recent experiments at the University of Iowa, eight trained pigeons were shown photographs of people displaying emotions of happiness, anger, surprise, and disgust. The birds learned to recognize the differences between these expressions. Not only that, but they were able to identify the same expressions in photographs of unfamiliar faces correctly. That means the pigeons understood what human expressions meant.

Some psychologists have theorized that only humans have developed unique nervous systems capable of recognizing subtle facial expressions. The pigeons cast doubt on that idea, however. The ability to recognize facial expressions of emotion is not necessarily inherent even in human babies but may have to be learned in much the same way as pigeons learn. Before these experiments, the research group at the University of Iowa conducted other experiments. They found that pigeons organize images of things into the same logical categories humans do. These findings would not surprise Charles Darwin, who long ago wrote about the continuity of mental development from animals to humans.

11. Which of the following is the best title for the selection?
   (A) Debunking Hidden Talents of Pigeons
   (B) Charles Darwin Vs. Modern Psychologists
   (C) Mental Continuity between Animals and Humans
   (D) How to Develop the Human Nervous System
   (E) Experiments with Birds and Humans

12. Which of the following best describes the author's opinion of the view that humans are superior to animals?
   (A) insightful
   (B) perspicacious
   (C) laudable
   (D) contemptible
   (E) dubious

13. As it is used in this passage, "inherent" most nearly means
    (A) immediate
    (B) instinctive
    (C) believable
    (D) coherent
    (E) enigmatic

14. When the author describes animal experiments, the tone of the passage is
    (A) pessimistic
    (B) suspicious
    (C) pompous
    (D) amusing
    (E) matter-of-fact

15. When the author says, "These findings would not surprise Charles Darwin," he means
    (A) Darwin has always known about pigeons' ability to recognize expressions.
    (B) Psychologists should have believed Darwin a long time ago.
    (C) The experiments with pigeons further confirm Darwin's evolutionary theories.
    (D) Animals can be trained to have the same mental capabilities as humans.
    (E) Many other ecologists found the same results in his experiments with other animals.

➜ GO ON TO THE NEXT PAGE

In the last months of writing a book, as the end comes in sight, she becomes possessed. She doesn't go anywhere, or talk about anything other than the book. She stops only to eat. Her sleep and work hours become erratic; often, she will wake up at three in the morning, write for several hours, and then go back to bed. She becomes more and more anxious; it feels to her like stage fright, unnaturally and intolerably prolonged, as though at last she were spinning all her plates at once, darting about from one to the other and terrified of making a mistake because she knows that if one plate spins off balance, they will all come crashing down.

She doesn't believe in inventing greatness or significance where none exists. This is why she likes historical fiction: she feels she can write about greatness only in historical moments that have already proved ripe for its flourishing. She believes that there are no great characters without a great time; ordinary times breed ordinary people (of the sort—dull, trapped, despairing—who inhabit modern novels).

She wants to sit and think in a sustained way about what it is that she or anyone else is doing when she writes historical fiction. What sort of person writes fiction about the past? It is helpful to be acquainted with violence because the past was violent. It is necessary to understand that the people who live there are not the same as people now. It is necessary to understand that the dead are real and have power over the living. It is helpful to have encountered the dead firsthand in the form of ghosts.

16. The narrator is describing a writer who is
    (A) immersed
    (B) soporific
    (C) possessive
    (D) turbulent
    (E) simple

17. In the second line, "only" most nearly means
    (A) alone
    (B) uniquely
    (C) just
    (D) entirely
    (E) narrowly

18. The last sentence of the first paragraph is an example of which literary device?
    (A) oxymoron
    (B) metaphor
    (C) alliteration
    (D) pun
    (E) simile

19. According to the passage, why does the writer become more and more anxious in the last months of writing?
    (A) Due to a fear of failure and making mistakes
    (B) Because of a dislike for historical moments
    (C) To create a sense of suspense in her writing
    (D) Because of a lack of interest in the book
    (E) To maintain a healthy work-life balance

20. The narrator's primary purpose in the passage is to
    (A) introduce a setting
    (B) clarify the steps involved in the writing
    (C) impart a lesson
    (D) resolve a question
    (E) introduce a character

21. What is the main idea of the passage?
    (A) The writer's daily routine
    (B) The challenges of writing historical fiction
    (C) The influence of the past on present actions
    (D) The writer's belief in greatness
    (E) The impact of stage fright on creativity

➜ GO ON TO THE NEXT PAGE

It seems the true source of creation for nineteenth-century French novelist Honore de Balzac was not sensitivity but imagination. Balzac's fiction originally sprang from an intuition he first discovered as a wretched little school boy locked in a dark closet of his boarding school: life is a prison, and only imagination can open its doors.

5　　Owing to his keen observation of detail and unfiltered representation of society, Balzac is regarded as one of the founders of realism in European literature. He is renowned for his multifaceted characters; even his lesser characters are complex, morally ambiguous, and fully human. Inanimate objects are imbued with character as well; the city of Paris, a backdrop for much of his writing, takes on many human
10　qualities.

That Balzac could be financially wise in his fiction while losing all his money in life was an irony duplicated in other matters. For instance, the very women who were drawn to him by the penetrating intuition of the female heart that he showed in his novels were appalled to discover how insensitive and awkward this man in real life could be.

22. The example in the last paragraph suggests that
    (A) Balzac could not write convincingly about financial matters
    (B) Balzac's work was not especially popular among female readers
    (C) Balzac's insights into character were not evident in his everyday life
    (D) people who knew Balzac personally could not respect him as a writer
    (E) readers found Balzac to have a deep sympathy for humankind

23. The author mentions Balzac's experience as a schoolboy in order to
    (A) point out a possible source of Balzac's powerful imagination
    (B) explain why Balzac was unable to conduct his financial affairs properly
    (C) exonerate the boarding school for Balzac's lackluster performance
    (D) foster the impression that Balzac was an unruly student
    (E) depict the conditions of boarding school life during Balzac's youth

→ GO ON TO THE NEXT PAGE

24. The word "multifaceted" most nearly means
    (A) ignorant
    (B) versatile
    (C) deceptive
    (D) impassioned
    (E) vehement

"The company had come to a halt, more sober men, as you may guess, than when they started. The most of them would by no means advance, but three of them, the boldest, or it may be the most drunken, rode forward down the goyal. Now, it opened into a broad space in which stood two of those great stones, still to be seen there, which were set by certain forgotten peoples in the days of old. The moon was shining bright upon the clearing, and there in the centre lay the unhappy maid where she had fallen, dead of fear and of fatigue. But it was not the sight of her body, nor yet was it that of the body of Hugo Baskerville lying near her, which raised the hair upon the heads of these three dare-devil roysterers, but it was that, standing over Hugo, and plucking at his throat, there stood a foul thing, a great, black beast, shaped like a hound, yet larger than any hound that ever mortal eye has rested upon. And even as they looked the thing tore the throat out of Hugo Baskerville, on which, as it turned its blazing eyes and dripping jaws upon them, the three shrieked with fear and rode for dear life, still screaming, across the moor. One, it is said, died that very night of what he had seen, and the other twain were but broken men for the rest of their days."

"Such is the tale, my sons, of the coming of the hound which is said to have plagued the family so sorely ever since. If I have set it down it is because that which is clearly known hath less terror than that which is but hinted at and guessed. Nor can it be denied that many of the family have been unhappy in their deaths, which have been sudden, bloody, and mysterious. Yet may we shelter ourselves in the infinite goodness of Providence, which would not forever punish the innocent beyond that third or fourth generation which is threatened in Holy Writ. To that Providence, my sons, I hereby commend you, and I counsel you by way of caution to forbear from crossing the moor in those dark hours when the powers of evil are exalted.

"[This from Hugo Baskerville to his sons Rodger and John, with instructions that they say nothing thereof to their sister Elizabeth.]"

When Dr. Mortimer had finished reading this singular narrative he pushed his spectacles up on his forehead and stared across at Mr. Sherlock Holmes. The latter yawned and tossed the end of his cigarette into the fire.

25. In the last sentence, the word "latter" most likely refers to
    (A) Hugo Baskerville
    (B) Sherlock Holmes
    (C) a spectator
    (D) Dr. Mortimer
    (E) there is not enough detail to ascertain

26. The author's tone in the last sentence is one of
    (A) disbelief
    (B) exhilarated
    (C) accusatory
    (D) apathetic
    (E) pessimistic

27. In line 13, "blazing eyes" provides an example of which literary device?
    (A) pun
    (B) metaphor
    (C) onomatopoeia
    (D) understatement
    (E) anticlimax

28. The author's primary purpose of the first two paragraphs is to
    (A) create suspense
    (B) give advice
    (C) describe a setting
    (D) resolve a plot
    (E) absolve a lesson

29. As it is written in line 24, "Providence" most nearly means
    (A) retribution
    (B) God's will
    (C) foresight
    (D) nemesis
    (E) vengeance

30. In line 14, "rode for dear life" provides an example of which literary device?
    (A) hyperbole
    (B) personification
    (C) alliteration
    (D) idiom
    (E) metaphor

→ GO ON TO THE NEXT PAGE

Scientists are not under the impression that animals can make calculations consciously. They say that those individuals whose genetic makeup is such that they tend to gamble successfully are, as a direct result, more likely to survive and therefore are able to propagate those same genes.

When a gnu goes down to the river to drink, it increases the risk of being eaten by crocodiles that make their living lurking for prey in the river. However, if the creature does not go down to the river, it will eventually die of thirst. Its best policy is to postpone drinking until it is very thirsty, then go and have one good long drink to last for some time. This would enable the animal to reduce the number of separate visits to the river. On the other hand, it has to spend a long time with its head down when it finally does go to the river to drink. Alternatively, the best gamble in the gnu's favor might be to drink smaller amounts more often, snatching quick gulps of water.

Every decision a survival machine makes is a gamble, and it is the business of genes to program brains in advance so that, on average, they make innocuous decisions.

31. Which of the following best describes the main point of the passage?
    (A) Statistically, predators make better decisions than their prey.
    (B) Gambling threatens an individual's survival.
    (C) Those animals that require large amounts of water daily have short life spans.
    (D) The program of the brain has become the central issue of genetic engineering.
    (E) Survival depends on genetic programming that allows an individual to make a decision.

32. According to the passage, the individual's life is influenced most by the individual's ability to
    (A) be determined
    (B) be conscientious
    (C) move fast
    (D) predict correctly
    (E) find easy prey

33. The tone of this passage is
    (A) sarcastic
    (B) colloquial
    (C) skeptical
    (D) informative
    (E) disapproving

34. According to the passage, animals mainly make decisions by their
    (A) intelligence
    (B) sympathy
    (C) conscience
    (D) intuition
    (E) principle

35. As used in the passage, "survival machine" refers to
    (A) life form
    (B) lethal weapon
    (C) disruptive technology
    (D) vulnerable prey
    (E) electronic device

→ GO ON TO THE NEXT PAGE

All the world's a stage,
And all the men and women merely players;
They have their exits and their entrances,
And one man in his time plays many parts,
His acts being seven ages. At first the infant,

Mewling and puking in the nurse's arms.
Then, the whining school-boy with his satchel
And shining morning face, creeping like snail
Unwillingly to school. And then the lover,
Sighing like furnace, with a woeful ballad

Made to his mistress' eyebrow. Then, a soldier,
Full of strange oaths, and bearded like the pard,
Jealous in honour, sudden, and quick in quarrel,
Seeking the bubble reputation
Even in the cannon's mouth. And then, the justice,

In fair round belly, with a good capon lined,
With eyes severe, and beard of formal cut,
Full of wise saws, and modern instances,
And so he plays his part. The sixth age shifts
Into the lean and slippered pantaloon,

With spectacles on nose and pouch on side,
His youthful hose, well saved, a world too wide
For his shrunk shank, and his big manly voice,
Turning again toward childish treble, pipes
And whistles in his sound. Last scene of all,

That ends this strange eventful history,
Is second childishness and mere oblivion,
Sans teeth, sans eyes, sans taste, sans everything.

36. In the context of this excerpt, a "stage" is
    (A) a classroom
    (B) a human life
    (C) a performing place
    (D) the world
    (E) an art studio

37. The poet uses the words "entrance and exit" as a comparison for
    (A) nature and human
    (B) birth and death
    (C) dream and reality
    (D) achievement and frustration
    (E) ending and beginning

38. What figure of speech does the word "stage" represent in this poem?
    (A) simile
    (B) personification
    (C) irony
    (D) metaphor
    (E) hyperbole

39. "Even in the cannon's mouth" most nearly means
    (A) The soldier is quick-tempered.
    (B) The soldier wants to hide in the cannon.
    (C) The soldier is ready to face all kinds of danger.
    (D) The soldier knows many wise saws and modern instances.
    (E) The soldier shouts like a furnace.

40. The poet uses the phrase "fair round belly" to emphasize
    (A) He is stout.
    (B) He is wise.
    (C) He seeks fame.
    (D) He is generous.
    (E) He is fair.

IF YOU FINISH BEFORE TIME IS CALLED,
YOU MAY CHECK YOUR WORK ON THIS SECTION ONLY.
DO NOT TURN TO ANY OTHER SECTION IN THE TEST.

SECTION 3

+ Verbal (60 Questions/ 30 Minutes) +

This section consists of two different types of questions: synonyms and analogies. There are directions and a sample question for each type.

Synonyms

Each of the following questions consists of one word followed by five words or phrases. You are to select the one word or phrase whose meaning is closest to the word in capital letters.

Sample Problem:

> CHILLY:
> (A) lazy
> (B) nice
> (C) dry
> (D) cold
> (E) sunny   Ⓐ Ⓑ Ⓒ ● Ⓔ

1. MALLEABLE:
   (A) docile
   (B) faded
   (C) temperate
   (D) curable
   (E) immobile

2. CAJOLE:
   (A) stay
   (B) attack
   (C) mount
   (D) entice
   (E) deceive

3. RELINQUISH:
   (A) revisit
   (B) reimburse
   (C) renounce
   (D) retrospect
   (E) retreat

4. TEMPER:
   (A) disposition
   (B) ballot
   (C) rebuttal
   (D) synthesis
   (E) deed

→ GO ON TO THE NEXT PAGE

5. TRIFLING:

   (A) appropriate
   (B) trivial
   (C) irregular
   (D) inborn
   (E) mediocre

6. IGNORANT:

   (A) ambiguous
   (B) creative
   (C) relevant
   (D) factual
   (E) unaware

7. EPOCH:

   (A) vie
   (B) stash
   (C) duct
   (D) safe
   (E) era

8. CONVEY:

   (A) quit
   (B) bare
   (C) keep
   (D) carry
   (E) refuse

9. SEQUESTER:

   (A) renounce
   (B) aim
   (C) relinquish
   (D) seclude
   (E) annex

10. COMPASSIONATE:

    (A) moderate
    (B) exacting
    (C) indulgent
    (D) demanding
    (E) sympathetic

11. PROWL:

    (A) become invisible
    (B) run very fast
    (C) tease lightly
    (D) eat greedily
    (E) move stealthily

12. EXOTIC:

    (A) outlandish
    (B) terrific
    (C) explicit
    (D) homely
    (E) minute

13. EPHEMERAL:

    (A) naive
    (B) ingenious
    (C) fleeting
    (D) mulish
    (E) extraordinary

14. HAPLESS:

    (A) distressed
    (B) inferior
    (C) unfortunate
    (D) reluctant
    (E) efficient

➜ GO ON TO THE NEXT PAGE

15. ADOPT:

　(A) affect

　(B) offer

　(C) diagnose

　(D) choose

　(E) reflect

16. KINDRED:

　(A) clan

　(B) trait

　(C) disposition

　(D) hospitality

　(E) qualification

17. GROVEL:

　(A) rotate

　(B) involve

　(C) abase

　(D) combine

　(E) remind

18. UNIQUE:

　(A) singular

　(B) boastful

　(C) nervous

　(D) orderly

　(E) special

19. BLATANT:

　(A) coy

　(B) flagrant

　(C) implicit

　(D) suitable

　(E) apprehensive

20. INTROSPECTION:

　(A) intervention

　(B) perspective

　(C) custom

　(D) factor

　(E) reflection

21. METAMORPHOSIS:

　(A) transformation

　(B) integrity

　(C) consistency

　(D) valiance

　(E) opulence

22. JOCULAR:

　(A) murky

　(B) unconventional

　(C) solemn

　(D) humorous

　(E) benevolent

23. COTERIE:

　(A) fallacy

　(B) affront

　(C) clique

　(D) insurgent

　(E) mutiny

24. GENUFLECT:

　(A) kowtow

　(B) heave

　(C) knead

　(D) stack

　(E) hoist

→ GO ON TO THE NEXT PAGE

25. REPROACH:
    (A) commend
    (B) laud
    (C) reprimand
    (D) exonerate
    (E) sanction

26. INTRICATE:
    (A) complicated
    (B) headstrong
    (C) quaint
    (D) mocking
    (E) enduring

27. TIMID:
    (A) remorseful
    (B) querulous
    (C) furious
    (D) timorous
    (E) imminent

28. FAUX:
    (A) favored
    (B) studied
    (C) repetitious
    (D) abundant
    (E) fake

29. THEATRICAL:
    (A) histrionic
    (B) novel
    (C) prudent
    (D) wizened
    (E) unleashed

30. LUDICROUS:
    (A) pleasant
    (B) rabid
    (C) unwilling
    (D) absurd
    (E) durable

→ GO ON TO THE NEXT PAGE

Analogies

The following questions ask you to find relationships between words. For each question, select the answer choice that best completes the meaning of the sentence.

Sample Problem:

> Kitten is to cat as
> (A) fawn is to colt
> (B) puppy is to dog
> (C) cow is to bull
> (D) wolf is to bear
> (E) hen is to rooster   Ⓐ ● Ⓒ Ⓓ Ⓔ

Choice (B) is the best answer because a kitten is a young cat just as a puppy is a young dog. Of all the answer choices, (B) states a relationship that is most like the relationship between kitten and cat.

---

31. Man is to sprint as horse is to
    (A) jog
    (B) saddle
    (C) hoof
    (D) gallop
    (E) slither

32. Cardiac is to heart as
    (A) thermal is to lung
    (B) cerebral is to brain
    (C) ventral is to back
    (D) dorsal is to abdomen
    (E) pulmonary is to blood vessel

33. Rectify is to mistake as
    (A) amend is to law
    (B) recall is to memory
    (C) reject is to offer
    (D) abscond is to funds
    (E) magnify is to fault

34. Chemistry is to science as
    (A) literature is to history
    (B) statistics is to mathematics
    (C) demography is to earth
    (D) novice is to master
    (E) dentist is to drill

→ GO ON TO THE NEXT PAGE

35. Stray is to path as
    (A) travel is to itinerary
    (B) ramble is to meeting
    (C) roam is to dinosaur
    (D) wander is to deviation
    (E) digress is to topic

36. Suggestible is to influence as
    (A) invincible is to defeat
    (B) impregnable is to bulwark
    (C) vulnerable is attack
    (D) guilty is to innocence
    (E) fraud is to trickster

37. Snake is to hiss as
    (A) rooster is to chirp
    (B) cat is to bleat
    (C) horse is to croak
    (D) owl is to hoot
    (E) frog is to neigh

38. Worker is to union as
    (A) project is to research
    (B) foundation is to building
    (C) handle is to bicycle
    (D) state is to federation
    (E) molecule is to atom

39. Counselor is to advice as
    (A) donor is to contribution
    (B) spendthrift is to poverty
    (C) heir is to heirloom
    (D) abolitionist is to slavery
    (E) protagonist is to novel

40. Void is to check as
    (A) dye is to fabric
    (B) rescind is to retreat
    (C) provoke is to order
    (D) erase is to smudge
    (E) annul is to contract

41. Incredulous is to skeptic as
    (A) praise is to critic
    (B) tenacious is to toil
    (C) miserly is to skinflint
    (D) admiring is to scribe
    (E) biased is to arbiter

42. Architect is to blueprint as
    (A) biologist is to lecture
    (B) dentist is to drill
    (C) teacher is to assignment
    (D) playwright is to script
    (E) butcher is to cleaver

43. Conundrum is to riddle as
    (A) horse is to saddle
    (B) labyrinth is to maze
    (C) mystery is to unraveling
    (D) enigma is to stigma
    (E) trick is to candor

44. Connoisseur is to expert as
    (A) dilettante is to amateur
    (B) hobbyist is to vocation
    (C) maven is to magnate
    (D) professional is to novice
    (E) master is to pupil

→ GO ON TO THE NEXT PAGE

45. Clamp is to hold as
    (A) shovel is to decelerate
    (B) dolly is to transport
    (C) pulley is to dig
    (D) scythe is to garner
    (E) trolley is to accelerate

46. Prologue is to epilogue as
    (A) chapter is to book
    (B) word is to sentence
    (C) climax is to anticlimax
    (D) dessert is to appetizer
    (E) overture is to finale

47. Euphonious is to sound as
    (A) fragrant is to smell
    (B) loud is to deafening
    (C) soft is to whisper
    (D) compassionate is to pity
    (E) jumbled is to object

48. Vacant is to occupants as
    (A) piqued is to infuriated
    (B) clamorous is to noise
    (C) outspoken is to politicians
    (D) impoverished is to money
    (E) sanitary is to clean

49. Mislead is to defraud as
    (A) lie is to certify
    (B) last is to crumble
    (C) cling is to stick
    (D) fume is to consider
    (E) collide is to slide

50. Arena is to spectators as
    (A) church is to congregation
    (B) ballroom is to boxers
    (C) practitioners is to gym
    (D) capitol is to pariahs
    (E) engineers is to studio

51. Armory is to munitions as shed is to
    (A) curator
    (B) tool
    (C) food
    (D) silo
    (E) library

52. Jaunt is to trip as
    (A) trek is to outing
    (B) debut is to premier
    (C) skit is to play
    (D) opera is to ditty
    (E) matinee is to understudy

53. Albino is to pigment as
    (A) biology is to lecture
    (B) drought is to water
    (C) doctor is to prescription
    (D) dentist is to drill
    (E) freshet is to flood

54. Adroit is to motion as
    (A) guarded is to emotion
    (B) confined is to restraint
    (C) clumsy is to skill
    (D) ubiquitous is to presence
    (E) articulate is to speech

→ GO ON TO THE NEXT PAGE

55. Hospitable is to belligerent as
    (A) harmonious is to mellifluous
    (B) grim is to austere
    (C) gregarious is to antisocial
    (D) benign is to agreeable
    (E) innovative is to technology

56. Tact is to diplomat as
    (A) rudeness is to conductor
    (B) flavor is to licorice
    (C) plan is to battle
    (D) agility is to gymnast
    (E) mission is to spy

57. Scoundrel is to virtue as
    (A) mogul is to vice
    (B) glutton is to moderation
    (C) vassal is to feudalism
    (D) gambler is to luck
    (E) benefactor is to funds

58. Monologue is to speech as
    (A) dessert is to meal
    (B) ditty is to encore
    (C) container is to pitcher
    (D) snack is to banquet
    (E) aria is to opera

59. Prudent is to rash as
    (A) discreet is to reckless
    (B) attentive is to focused
    (C) considerate is to incensed
    (D) envious is to covetous
    (E) controversial is to argumentative

60. Forgery is to imitation as
    (A) bounty is to hunter
    (B) feat is to milestone
    (C) collusion is to cooperation
    (D) euphoria is to emotion
    (E) epiphany is to realization

IF YOU FINISH BEFORE TIME IS CALLED,
YOU MAY CHECK YOUR WORK ON THIS SECTION ONLY.
DO NOT TURN TO ANY OTHER SECTION IN THE TEST.

SECTION 4

+ Quantitative (Math) (25 Questions / 30 Minutes) +

Following each problem in this section, there are five suggested answers. Work each problem in your head or in the blank space provided at the right of the page. Then look at the five suggested answers and decide which one is best.

Note: Figures that accompany problems in this section are drawn as accurately as possible EXCEPT when it is stated in a specific problem that its figure is not drawn to scale.

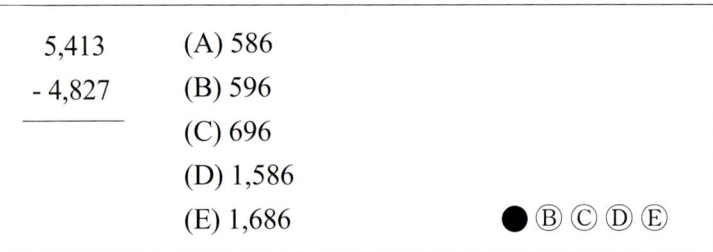

USE THIS SPACE FOR FIGURING

1. If $\dfrac{4}{12} = \dfrac{4}{x+2}$, what is the value of x?

    (A) 2
    (B) 4
    (C) 6
    (D) 8
    (E) 10

2. How many 2-liter jars are needed to hold 6P liters of juice?

    (A) $P+4$
    (B) $P \times P$
    (C) $3P$
    (D) P
    (E) $\dfrac{P}{3}$

→ GO ON TO THE NEXT PAGE

3. Peter bought a stereo for x dollars and sold it at a 5 percent profit. Which of the following gives the amount of Peter's profit?

(A) $0.005x$
(B) $0.05x$
(C) $0.5x$
(D) $1.5x$
(E) $0.95x$

4. The ratio of a to b to c to d to e is 5 to 4 to 3 to 2 to 1. If $a = 45$, what is the value of c?

(A) 9
(B) 11
(C) 15
(D) 18
(E) 27

5. The sum of four consecutive odd integers a, b, c, and d is 32. What is the median of the set $\{a, b, c, d, 24\}$?

(A) 5
(B) 7
(C) 9
(D) 12
(E) 24

→ GO ON TO THE NEXT PAGE

6. Which of the following is equal in value to 1 plus (100 percent of 1)?
   (A) 100 percent of 1
   (B) 105 percent of 1
   (C) 110 percent of 1
   (D) 200 percent of 1
   (E) 201 percent of 1

7. At halftime, Team A was 12 points behind Team B, but Team A won by 5 points. How many points did Team A score after halftime if Team B scored 21 points in the second half?
   (A) 16
   (B) 17
   (C) 23
   (D) 38
   (E) 44

8. One circle has a radius of $\frac{1}{2}$ and another circle has a radius of 1. What is the ratio of the area of the larger circle to the area of the smaller circle?
   (A) 2:1
   (B) 3:1
   (C) 3:2
   (D) 4:1
   (E) 4:3

→ GO ON TO THE NEXT PAGE

9. Steph is currently 12 years old. Jason is half the age of Steph. When Steph is 30, how old will Jason be?

   (A) 6
   (B) 12
   (C) 18
   (D) 20
   (E) 24

10. In the correctly worked addition problem below, *A* and *B* represent two different digits. What digit does *A* represent?

$$\begin{array}{r} AB \\ + BA \\ \hline 1A2 \end{array}$$

   (A) 3
   (B) 4
   (C) 5
   (D) 6
   (E) 7

⟨Kids Apparel Company's June Sale⟩

	Short-sleeves	Long-sleeves	Total
Orange	3,600		
Green		1,500	
Total		5,500	10,000

11. A kids' dress company sells only orange dresses and green dresses, both of which are available as either short-sleeves or long-sleeves. Based on the information in the table above, how many green dresses did the company sell in June?

    (A) 900
    (B) 2,400
    (C) 4,000
    (D) 4,500
    (E) 5,200

12. When twice a number is decreased by 7, the result is 123. What is the number?

    (A) 35
    (B) 40
    (C) 52
    (D) 65
    (E) 130

→ GO ON TO THE NEXT PAGE

13. A computer program randomly selects a positive two-digit number. If the number selected is odd, twice that number is printed. If the number selected is even, the number itself is printed. If the number printed is 34, which of the following could have been the number selected?

    I. 17
    II. 22
    III. 34

    (A) I only
    (B) II only
    (C) I and III only
    (D) II and III only
    (E) I, II, and III

14. If a is an even integer and b is an odd integer, which of the following must be even?

    (A) $ab + 1$
    (B) $a^2 + 1$
    (C) $a^2 + b^2$
    (D) $a^2b^2 + 1$
    (E) $b^2 + 3$

➔ GO ON TO THE NEXT PAGE

15. Which figure has a path that can be traveled without lifting the pencil or retracing?

(A)

(B)

(C)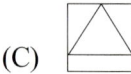

(D)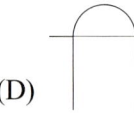

(E)

16. Johnny is collecting nickels. He saves one nickel on the first day, two on the second day, and three on the third day. If this pattern continues, how much money will Johnny have saved at the end of 30 days?
(A) $22.00
(B) $22.25
(C) $23.00
(D) $23.25
(E) $24.00

17. Find the *x* intercept for the line $3x+2y=12$.

   (A) -4
   (B) 0
   (C) 3
   (D) 4
   (E) 6

18. In a survey, each of 1,000 people was found to have a checking account, a savings account, or both. If 600 people have checking accounts and 600 have savings accounts, how many people have both a checking account and a savings account?

   (A) 50
   (B) 100
   (C) 150
   (D) 200
   (E) 250

19. In Figure 1, C is the circle's center and ∠ACB is right. Vertices A and B of the triangle are on the circle. If the area of the triangle ACB is 18, then what is the area of the shaded region?

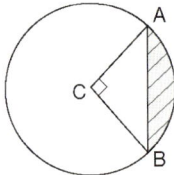

Figure 1

(A) $18 - 9\pi$
(B) $9\pi - 18$
(C) $36\pi - 18$
(D) $9\pi - 6$
(E) It cannot be determined from the information given.

20. A cylindrical clam chowder soup serving four people has a base diameter of 8 inches and a height of 10 inches. The soup company wants to introduce the soup in single-serving cans as well. If the company keeps the height of the new can at 10 inches, what should its new base diameter equal?

(A) 1
(B) $\sqrt{2}$
(C) 2
(D) 4
(E) $2\sqrt{2}$

21. In the xy-coordinate plane, the line passing through the points (1,2) and (a, -4) has slope of -3. What is the value of a?

    (A) -6
    (B) -4
    (C) 0
    (D) 1
    (E) 3

22. A trucker took between $2\frac{1}{2}$ and 4 hours to make a 200-mile trip. The average speed, in miles per hour, must have been between

    (A) 30 and 50
    (B) 50 and 80
    (C) 50 and 100
    (D) 80 and 100
    (E) 100 and 120

23. If $4 - x$ is less than $\frac{1}{2}$, which of the following could be x?

(A) $\frac{9}{3}$

(B) $\frac{1}{3}$

(C) $\frac{7}{2}$

(D) $1\frac{1}{4}$

(E) $\frac{9}{2}$

24. The mass requires to trigger a mouse trap is 175g. If a mouse is 5 oz, what is the largest amount of cheese the mouse could carry without setting off the trap? (1oz.=28g)

(A) 147g

(B) 140g

(C) 35g

(D) 34g

(E) 23.25g

→ GO ON TO THE NEXT PAGE

25. A circle, a square, and an equilateral triangle all have the same perimeter. Which of the following lists the shapes in decreasing order of area?

(A) circle, square, triangle
(B) circle, triangle, square
(C) triangle, circle, square
(D) triangle, square, circle
(E) square, circle, triangle

IF YOU FINISH BEFORE TIME IS CALLED,
YOU MAY CHECK YOUR WORK ON THIS SECTION ONLY.
DO NOT TURN TO ANY OTHER SECTION IN THE TEST.

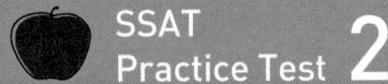

SSAT Practice Test 2

SSAT
Practice Test 2

UPPER LEVEL (Grade 8-11)

Section	Time Allotted (Number of Questions)
Writing Sample	25 minutes (1Q)
Break	10 minutes
Quantitative (Section 1)	30 minutes (25Q)
Reading (Section 2)	40 minutes (40Q)
Break	10 minutes
Verbal (Section 3)	30 minutes (60Q)
Quantitative (Section 4)	30 minutes (25Q)
Experimental (Section 5)	15 minutes (16Q)
Totals	3 hours, 10 minutes

* Of the 167 items including the writing sample, only 150 questions are scored.

ANSWER SHEET 2

Be sure each mark completely fills the answer space.

Start with number 1 for each new section of the test. You may find more answer spaces than you need. If so, please leave them blank.

Section 1

1 Ⓐ Ⓑ Ⓒ Ⓓ Ⓔ   6 Ⓐ Ⓑ Ⓒ Ⓓ Ⓔ   11 Ⓐ Ⓑ Ⓒ Ⓓ Ⓔ   16 Ⓐ Ⓑ Ⓒ Ⓓ Ⓔ   21 Ⓐ Ⓑ Ⓒ Ⓓ Ⓔ
2 Ⓐ Ⓑ Ⓒ Ⓓ Ⓔ   7 Ⓐ Ⓑ Ⓒ Ⓓ Ⓔ   12 Ⓐ Ⓑ Ⓒ Ⓓ Ⓔ   17 Ⓐ Ⓑ Ⓒ Ⓓ Ⓔ   22 Ⓐ Ⓑ Ⓒ Ⓓ Ⓔ
3 Ⓐ Ⓑ Ⓒ Ⓓ Ⓔ   8 Ⓐ Ⓑ Ⓒ Ⓓ Ⓔ   13 Ⓐ Ⓑ Ⓒ Ⓓ Ⓔ   18 Ⓐ Ⓑ Ⓒ Ⓓ Ⓔ   23 Ⓐ Ⓑ Ⓒ Ⓓ Ⓔ
4 Ⓐ Ⓑ Ⓒ Ⓓ Ⓔ   9 Ⓐ Ⓑ Ⓒ Ⓓ Ⓔ   14 Ⓐ Ⓑ Ⓒ Ⓓ Ⓔ   19 Ⓐ Ⓑ Ⓒ Ⓓ Ⓔ   24 Ⓐ Ⓑ Ⓒ Ⓓ Ⓔ
5 Ⓐ Ⓑ Ⓒ Ⓓ Ⓔ   10 Ⓐ Ⓑ Ⓒ Ⓓ Ⓔ   15 Ⓐ Ⓑ Ⓒ Ⓓ Ⓔ   20 Ⓐ Ⓑ Ⓒ Ⓓ Ⓔ   25 Ⓐ Ⓑ Ⓒ Ⓓ Ⓔ

Section 2

1 Ⓐ Ⓑ Ⓒ Ⓓ Ⓔ   9 Ⓐ Ⓑ Ⓒ Ⓓ Ⓔ   17 Ⓐ Ⓑ Ⓒ Ⓓ Ⓔ   25 Ⓐ Ⓑ Ⓒ Ⓓ Ⓔ   33 Ⓐ Ⓑ Ⓒ Ⓓ Ⓔ
2 Ⓐ Ⓑ Ⓒ Ⓓ Ⓔ   10 Ⓐ Ⓑ Ⓒ Ⓓ Ⓔ   18 Ⓐ Ⓑ Ⓒ Ⓓ Ⓔ   26 Ⓐ Ⓑ Ⓒ Ⓓ Ⓔ   34 Ⓐ Ⓑ Ⓒ Ⓓ Ⓔ
3 Ⓐ Ⓑ Ⓒ Ⓓ Ⓔ   11 Ⓐ Ⓑ Ⓒ Ⓓ Ⓔ   19 Ⓐ Ⓑ Ⓒ Ⓓ Ⓔ   27 Ⓐ Ⓑ Ⓒ Ⓓ Ⓔ   35 Ⓐ Ⓑ Ⓒ Ⓓ Ⓔ
4 Ⓐ Ⓑ Ⓒ Ⓓ Ⓔ   12 Ⓐ Ⓑ Ⓒ Ⓓ Ⓔ   20 Ⓐ Ⓑ Ⓒ Ⓓ Ⓔ   28 Ⓐ Ⓑ Ⓒ Ⓓ Ⓔ   36 Ⓐ Ⓑ Ⓒ Ⓓ Ⓔ
5 Ⓐ Ⓑ Ⓒ Ⓓ Ⓔ   13 Ⓐ Ⓑ Ⓒ Ⓓ Ⓔ   21 Ⓐ Ⓑ Ⓒ Ⓓ Ⓔ   29 Ⓐ Ⓑ Ⓒ Ⓓ Ⓔ   37 Ⓐ Ⓑ Ⓒ Ⓓ Ⓔ
6 Ⓐ Ⓑ Ⓒ Ⓓ Ⓔ   14 Ⓐ Ⓑ Ⓒ Ⓓ Ⓔ   22 Ⓐ Ⓑ Ⓒ Ⓓ Ⓔ   30 Ⓐ Ⓑ Ⓒ Ⓓ Ⓔ   38 Ⓐ Ⓑ Ⓒ Ⓓ Ⓔ
7 Ⓐ Ⓑ Ⓒ Ⓓ Ⓔ   15 Ⓐ Ⓑ Ⓒ Ⓓ Ⓔ   23 Ⓐ Ⓑ Ⓒ Ⓓ Ⓔ   31 Ⓐ Ⓑ Ⓒ Ⓓ Ⓔ   39 Ⓐ Ⓑ Ⓒ Ⓓ Ⓔ
8 Ⓐ Ⓑ Ⓒ Ⓓ Ⓔ   16 Ⓐ Ⓑ Ⓒ Ⓓ Ⓔ   24 Ⓐ Ⓑ Ⓒ Ⓓ Ⓔ   32 Ⓐ Ⓑ Ⓒ Ⓓ Ⓔ   40 Ⓐ Ⓑ Ⓒ Ⓓ Ⓔ

Section 3

1 Ⓐ Ⓑ Ⓒ Ⓓ Ⓔ   13 Ⓐ Ⓑ Ⓒ Ⓓ Ⓔ   25 Ⓐ Ⓑ Ⓒ Ⓓ Ⓔ   37 Ⓐ Ⓑ Ⓒ Ⓓ Ⓔ   49 Ⓐ Ⓑ Ⓒ Ⓓ Ⓔ
2 Ⓐ Ⓑ Ⓒ Ⓓ Ⓔ   14 Ⓐ Ⓑ Ⓒ Ⓓ Ⓔ   26 Ⓐ Ⓑ Ⓒ Ⓓ Ⓔ   38 Ⓐ Ⓑ Ⓒ Ⓓ Ⓔ   50 Ⓐ Ⓑ Ⓒ Ⓓ Ⓔ
3 Ⓐ Ⓑ Ⓒ Ⓓ Ⓔ   15 Ⓐ Ⓑ Ⓒ Ⓓ Ⓔ   27 Ⓐ Ⓑ Ⓒ Ⓓ Ⓔ   39 Ⓐ Ⓑ Ⓒ Ⓓ Ⓔ   51 Ⓐ Ⓑ Ⓒ Ⓓ Ⓔ
4 Ⓐ Ⓑ Ⓒ Ⓓ Ⓔ   16 Ⓐ Ⓑ Ⓒ Ⓓ Ⓔ   28 Ⓐ Ⓑ Ⓒ Ⓓ Ⓔ   40 Ⓐ Ⓑ Ⓒ Ⓓ Ⓔ   52 Ⓐ Ⓑ Ⓒ Ⓓ Ⓔ
5 Ⓐ Ⓑ Ⓒ Ⓓ Ⓔ   17 Ⓐ Ⓑ Ⓒ Ⓓ Ⓔ   29 Ⓐ Ⓑ Ⓒ Ⓓ Ⓔ   41 Ⓐ Ⓑ Ⓒ Ⓓ Ⓔ   53 Ⓐ Ⓑ Ⓒ Ⓓ Ⓔ
6 Ⓐ Ⓑ Ⓒ Ⓓ Ⓔ   18 Ⓐ Ⓑ Ⓒ Ⓓ Ⓔ   30 Ⓐ Ⓑ Ⓒ Ⓓ Ⓔ   42 Ⓐ Ⓑ Ⓒ Ⓓ Ⓔ   54 Ⓐ Ⓑ Ⓒ Ⓓ Ⓔ
7 Ⓐ Ⓑ Ⓒ Ⓓ Ⓔ   19 Ⓐ Ⓑ Ⓒ Ⓓ Ⓔ   31 Ⓐ Ⓑ Ⓒ Ⓓ Ⓔ   43 Ⓐ Ⓑ Ⓒ Ⓓ Ⓔ   55 Ⓐ Ⓑ Ⓒ Ⓓ Ⓔ
8 Ⓐ Ⓑ Ⓒ Ⓓ Ⓔ   20 Ⓐ Ⓑ Ⓒ Ⓓ Ⓔ   32 Ⓐ Ⓑ Ⓒ Ⓓ Ⓔ   44 Ⓐ Ⓑ Ⓒ Ⓓ Ⓔ   56 Ⓐ Ⓑ Ⓒ Ⓓ Ⓔ
9 Ⓐ Ⓑ Ⓒ Ⓓ Ⓔ   21 Ⓐ Ⓑ Ⓒ Ⓓ Ⓔ   33 Ⓐ Ⓑ Ⓒ Ⓓ Ⓔ   45 Ⓐ Ⓑ Ⓒ Ⓓ Ⓔ   57 Ⓐ Ⓑ Ⓒ Ⓓ Ⓔ
10 Ⓐ Ⓑ Ⓒ Ⓓ Ⓔ   22 Ⓐ Ⓑ Ⓒ Ⓓ Ⓔ   34 Ⓐ Ⓑ Ⓒ Ⓓ Ⓔ   46 Ⓐ Ⓑ Ⓒ Ⓓ Ⓔ   58 Ⓐ Ⓑ Ⓒ Ⓓ Ⓔ
11 Ⓐ Ⓑ Ⓒ Ⓓ Ⓔ   23 Ⓐ Ⓑ Ⓒ Ⓓ Ⓔ   35 Ⓐ Ⓑ Ⓒ Ⓓ Ⓔ   47 Ⓐ Ⓑ Ⓒ Ⓓ Ⓔ   59 Ⓐ Ⓑ Ⓒ Ⓓ Ⓔ
12 Ⓐ Ⓑ Ⓒ Ⓓ Ⓔ   24 Ⓐ Ⓑ Ⓒ Ⓓ Ⓔ   36 Ⓐ Ⓑ Ⓒ Ⓓ Ⓔ   48 Ⓐ Ⓑ Ⓒ Ⓓ Ⓔ   60 Ⓐ Ⓑ Ⓒ Ⓓ Ⓔ

Section 4

1 Ⓐ Ⓑ Ⓒ Ⓓ Ⓔ   6 Ⓐ Ⓑ Ⓒ Ⓓ Ⓔ   11 Ⓐ Ⓑ Ⓒ Ⓓ Ⓔ   16 Ⓐ Ⓑ Ⓒ Ⓓ Ⓔ   21 Ⓐ Ⓑ Ⓒ Ⓓ Ⓔ
2 Ⓐ Ⓑ Ⓒ Ⓓ Ⓔ   7 Ⓐ Ⓑ Ⓒ Ⓓ Ⓔ   12 Ⓐ Ⓑ Ⓒ Ⓓ Ⓔ   17 Ⓐ Ⓑ Ⓒ Ⓓ Ⓔ   22 Ⓐ Ⓑ Ⓒ Ⓓ Ⓔ
3 Ⓐ Ⓑ Ⓒ Ⓓ Ⓔ   8 Ⓐ Ⓑ Ⓒ Ⓓ Ⓔ   13 Ⓐ Ⓑ Ⓒ Ⓓ Ⓔ   18 Ⓐ Ⓑ Ⓒ Ⓓ Ⓔ   23 Ⓐ Ⓑ Ⓒ Ⓓ Ⓔ
4 Ⓐ Ⓑ Ⓒ Ⓓ Ⓔ   9 Ⓐ Ⓑ Ⓒ Ⓓ Ⓔ   14 Ⓐ Ⓑ Ⓒ Ⓓ Ⓔ   19 Ⓐ Ⓑ Ⓒ Ⓓ Ⓔ   24 Ⓐ Ⓑ Ⓒ Ⓓ Ⓔ
5 Ⓐ Ⓑ Ⓒ Ⓓ Ⓔ   10 Ⓐ Ⓑ Ⓒ Ⓓ Ⓔ   15 Ⓐ Ⓑ Ⓒ Ⓓ Ⓔ   20 Ⓐ Ⓑ Ⓒ Ⓓ Ⓔ   25 Ⓐ Ⓑ Ⓒ Ⓓ Ⓔ

Writing Sample

Schools would like to get to know you better through an essay you write. If you choose to write a personal essay, base your essay on the topic presented in A. If you choose to write a general essay, base your essay on the topic presented in B

> A. Is honesty always the best policy, or are there some situations in which it is better not to tell the truth? Support your answer with reasons and examples.

> B. What are the pros and cons of AI technology in our day-to-day life?

Use this page and the next page to complete your writing sample.

Continue on the next page

SECTION 1

+ Quantitative (Math) (25 Questions / 30 Minutes) +

Following each problem in this section, there are five suggested answers. Work each problem in your head or in the blank space provided at the right of the page. Then look at the five suggested answers and decide which one is best.

<u>Note</u>: Figures that accompany problems in this section are drawn as accurately as possible EXCEPT when it is stated in a specific problem that its figure is not drawn to scale.

Sample Problem:

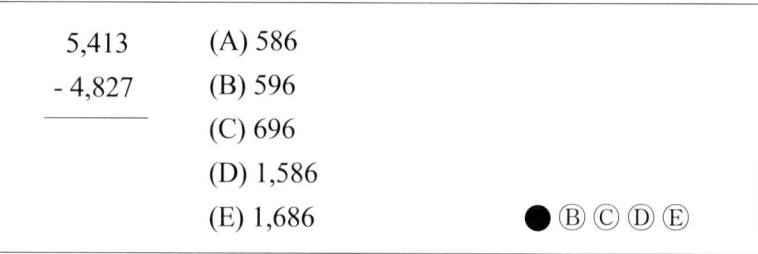

USE THIS SPACE FOR FIGURING

1. 14 × 3 × 6 × 1 is equal to the product of 9 and

   (A) 24
   (B) 25
   (C) 26
   (D) 27
   (E) 28

2. Logan and Alexander are playing a board game. On Alexander's turn, he is 9 squares behind Logan. If Alexander rolls a 5 and a 6 and moves forward that number of spaces, he will be

   (A) 2 squares ahead of Logan
   (B) 3 squares behind Logan
   (C) 4 squares behind Logan
   (D) 3 squares ahead of Logan
   (E) 20 squares ahead of Logan

→ GO ON TO THE NEXT PAGE

3. Ethan bought four dozen marbles on sale for $96. What was the cost per marble?

   (A) $1
   (B) $2
   (C) $8
   (D) $24
   (E) $32

4. A bed priced at $1,500 was sold for $960. What was the rate of discount?

   (A) 4%
   (B) 18%
   (C) 27%
   (D) 36%
   (E) 43%

5. A certain bank pays interest on money market accounts at 4% annually. If Marta deposits $7,200, find the interest earned after two years.

   (A) $28
   (B) $288
   (C) $576
   (D) $7,988
   (E) $7,776

→ GO ON TO THE NEXT PAGE

USE THIS SPACE FOR FIGURING

6. A train travels 120 miles at an average rate of 60 mph and returns along the same route at an average rate of 30 mph. What is the average rate of speed for the entire trip?

   (A) 35 mph
   (B) 40 mph
   (C) 45 mph
   (D) 50 mph
   (E) 55 mph

7. If $A \times B = 2.8$ and $B = 100$, then A is closest to which of the following?

   (A) 0.02
   (B) 0.03
   (C) 0.3
   (D) 28
   (E) 30

8. Matthew's coin collection consists of quarters and nickels and has a value of $1.10. The total number of coins is 10. Find the number of nickels in the collection.

   (A) 0.25
   (B) 1
   (C) 3
   (D) 5
   (E) 7

→ GO ON TO THE NEXT PAGE

Practice Test 2　81

9. A pole sticking out of the ground vertically is 3 feet tall and casts a shadow of 6 feet. At the same time, a tree next to the pole casts a shadow of 12 feet. How tall is the tree?
   (A) 6 feet
   (B) 12 feet
   (C) 24 feet
   (D) 48 feet
   (E) 56 feet

10. Four roommates each contribute $5 per week to a savings fund to buy an air purifier for their apartment. To save the same amount each week, how much would each person pay per week if a fifth roommate also contributed?
    (A) $1
    (B) $2
    (C) $3
    (D) $4
    (E) $5

11. If $(3 + x) \times (5 + y) = 1$ and x is greater than zero, then y must be
    (A) even
    (B) odd
    (C) positive
    (D) negative
    (E) greater than zero

12. The "3" in place x in the number below has a value. How many times is the value of the "3" in place y?

    7,5<u>3</u>1.<u>3</u>17
       x y

    (A) 1
    (B) 10
    (C) 100
    (D) 1,000
    (E) 10,000

13. Alex has two shelves of books. The first shelf has e books and the second has 8 more books than the first. If he moves 12 books from the second shelf to the first and then adds 7 new books to the second shelf, how many books would the second shelf now have?

    (A) $e - 12$
    (B) $e - 8$
    (C) $e - 7$
    (D) $e + 3$
    (E) $e + 7$

14. Ryan has five coins in his pocket, including quarters, dimes, and nickels. He knows that only one coin is a quarter, and he has at least one of each. What is the maximum amount of money he could be holding?

    (A) $1.25
    (B) $0.65
    (C) $0.60
    (D) $0.50
    (E) $0.45

15. Chloe has a handful of quarters, dimes, and nickels. Which of the following is NOT a possible value for the number of cents she carries?

    (A) 25
    (B) 30
    (C) 37
    (D) 40
    (E) 45

16. Evaluate: $(1.7 \times 10^{-5})(2.3 \times 10^{7})$

    (A) 3.91×10^{-2}
    (B) 3.91×10^{2}
    (C) 4.00×10^{2}
    (D) 4.00×10^{-2}
    (E) 4.00×10^{-35}

17. The points (-6, 23) and (6, -10) are on a line. Which of the following points is also on that line?

    (A) (-2, 12)
    (B) (-1, 9)
    (C) (0, -8)
    (D) (-3, 23)
    (E) (5, 15)

→ GO ON TO THE NEXT PAGE

18. The perimeter of the rectangle is 32 meters with a length of 12. Find its area to the nearest square meter.

   (A) 12 m^2
   (B) 24 m^2
   (C) 34 m^2
   (D) 36 m^2
   (E) 48 m^2

19. Step 1: Choose any number does not equal zero.
    Step 2: Multiply the number by 10
    Step 3: ???

    Jennie tells her friends that if they tell her the answer they get after step 3, she can tell them the number they chose originally. How does she do this for Step 3?

    (A) She subtracts 10 from the answer and then multiplies it by 2
    (B) She multiplies the answer by 20
    (C) She adds 30 to the answer and subtracts 50
    (D) She divides the answer to itself
    (E) She divides the answer by 100 and multiply by 10

20. $\dfrac{5}{x} = \dfrac{2x}{10}$

In the equation above, which of the following is a possible value of x?

(A) 1
(B) 2
(C) 4
(D) 5
(E) There is no value of x that will make this true.

21. Lawrence High School has 3,500 students. Each student must take only one foreign language. This year, 30% of the students are taking German, and 60% are taking Spanish. The remaining students are taking either French, Latin, or Russian. If there are 148 students in the Latin class and 50 students in the Russian class, how many students are taking French?

(A) 72
(B) 152
(C) 198
(D) 1,050
(E) 2,100

22. Over a semester, a student takes nine tests. She earns grades of 78, 94, 83, 90, 99, 74, 94, 88, 100. What is her median test score?

(A) 78
(B) 80
(C) 88
(D) 90
(E) 94

→ GO ON TO THE NEXT PAGE

23. The average of 12 statistical entries is 15.46. If a single entry is increased by 1.5 to correct an error, by what amount is the average increased?
    (A) 0.01
    (B) 0.15
    (C) 0.10
    (D) 0.125
    (E) 0.005

24. What is the smallest value of n that makes $(\frac{2}{5})^n$ less than 10%
    (A) 7
    (B) 6
    (C) 5
    (D) 4
    (E) 3

25. If one grey square represents one unit of area in Figure 1, the polygon on the left contains how many fewer units of an area than the polygon on the right?

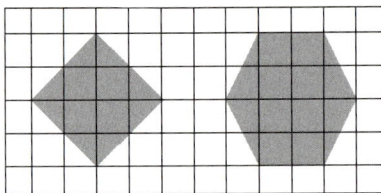

Figure 1

(A) 0
(B) 2
(C) 4
(D) 6
(E) 8

IF YOU FINISH BEFORE TIME IS CALLED,
YOU MAY CHECK YOUR WORK ON THIS SECTION ONLY.
DO NOT TURN TO ANY OTHER SECTION IN THE TEST.

SECTION 2

+ Reading (40 Questions / 40 Minutes) +

Read each passage carefully and then answer the questions about it. For each question, decide on the basis of the passage which one of the choices best answers the question.

The term "humpback" describes the form of a whale's back. They swim slowly and have the propensity to migrate. They typically travel in groups of two or three. Whales tend to be very peaceful animals. The out-of-water posture, lengthy fore flippers, and intricate calls of humpback whales are a few well-known characteristics.

5   The humpback whale song is a series of sounds that typically lasts 10-15 minutes and is repeated over time. The song consists of several different themes (often four to six) sung in a continuous loop. Each theme is composed of sound units distinctly arranged as a phrase, which is repeated for several minutes. For roughly six months out of the year, male humpback whales sing nonstop, while it is not entirely clear why researchers

10 believe they sing as both a way to attract females and to ward off encroaching male whales.

Whale songs are typically sung 50 to 60 feet below the water's surface for between 20 and 40 minutes at a time. Common humpback whales have a sound frequency ranging from 20 Hz to 10,000 Hz, most of which are within the audible range of the

15 human ear hearing distance. Humpback whales almost 9,000 miles apart have been caught singing the same song. According to new research, Humpback whales throughout the entire South Pacific Ocean are connected to each other via shared song.

1. The most suitable title for this passage is
   (A) A Song to be Sung
   (B) The Humpback's Cantata
   (C) Humpbacks In the Wild
   (D) The Strong Bonds
   (E) A Shared Joy

2. The author's primary purpose in the passage is to
   (A) provide generic information about humpback whales
   (B) list the characteristics of humpback whales
   (C) specifically discuss humpback whale songs
   (D) compare frequencies of the humpback whale songs
   (E) discuss the occurrences of humpback whales

3. The author's description of the humpback whale is attributed to
   (A) personal experience
   (B) familial stories
   (C) completed research
   (D) illustrations
   (E) a literature review

4. As used in line 12, "encroaching" most nearly means
   (A) incompetent
   (B) alarming
   (C) indefatigable
   (D) defensive
   (E) intruding

5. Why do researchers believe male humpback whales sing?
   (A) To communicate with other species.
   (B) To showcase their territorial dominance.
   (C) As a response to migratory patterns.
   (D) To attract females and deter rival males.
   (E) To signal distress to other whales.

→ GO ON TO THE NEXT PAGE

Daisy took her face in her hands as if feeling its lovely shape, and her eyes moved gradually out into the velvet dusk. I saw that turbulent emotions possessed her, so I asked what I thought would be some sedative questions about her little girl.

"We don't know each other very well, Nick," she said suddenly. "Even if we are cousins. You didn't come to my wedding."

"I wasn't back from the war."

"That's true." She hesitated. "Well, I've had a very bad time, Nick, and I'm pretty cynical about everything."

Evidently she had reason to be. I waited but she didn't say any more, and after a moment I returned rather feebly to the subject of her daughter.

"I suppose she talks, and—eats, and everything."

"Oh, yes." She looked at me absently. "Listen, Nick; let me tell you what I said when she was born. Would you like to hear?"

"Very much."

"It'll show you how I've gotten to feel about—things. Well, she was less than an hour old and Tom was God knows where. I woke up out of the ether with an utterly abandoned feeling, and asked the nurse right away if it was a boy or a girl. She told me it was a girl, and so I turned my head away and wept. 'all right,' I said, 'I'm glad it's a girl. And I hope she'll be a fool—that's the best thing a girl can be in this world, a beautiful little fool."

"You see, I think everything's terrible anyhow," she went on in a convinced way. "Everybody thinks so—the most advanced people. And I KNOW. I've been everywhere and seen everything and done everything." Her eyes flashed around her in a defiant way, rather like Tom's, and she laughed with thrilling scorn. "Sophisticated—God, I'm sophisticated!"

The instant her voice broke off, ceasing to compel my attention, my belief, I felt the basic insincerity of what she had said. It made me uneasy, as though the whole evening had been a trick of some sort to exact a contributory emotion from me. I waited, and sure enough, in a moment she looked at me with an absolute smirk on her lovely face, as if she had asserted her membership in a rather distinguished secret society to which she and Tom belonged.

6. How did Daisy at first respond to Nick's original questions about her daughter?
   (A) Daisy felt calmed by the questions.
   (B) Daisy began telling Nick the story of her daughter's birth.
   (C) Daisy told Nick she did not feel close enough to him to talk about it.
   (D) Daisy asked Nick what had happened in the war.
   (E) Daisy told Nick she did not know her daughter that well.

7. The passage primarily emphasizes
   (A) Daisy's sense of forsakenness
   (B) Daisy's ingenuous viewpoint akin to childhood innocence
   (C) Daisy's cynical outlook on life
   (D) Daisy's behavior marked by apparent contradictions concerning Tom
   (E) Daisy's romantically imbued perspective

8. As used in line 3, the word "sedative" means
   (A) calming
   (B) disturbing
   (C) personal
   (D) childish
   (E) emotional

9. In the context of the passage, the word "scorn" means
   (A) contempt
   (B) excitement
   (C) happiness
   (D) sophistication
   (E) emotion

10. Why did Nick wait to respond to Daisy after she cried out, "Sophisticated—God, I'm sophisticated"?
    (A) He thought she might need more time to finish.
    (B) He was worried she was going to start crying.
    (C) He felt sad himself after hearing her story.
    (D) He felt Daisy was trying to fool him.
    (E) He had not paid attention to what she had been saying.

11. What does Daisy's verbiage imply about her feelings towards her husband Tom?
    (A) She was disappointed he was not present for his daughter's birth.
    (B) She felt closer to Tom because they had a daughter together.
    (C) She felt they both belonged to a rather unremarkable society.
    (D) She felt Tom would have been happier had the baby been a boy.
    (E) She was angry with Tom because he believes he is sophisticated.

➜ GO ON TO THE NEXT PAGE

12. In which literary device does the sentence "I hope she'll be a fool-that's the best thing a girl can be in this wolrd, a beautiful little fool." exemplify?

(A) irony
(B) foreshadowing
(C) onomatopoeia
(D) antithesis
(E) pun

13. What does the metaphorical expression "her membership in a rather distinguished secret society" suggest about Daisy's perception of herself and Tom?

(A) Daisy views her relationship with Nick as a mysterious and confidential bond.
(B) Daisy views her relationship with Tom as burdensome.
(C) Daisy sees herself and Tom as part of an elite and exclusive group, emphasizing their privileged status.
(D) Daisy considers her association with Tom as supportive and respectful.
(E) Daisy believes in the uniqueness of her relationship with Tom, emphasizing their distinctiveness.

➜ GO ON TO THE NEXT PAGE

This book is the result of twelve years of experience in teaching university students to write special feature articles for newspapers and popular magazines. By applying the methods outlined in the following pages, young men and women have been able to prepare articles that have been accepted by many newspaper and magazine editors. The success that these students have achieved leads the author to believe that others who desire to write special articles may be aided by the suggestions given in this book.

Although innumerable books on short-story writing have been published, no attempt has hitherto been made to discuss in detail the writing of special feature articles. In the absence of any generally accepted method of approach to the subject, it has been necessary to work out a systematic classification of the various types of articles and of the different kinds of titles, beginnings, and similar details, as well as to supply names by which to identify them.

A careful analysis of current practice in the writing of special feature stories and popular magazine articles is the basis of the methods presented. In this analysis, an effort has been made to show the application of the principles of composition to the writing of articles. Examples taken from representative newspapers and magazines are freely used to illustrate the methods discussed. To encourage students to analyze typical articles, the second part of the book is devoted to a collection of newspaper and magazine articles of various types, with an outline for their analysis of them.

Particular emphasis is placed on methods of popularizing such knowledge as is not available to the general reader. This has been done in the belief that it is important for the average person to know of the progress that is being made in every field of human endeavor, in order that he may, if possible, apply the results to his own affairs. The problem, therefore, is to show aspiring writers how to present discoveries, inventions, new methods, and every significant advance in knowledge, in an accurate and attractive form.

14. The best title for this selection is
    (A) How to Write Special Feature Articles
    (B) How to be a Journalist
    (C) How to Analyze Portfolios
    (D) How to Write a Short Stories
    (E) How to be a Magazine Editor

15. As used in line 25, the word "endeavor" means
    (A) strife
    (B) temptation
    (C) effort
    (D) gossip
    (E) devotion

16. The author's tone is best described as
    (A) dissuasive
    (B) jubilant
    (C) ambivalent
    (D) somber
    (E) informative

17. This passage can most likely be found in a (an)
    (A) preface
    (B) inaugural address
    (C) epilogue
    (D) propaganda
    (E) valediction

18. According to the passage, what is the main difference between this book and other books on short-story writing?
    (A) It thoroughly addresses the writing of special feature articles.
    (B) It encourages students to analyze typical articles.
    (C) It has a wide range of readers.
    (D) It presents a collection of newspaper and magazine articles of various types.
    (E) This book emphasizes special feature articles should present the author's intense emotions.

➜ GO ON TO THE NEXT PAGE

> Not they who soar, but they who plod
> Their rugged way, unhelped, to God
> Are heroes; they who higher fare,
> And, flying, fan the upper air,
> 5   Miss all the toil that hugs the sod.
> 'Tis they whose backs have felt the rod,
> Whose feet have pressed the path unshod,
> May smile upon defeated care,
> Not they who soar.
> 10
> High up there are no thorns to prod,
> Nor boulders lurking 'neath the clod
> To turn the keenness of the share,
> For flight is ever free and rare;
> 15   But heroes they the soil who've trod,
> Not they who soar!

19. What is the poem's tone?

(A) playful
(B) pessimistic
(C) inspirational
(D) nostalgic
(E) sarcastic

20. What is the main idea of the poem?

(A) Those who fly high and take shortcuts are the villains.
(B) True heroes are those who endure life's challenges and toil on the ground.
(C) Those who soar high in the sky can get help from Gods.
(D) Those who miss all the toil are desirable.
(E) Those who plod are unabashed.

21. Who are the heroes in the poem?
    (A) Those who fly high and take shortcuts.
    (B) Those who whipped the enslaved people
    (C) Those who soar high in the sky.
    (D) Those whose feet have pressed the pavements.
    (E) Those who work hard and persevere in life.

22. What does the author imply about those who soar?
    (A) They are well-to-do with financial opulence.
    (B) They are proud black people.
    (C) They are unidentified and fearful creatures.
    (D) They kept all scores and rewards.
    (E) They miss out on the valuable experience of struggle.

23. What does the author mean by "the toil that hugs the sod"?
    (A) The agony and distress of prisoners
    (B) The heart pounding just before receiving an award
    (C) The joys and sorrows of daily life
    (D) The difficulties and challenges of life
    (E) The excitement ahead of a new start

24. As used in line 1, the word "plod" is most likely refers to
    (A) trudge
    (B) skitter
    (C) trot
    (D) leap
    (E) gallop

25. When the poem states, "they who higher fare," it most nearly means
    (A) Those who harass innocent people
    (B) Those who have had an easy Life
    (C) Those who are bondmen.
    (D) Those who are plebeians.
    (E) Those who are indifferent to politics.

26. As used in line 12, in this poem, the "boulders" represent
    (A) the hidden treasures
    (B) the blackmail from extortionists
    (C) the hardships of slavery
    (D) the gratitude to God
    (E) the nature's device to trip travelers

→ GO ON TO THE NEXT PAGE

It was about the beginning of September, 1664, that I, among the rest of my neighbors, heard in ordinary discourse that the plague was returned again in Holland; for it had been very violent there, and particularly at Amsterdam and Rotterdam, in the year 1663, whither, they say, it was brought, some said from Italy, others from the Levant, among some goods which were brought home by their Turkey fleet; others said it was brought from Candia; others from Cyprus. It mattered not from whence it came; but all agreed it was come into Holland again.

We had no such thing as printed newspapers in those days to spread rumors and reports of things, and to improve them by the invention of men, as I have lived to see practiced since. But such things as these were gathered from the letters of merchants and others who corresponded abroad, and from them was handed about by word of mouth only; so that things did not spread instantly over the whole nation, as they do Now.

But it seems that the Government had a true account of it, and several councils were held about ways to prevent its coming over; but all was kept very private. Hence it was that this rumor died off again, and people began to forget it as a thing we were very little concerned in, and that we hoped was not true; till the latter end of November or the beginning of December 1664 when two men, said to be Frenchmen, died of the plague in Long Acre, or rather at the upper end of Drury Lane. The family they were in endeavored to conceal it as much as possible, but as it had gotten some vent in the discourse of the neighborhood, the Secretaries of State got knowledge of it; and concerning themselves to inquire about it, in order to be certain of the truth, two physicians and a surgeon were ordered to go to the house and make an inspection.

This they did; and finding evident tokens of the sickness upon both the bodies that were dead, they gave their opinions publicly that they died of the plague.

27. How did the government find out about the plague outbreak in Long Acre?
    (A) By word of mouth
    (B) Through the printed newspapers
    (C) Through the letters of merchants
    (D) Through the inquiries of the Secretaries of State
    (E) Through the broadcasts of the radio

28. This passage is primarily about
    (A) the statics of casualties of plague
    (B) the journey to Italy
    (C) the first printed newspaper
    (D) true or lie
    (E) the outbreak of plague

29. What was the role of the two physicians and a surgeon?
    (A) To spread the rumors about the plague
    (B) To conceal the truth about the plague
    (C) To determine the truth about the plague
    (D) To improve the reports of the plague
    (E) To prevent the spread of the plague

30. What was the source of information about the outbreak of plague in 1664 in Holland?
    (A) telegrams
    (B) letters
    (C) newspapers
    (D) radio
    (E) television

31. What was the opinion of the physicians and surgeons after their inspection of the bodies?
    (A) The bodies showed no signs of sickness
    (B) The bodies showed tokens of some other illness
    (C) The bodies showed evident tokens of the plague
    (D) The opinion was not mentioned
    (E) The bodies showed nothing explicitly.

→ GO ON TO THE NEXT PAGE

The mastery of English spelling is a serious undertaking. First, we must memorize from one to three thousand irregularly spelled words. The best way to accomplish this is to classify them as much as possible and practice methods of association which will aid in the drudgery of the memorization process.

5   Homonyms are one example of irregular English words. These words are pronounced alike but spelled differently. They can be studied only in connection with their meaning, since the meaning and grammatical use in the sentence is our only link to their form. Therefore, we have to go considerably beyond the mere mechanical association of letters.

10 Besides the two or three thousand common irregular words, the dictionary contains over two hundred thousand other words. Of course none of us can possibly have an occasion to use all of those words; but at the same time, every one of us may sooner or later found ourselves wanting to use any one of them. Because we cannot tell beforehenad what words we shall need, we should be prepared to write any or all of

15 them at the drop of a hat.

Of course we may refer to the dictionary, but this is not always possible. It would be an immense advantage to us if we could find a key to the spelling of these numerous but infrequently used words.

32. What is the primary idea of the passage?
    (A) The importance of memorizing common irregular words.
    (B) The challenges of mastering English spelling and strategies for overcoming them.
    (C) The significance of homonyms in language learning.
    (D) The mechanical association of letters in spelling.
    (E) The impracticality of using all words in the dictionary.

33. The "drudgery" mentioned in line 4 means
    (A) interval
    (B) force
    (C) hindrance
    (D) liaison
    (E) toil

34. How is the phrase "at the drop of a hat" employed in the passage?
    (A) Alluding to an unanticipated descent of headwear
    (B) Implying a disdain for headwear
    (C) Denoting an instantaneous and impromptu reaction
    (D) Characterizing a methodical and unhurried course of action
    (E) Conveying a penchant for donning headgear

35. Considering the content of the passage, one might expect the author to discuss which of the following topics next?
    (A) The Easy Way to Remember Numerous but Infrequently Used Words
    (B) The Impact of Learning Many Foreign Languages
    (C) The Linguistic History of English
    (D) The Most Efficient Way of Increasing Vocabulary
    (E) The Grammatical Uses of Sentences

36. The tone of the author is
    (A) evaluative
    (B) reminiscent
    (C) satirical
    (D) didactic
    (E) querulous

The evening began with a capital farce, Away with Melancholy, and then came the great play, Henry VIII, the greatest theatrical treat I ever had or expected to have. I had no idea that anything so superb as the scenery and dresses were ever to be seen on the stage. Kean was magnificent as Cardinal Wolsey, Mrs. Kean a worthy successor to Mrs. Siddons in Queen Catherine, and all the accessories without exception were good – but oh, that exquisite vision of Queen Catherine! I almost held my breath to watch: the illusion was perfect, and I felt as if in a dream all the time it lasted. It was like a delicious reverie, or the most beautiful poetry. This is the true end and object of acting – to raise the mind above itself, and out of its petty everyday cares – never shall I forget that wonderful evening, that exquisite vision – sunbeams broke in through the roof, and gradually revealed two angel forms, floating in front of the carved work on the ceiling: the column of sunbeams shone down upon the sleeping queen, and gradually down it floated a troop of angelic forms, transparent, and carrying palm branches in their hands: they waved these over the sleeping queen, with oh! such a sad and solemn grace. So could I fancy (if the thought be not profane) would real angels seem to our mortal vision, though doubtless our conception is poor and mean to the reality. She, in an ecstasy, raises her arms towards them, and to sweet slow music they vanish as marvelously as they came. Then the profound silence of the audience burst at once into a rapture of applause, but even that scarcely marred the effect of the beautiful, sad waking words of the Queen, "Spirits of peace, where are ye?" I had never enjoyed anything so much in my life before: and never felt so inclined to shed tears at anything fictitious, save perhaps at that poetical gem of Dickens, the death of little Paul.

37. Which of the following best describes the author's opinion of Mrs. Kean?
    (A) A fortunate heir
    (B) A musical starlet
    (C) A victimized underscore
    (D) A great choreographer
    (E) A brilliant actress

38. The "petty cares" referred to in the passage were
    (A) trivial things
    (B) magnificent sceneries
    (C) pretty angels
    (D) actors on the stage
    (E) Dickens and Paul

39. The author's tone can be described as
    (A) dispassionate
    (B) good-natured
    (C) laudatory
    (D) smug
    (E) sarcastic

40. Which of the following is the best title for this passage?
    (A) A Touching Scene
    (B) Fabulous Garments
    (C) A Trite Synopsis
    (D) A Great Play of My Life
    (E) From Elation to Discontent

IF YOU FINISH BEFORE TIME IS CALLED,
YOU MAY CHECK YOUR WORK ON THIS SECTION ONLY.
DO NOT TURN TO ANY OTHER SECTION IN THE TEST.

SECTION 3

+ Verbal (60 Questions/ 30 Minutes) +

This section consists of two different types of questions: synonyms and analogies. There are directions and a sample question for each type.

Synonyms

Each of the following questions consists of one word followed by five words or phrases. You are to select the one word or phrase whose meaning is closest to the word in capital letters.

Sample Problem:

> CHILLY:
> (A) lazy
> (B) nice
> (C) dry
> (D) cold
> (E) sunny
>
> Ⓐ Ⓑ Ⓒ ● Ⓔ

---

1. DISQUIET:
   (A) protractor
   (B) fledgling
   (C) unsettle
   (D) sprint
   (E) boon

2. SPLICE:
   (A) join
   (B) subdue
   (C) purloin
   (D) encumber
   (E) mingle

3. BEWILDERED:
   (A) rounded
   (B) wan
   (C) succinct
   (D) nebulous
   (E) perplexed

4. JUMBLE:
   (A) mixture
   (B) theme
   (C) premium
   (D) edifice
   (E) paragon

→ GO ON TO THE NEXT PAGE

5. BIZARRE:
   (A) serene
   (B) peculiar
   (C) conspicuous
   (D) pungent
   (E) market

6. RETORT:
   (A) leisurely walk
   (B) unyielding wand
   (C) formidable foe
   (D) snappy answer
   (E) treasure found

7. SHIMMER:
   (A) force
   (B) gleam
   (C) mentor
   (D) vertigo
   (E) reminiscence

8. NUDGE:
   (A) push
   (B) fluctuate
   (C) reconcile
   (D) deprive
   (E) assent

9. MUFFLE:
   (A) recompense
   (B) falter
   (C) assume
   (D) wrap
   (E) encounter

10. REPUDIATE:
    (A) taunt
    (B) placate
    (C) condone
    (D) relinquish
    (E) glimpse

11. FACSIMILE:
    (A) endurance
    (B) replica
    (C) hoax
    (D) vigil
    (E) send

12. ADVERSE:
    (A) unfledged
    (B) inadequate
    (C) tenacious
    (D) profound
    (E) hostile

13. AFFRONT:
    (A) accolade
    (B) insult
    (C) retreat
    (D) creed
    (E) assessment

14. GAUNT:
    (A) inaudible
    (B) enunciated
    (C) stout
    (D) rotund
    (E) emaciated

➜ GO ON TO THE NEXT PAGE

15. INDIGENOUS :

    (A) roaming
    (B) mobile
    (C) recurrent
    (D) native
    (E) fragile

16. SCANTY:

    (A) meager
    (B) ludicrous
    (C) robust
    (D) mindful
    (E) compelling

17. FASTIDIOUS:

    (A) listless
    (B) contagious
    (C) demonstrative
    (D) offensive
    (E) meticulous

18. TENTATIVE:

    (A) graceful
    (B) impudent
    (C) uncertain
    (D) furtive
    (E) convenient

19. SEGREGATE:

    (A) prevail
    (B) feign
    (C) impart
    (D) generate
    (E) isolate

20. AMENABLE:

    (A) abridged
    (B) revised
    (C) brief
    (D) genuine
    (E) compliant

21. THERAPEUTIC:

    (A) strenuous
    (B) healing
    (C) depressed
    (D) lenient
    (E) concurrent

22. DECIMATE:

    (A) annihilate
    (B) elicit
    (C) fortify
    (D) pamper
    (E) grieve

23. RESCIND:

    (A) nullify
    (B) resort
    (C) decoy
    (D) supersede
    (E) appease

24. PORTAL:

    (A) postscript
    (B) utensil
    (C) vista
    (D) gate
    (E) excess

➜ GO ON TO THE NEXT PAGE

25. TOKEN:
    (A) visage
    (B) surplus
    (C) fare
    (D) symbol
    (E) zealot

26. SUBSTANTIATE:
    (A) prove
    (B) debilitate
    (C) enervate
    (D) confer
    (E) subordinate

27. ADROIT:
    (A) concrete
    (B) accommodating
    (C) nimble
    (D) submissive
    (E) transitory

28. PONDER:
    (A) meditate
    (B) subdue
    (C) supplant
    (D) abridge
    (E) trim

29. ZEAL:
    (A) twinge
    (B) compassion
    (C) adversity
    (D) mercy
    (E) ardor

30. ACQUIESCE:
    (A) collate
    (B) rebel
    (C) concede
    (D) shuffle
    (E) defy

→ GO ON TO THE NEXT PAGE

Analogies

The following questions ask you to find relationships between words. For each question, select the answer choice that best completes the meaning of the sentence.

Sample Problem:

> Kitten is to cat as
> (A) fawn is to colt
> (B) puppy is to dog
> (C) cow is to bull
> (D) wolf is to bear
> (E) hen is to rooster

Choice (B) is the best answer because a kitten is a young cat just as a puppy is a young dog. Of all the answer choices, (B) states a relationship that is most like the relationship between <u>kitten</u> and <u>cat</u>.

---

31. Caricature is to portrait as
    (A) illustration is to idea
    (B) cake is to batter
    (C) caravan is to route
    (D) editorial is to magazine
    (E) hyperbole is to statement

32. Distance is to yard as
    (A) foot is to acre
    (B) celerity is to speed
    (C) volume is to pint
    (D) depth is to pound
    (E) speed is to fathom

33. School is to fish as
    (A) pea is to pods
    (B) pride of lions
    (C) corn is to husks
    (D) swarm is to trees
    (E) monkey is to troops

34. Scalpel is to surgeon as
    (A) road is to pavement
    (B) compass is to pilgrim
    (C) cleaver is to butcher
    (D) cockpit is to pilot
    (E) bludgeon is to club

35. Towering is to height as
    (A) winding is to road
    (B) shrinking is to width
    (C) hulking is to size
    (D) appealing is to intellect
    (E) meandering is to stream

36. Foot is to sole as
    (A) hand is to palm
    (B) arm is to elbow
    (C) finger is to digit
    (D) skull is to head
    (E) tooth is to jaw

→ GO ON TO THE NEXT PAGE

37. Mutton is to sheep as
    (A) venison is to chick
    (B) buck is to stallion
    (C) beef is to ewe
    (D) pork is to cutlet
    (E) veal is to calf

38. Obituary is to article as
    (A) fable is to labyrinth
    (B) medley is to chant
    (C) elegy is to poem
    (D) overture is to opera
    (E) verse is to prose

39. Anthem is to song as
    (A) fan is to ventilation
    (B) rake is to leaves
    (C) mop is to floor
    (D) still life is to painting
    (E) cartoon is to strip

40. Scroll is to parchment as
    (A) inkwell is to pen
    (B) book is to paper
    (C) enmity is to amity
    (D) gourmand is to food
    (E) ream is to letters

41. Crane is to raise as shovel is to
    (A) pound
    (B) cringe
    (C) snip
    (D) excavate
    (E) dispose

42. Goat is to kid as
    (A) lamb is to feather
    (B) baby is to crawl
    (C) amber is to jade
    (D) bear is to cub
    (E) cygnet is to swan

43. Senior citizens is to geriatrics as
    (A) children is to pediatrics
    (B) scald is to dermatology
    (C) biodegraded is to biology
    (D) insects is to ornithology
    (E) words is to petrology

44. Newspaper is to inform as
    (A) drama is to caution
    (B) script is to playwright
    (C) novel is to entertain
    (D) fiction is to peruse
    (E) periodical is to concede

45. Recede is to retreat as
    (A) subvert is to inquire
    (B) affirm is to abjure
    (C) depict is to portray
    (D) depart is to arrive
    (E) accord is to genre

46. Movement is to symphony as
    (A) chapter is to book
    (B) archive it to portfolio
    (C) jury is to juror
    (D) diameter is to perimeter
    (E) scene is to director

➜ GO ON TO THE NEXT PAGE

47. Quill is to porcupine as

   (A) leg is to stork
   (B) tree is to grove
   (C) grizzly is to hibernate
   (D) odor is to skunk
   (E) habitat is to chameleon

48. Racquet is to tennis as

   (A) tutu is to ballet
   (B) puck is to hockey
   (C) club is to golf
   (D) lane is to bowling
   (E) gridiron is to football

49. Engine is to automobile as

   (A) sailing is to boat
   (B) navigation is to paddle
   (C) poppy is to lily
   (D) fur is to seal
   (E) locomotive is to train

50. Trickle is to gush as

   (A) tempo is to pace
   (B) scorch is to immerse
   (C) flicker is to blaze
   (D) crease is to fold
   (E) gasp is to garble

51. Beneficial is to helpful as

   (A) ecumenical is to bigoted
   (B) dubious is to skeptical
   (C) decent is to unseemly
   (D) bland is to significant
   (E) luminescent is to somber

52. Singer is to choir as

   (A) domicile is to chairperson
   (B) horse is to harness
   (C) dog is to leash
   (D) cast is to actors
   (E) teacher is to faculty

53. Daydream is to hallucination as

   (A) canyon is to gully
   (B) dragon is to python
   (C) cataract is to cascade
   (D) unicorn is to horse
   (E) cave is to cavern

54. Limousine is to jalopy as

   (A) tepee is to boat
   (B) condominium is to apartment
   (C) edifice is to facade
   (D) mansion is to hovel
   (E) cottage is to bungalow

55. Joust is to lance as

   (A) comment is to speech
   (B) patron is to supporter
   (C) debate is to speech
   (D) electricity is to wire
   (E) poem is to narrative

56. Misdemeanor is to felony as

   (A) confer is to mentor
   (B) purloin is to is to curator
   (C) comprise is to constitute
   (D) filch is to embezzle
   (E) bravado is to arrogance

→ GO ON TO THE NEXT PAGE

57. Timeless is to ephemeral as

   (A) interminable is to transient

   (B) faint-hearted is to fair-minded

   (C) adroit is to proficient

   (D) awkward is to gauche

   (E) malicious is to spiteful

58. Jog is to sprint as

   (A) trot is to tread

   (B) era is to epoch

   (C) glimpse is to stare

   (D) insomnia is to sleep

   (E) sovereign is to authority

59. Cobbler is to awl as

   (A) laconic is to words

   (B) tailor is to scissors

   (C) dancer is to choreography

   (D) plumber is to pipe

   (E) locker is to clothes

60. Tune is to symphony as

   (A) gimmick is to finesse

   (B) sleep is to coma

   (C) impurity is to refinery

   (D) sink is to founder

   (E) clinch is to clarification

IF YOU FINISH BEFORE TIME IS CALLED,
YOU MAY CHECK YOUR WORK ON THIS SECTION ONLY.
DO NOT TURN TO ANY OTHER SECTION IN THE TEST.

SECTION 4

+ Quantitative (Math) (25 Questions / 30 Minutes) +

Following each problem in this section, there are five suggested answers. Work each problem in your head or in the blank space provided at the right of the page. Then look at the five suggested answers and decide which one is best.

Note: Figures that accompany problems in this section are drawn as accurately as possible EXCEPT when it is stated in a specific problem that its figure is not drawn to scale.

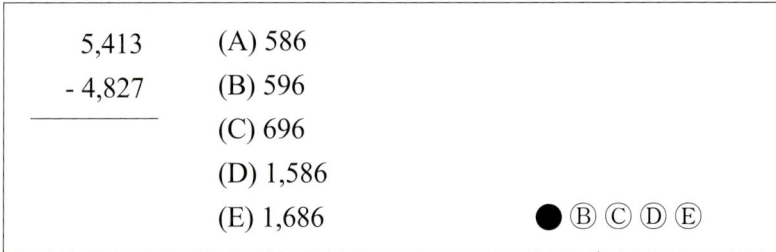

USE THIS SPACE FOR FIGURING

1. How much larger than 20 is 28?

    (A) 0
    (B) 2
    (C) 4
    (D) 6
    (E) 8

2. If a and b are positive numbers and c is a negative number, $ac - b$ must be

    (A) positive
    (B) negative
    (C) zero
    (D) even
    (E) odd

→ GO ON TO THE NEXT PAGE

3. Which of the following number is divisible by 3?

   (A) 125
   (B) 324
   (C) 301
   (D) 407
   (E) 908

4. 13 is one-third of what number?

   (A) 3
   (B) 13
   (C) 27
   (D) 39
   (E) 48

5. A building has $\frac{3}{7}$ of its floors below ground. What is the ratio of the number of floor below ground to the number of floors above ground?

   (A) 3:4
   (B) 4:3
   (C) 3:7
   (D) 4:7
   (E) 3:10

➜ GO ON TO THE NEXT PAGE

6. If snow is falling at the rate of one foot every three hours, how many feet of snow will fall in 9 hours

   (A) 3'
   (B) 6'
   (C) 9'
   (D) 12'
   (E) 15'

7. The charge for phone call is x cents for the first 2 minutes and y cents for each minute after that. What is the cost, in cents, of a phone call lasting exactly m minutes?

   (A) $m - 2$
   (B) $x - 2$
   (C) $x + (m - 2)$
   (D) $x + y(m - 2)$
   (E) $x + (ym - 2)$

→ GO ON TO THE NEXT PAGE

Questions 8-9 refers to the table in Figure 1.

Figure 1

```
**1 = 3
**2 = 6
**3 = 9
**4 = 12
**5 = 15
```

8. According to Figure 1, what would **10 equal?

   (A) 6
   (B) 8
   (C) 10
   (D) 30
   (E) 40

9. Which of following is equal to 27?

   (A) (**3)
   (B) (**3)(**1)
   (C) (**3)(**2)
   (D) (**3)(**4)
   (E) (**3)(**5)

➜ GO ON TO THE NEXT PAGE

Practice Test 2   115

10. There are exactly 12 rows of chairs in a room, with the same number in each row. If only one person can sit in each chair and people are sitting in all but 8 of the chairs, which can be the number of people seated?

    (A) 50
    (B) 54
    (C) 68
    (D) 100
    (E) 106

11. A French bistro offered its menu at 30% off the regular price for mother's day. Alex and his family decided to have dinner there to take advantage of the sale. Since it was Alex's birthday, the restaurant decided to give him an extra 20% off their meal. What percent of the regular menu price did Alex end up paying for his meal?

    (A) 22%
    (B) 30%
    (C) 56%
    (D) 72%
    (E) 88%

12. Colleen has eight pieces of candy while Adam has 14. How many pieces of candy should Adam give Colleen so each of them has an equal amount?

    (A) 2
    (B) 3
    (C) 5
    (D) 6
    (E) 9

→ GO ON TO THE NEXT PAGE

13. A polygon has perimeter of 72 and the average length is 6. How many sides does the polygon have?

    (A) 11
    (B) 12
    (C) 13
    (D) 91
    (E) 588

14. If the average of a set of 25 consecutive whole numbers is 57, then the largest number is how much greater than the smallest?

    (A) 16
    (B) 18
    (C) 22
    (D) 24
    (E) 26

15. $\frac{1}{4}$ of $\frac{2}{3}$ is what fraction?

    (A) $\frac{1}{6}$
    (B) $\frac{1}{3}$
    (C) $\frac{8}{3}$
    (D) $\frac{3}{8}$
    (E) $\frac{3}{7}$

➜ GO ON TO THE NEXT PAGE

USE THIS SPACE FOR FIGURING

16. When Austin bikes to train for his marathon, the 80-mile trip takes between 2.5 and 4 hours. In miles per hour, his average speed must be between
    (A) 8 and 10
    (B) 12 and 16
    (C) 20 and 32
    (D) 22 and 24
    (E) 22 and 36

17. Which is NOT a way to find 19,750 × 1.25?
    (A) (19,750 × 5) / 4
    (B) 19,750 × 5 / 4
    (C) (1,975,000 × 1.25) / 100
    (D) 1,975 × 12.5
    (E) 19,750 (1 × .25)

➜ GO ON TO THE NEXT PAGE

18. Figure 2 shows a square piece of cardboard. If 4 equal squares, each with whole number dimensions, are cut from the 4 corners as represented by the dashed lines, and the cardboard is then folded to make a box with a base of perimeters 24 inches. Which of the following could be the area of the original square piece of cardboard?

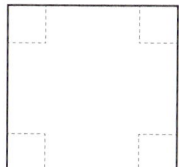

Figure 2

(A) 25
(B) 36
(C) 51
(D) 64
(E) 93

19. If two triangle overlap, the overlapping region can have

   I. fewer sides than a triangle
   II. more sides than a triangle
   III. the same number of sides as a triangle

(A) I only
(B) II only
(C) III only
(D) I and II only
(E) II and III only

20. If y is an integer and $y > 12$, which of the following is the smallest?

   (A) $\dfrac{(y+4)}{y}$

   (B) $\dfrac{2}{(y+2)}$

   (C) y^2

   (D) $2\sqrt{y}$

   (E) $y\sqrt{49}$

21. A length was given at 3 feet instead of 3 inches. How many times too long was it?

   (A) 3
   (B) 10
   (C) 12
   (D) 300
   (E) 900

22. If $x > 2$, which of the following is the least?

   (A) $\dfrac{x}{(x+2)}$

   (B) $x - 2$

   (C) $x + 2$

   (D) $2x - 1$

   (E) $\dfrac{x+2}{x}$

→ GO ON TO THE NEXT PAGE

USE THIS SPACE FOR FIGURING

23. A Christine started her hike in a valley that measured 5 meters below sea level. If three hours later, she had climbed up 12 meters from her starting point, then she had climbed to
    (A) 18 meters below sea level
    (B) 7 meters below sea level
    (C) 16 meters below sea level
    (D) 8 meters above sea level
    (E) 7 meters above sea level

24. If the polygon has a perimeter of 154, and the average length of each side is 11, how many sides does the polygon have?
    (A) 12
    (B) 13
    (C) 14
    (D) 15
    (E) 166

→ GO ON TO THE NEXT PAGE

25. A certain copier prints 700 sheets every 12 minutes. How long will it take the copier to print 12,000 sheets at that rate?

(A) Less than 2 hours
(B) Between 2 and 2.5 hours
(C) Between 2.5 and 3 hours
(D) Between 3 and 3.5 hours
(E) Between 3.5 and 4 hours

IF YOU FINISH BEFORE TIME IS CALLED,
YOU MAY CHECK YOUR WORK ON THIS SECTION ONLY.
DO NOT TURN TO ANY OTHER SECTION IN THE TEST.

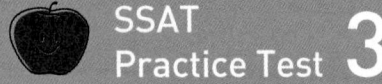

SSAT Practice Test 3

SSAT
Practice Test 3

UPPER LEVEL (Grade 8–11)

Section	Time Allotted (Number of Questions)
Writing Sample	25 minutes (1Q)
Break	10 minutes
Quantitative (Section 1)	30 minutes (25Q)
Reading (Section 2)	40 minutes (40Q)
Break	10 minutes
Verbal (Section 3)	30 minutes (60Q)
Quantitative (Section 4)	30 minutes (25Q)
Experimental (Section 5)	15 minutes (16Q)
Totals	3 hours, 10 minutes

* Of the 167 items including the writing sample, only 150 questions are scored.

ANSWER SHEET 3

Be sure each mark completely fills the answer space.

Start with number 1 for each new section of the test. You may find more answer spaces than you need. If so, please leave them blank.

Section 1

Section 2

Section 3

Section 4

Writing Sample

Schools would like to get to know you better through an essay you write. If you choose to write a personal essay, base your essay on the topic presented in A. If you choose to write a general essay, base your essay on the topic presented in B.

> A. If you could do something over again, what would it be and why?

> B. Should high school students be required to study a foreign language?

Use this page and the next page to complete your writing sample.

Continue on the next page

SECTION 1

+ Quantitative (Math) (25 Questions / 30 Minutes) +

Following each problem in this section, there are five suggested answers. Work each problem in your head or in the blank space provided at the right of the page. Then look at the five suggested answers and decide which one is best.

Note: Figures that accompany problems in this section are drawn as accurately as possible EXCEPT when it is stated in a specific problem that its figure is not drawn to scale.

Sample Problem:

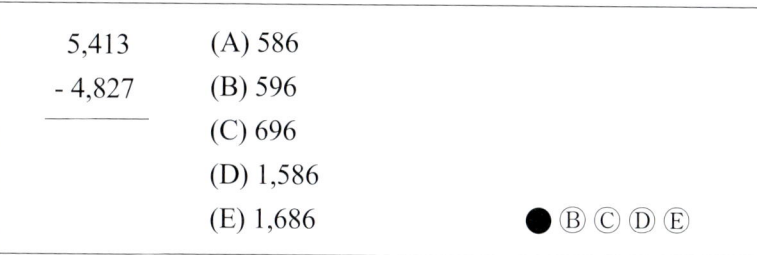

USE THIS SPACE FOR FIGURING

1. Point A (5, -2) is translated 3 units to the left and then reflected over the y-axis onto point A'. What are the coordinates of point A'?

    (A) (-2, 3)
    (B) (-8, -2)
    (C) (-2, -2)
    (D) (5, -5)
    (E) (-5, 2)

→ GO ON TO THE NEXT PAGE

Practice Test 3 **131**

2. What is the remainder when 47 is divided by 8?

   (A) 0
   (B) 3
   (C) 5
   (D) 7
   (E) 9

3. What is the tens digit of 12,497?

   (A) 1
   (B) 2
   (C) 4
   (D) 7
   (E) 9

4. Find the values of $7(a + b)$, if
   $a = 2b - 6$ and $4a + 2b = 16$.

   (A) 9
   (B) 12
   (C) 24
   (D) 36
   (E) 42

→ GO ON TO THE NEXT PAGE

5. Point M, N, O, and P lie on a line, in that order. N is the midpoint of MP and O is the midpoint of NP. If MP = 24, then what is OP?

   (A) 12
   (B) 6
   (C) 7
   (D) 9
   (E) It cannot be determined from the information given

6. 27 is what percent of 3?

   (A) 9%
   (B) 90%
   (C) 900%
   (D) 9000%
   (E) None of above

7. If a $1,200 dress is increased in price by 25%, what is the new selling price?

   (A) $1,105
   (B) $1,225
   (C) $900
   (D) $1,200
   (E) $1,500

→ GO ON TO THE NEXT PAGE

8. There are 243 people in a room, and the ratio of men to women to children in the room is 4:3:2. How many people are adults?

    (A) 27
    (B) 54
    (C) 81
    (D) 108
    (E) 189

9. Every inch on a map represents 90 yards. Approximately how many inches on the map will a 480-yard-long distance be?

    (A) 3.2 inches
    (B) 5.3 inches
    (C) 8.7 inches
    (D) 12.4 inches
    (E) 22.9 inches

10. David can weed a garden in 3 hours. If Richard can weed the same garden in 2 hours, how long will it take them to weed the garden at these rates, working together but independently?

    (A) 7 min.
    (B) 12 min.
    (C) 46 min.
    (D) 60 min.
    (E) 72 min.

→ GO ON TO THE NEXT PAGE

11. The average daily temperature for the first week of May was 31 degrees. If the average temperature for the first six days was 30 degrees, what was the temperature on the seventh day?

    (A) 217 degrees
    (B) 61 degrees
    (C) 37 degrees
    (D) 180 degrees
    (E) 250 degrees

12. 25% of $200 is equal to

    (A) 15% of $150
    (B) 25% of $90
    (C) 30% of $60
    (D) 100% of $50
    (E) 150% of $35

13. 28 students signed up to be camp staffs. No two buses for camp can have the same number of staff. If at least two staff must be on each bus and no more than 8 staff can be assigned to a bus, then what is the least number of buses needed for camp?

    (A) 4
    (B) 5
    (C) 6
    (D) 7
    (E) 8

→ GO ON TO THE NEXT PAGE

USE THIS SPACE FOR FIGURING

14. If $\dfrac{(2+2)}{(3+4)} = \dfrac{\forall}{42}$, then $\forall =$

   (A) 16
   (B) 19
   (C) 21
   (D) 24
   (E) 30

15. Ian shows his class how to cut out paper shapes. If the students cut through both layers of the folded sheets of paper as shown in Figure 1, they can produce any of the following shapes EXCEPT:

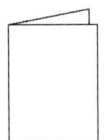

Figure 1

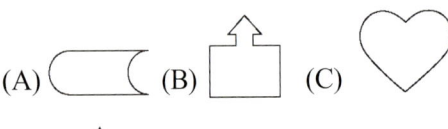

➜ GO ON TO THE NEXT PAGE

16. A new table design has an octagonal shape and a perimeter of 192 inches. How long is each side of the table, in feet?

    (A) 2
    (B) 12
    (C) 24
    (D) 48
    (E) 8

17. An independent school association reported that its schools provided financial aid to 79,000 students, or 82.7 percent of their total enrollment. According to the report, the total enrollment is between

    (A) 50,000 and 100,000
    (B) 100,000 and 150,000
    (C) 150,000 and 200,000
    (D) 200,000 and 250,000
    (E) 250,000 and 300,000

18. In Joseph's car race, he circled the track 30 times in 12 minutes and 15 seconds. What was Joseph's average time for race lap in seconds?

    (A) 22.5
    (B) 24
    (C) 24.5
    (D) 25
    (E) 25.5

19. If one-third of the weight of a jet is 6 tons, the weight of 8 identical planes can be found by multiplying 6 by

(A) $\frac{1}{3}$
(B) $\frac{8}{3}$
(C) 8
(D) 16
(E) 24

20. A distance of 20km separates cities A and B. Ramon left City A and biked the first half at 10km/hour; then he walked the rest of the distance. Ramon took 3 hours to travel from A to B, how fast does he walk?

(A) 3.2 km/hour
(B) 5 km/hour
(C) 6.1 km/hour
(D) 12 km/hour
(E) 30 km/hour

21. In 2011, the population of Town A was 9,600 and the population of Town B was 8,600. Since then, each year the population of Town B has increased by 100. Assuming that in each case, the rate continues, in what year will the two populations be equal?

(A) 2017
(B) 2018
(C) 2019
(D) 2020
(E) 2021

Questions 22-23 refer to the following definition.

For all real numbers x and y,

$A \bigstar B = (A \times B) - (A + B)$

22. $2 \bigstar 7 =$

(A) 3
(B) 4
(C) 5
(D) 6
(E) 7

23. If $Z \bigstar 5 = 27$, then $Z =$

(A) 5
(B) 8
(C) 10
(D) 12
(E) 19

→ GO ON TO THE NEXT PAGE

24. Over a semester, a student takes 9 tests. She earns grades of 83, 82, 99, 73, 94, 88, 82, 98, 100, 100, 74, 82, 85. What is the mode for her test scores?

(A) 78
(B) 80
(C) 82
(D) 88
(E) 100

25. Find the solution to the system of equations.

$y1 = \dfrac{5}{2}X - 3$

$y2 = \dfrac{1}{2}X + 2$

(A) $(\dfrac{1}{2}, 2)$

(B) $(0, -3)$

(C) $(\dfrac{5}{3}, \dfrac{7}{6})$

(D) $(\dfrac{1}{2}, -\dfrac{1}{2})$

(E) $(2, \dfrac{1}{2})$

IF YOU FINISH BEFORE TIME IS CALLED,
YOU MAY CHECK YOUR WORK ON THIS SECTION ONLY.
DO NOT TURN TO ANY OTHER SECTION IN THE TEST.

SECTION 2

+ Reading (40 Questions / 40 Minutes) +

Read each passage carefully and then answer the questions about it. For each question, decide on the basis of the passage which one of the choices best answers the question.

Magnetism is undoubtedly one of the most desirable possessions of the successful pianist. Only some psychologists attempt to fully undercover what magnetism is and how it is derived. We all have our theories, just why one pianist who often blunders as readily as a Rubinstein, who displays his many shortcomings at every concert, can invariably draw larger audiences and arouse more applause than his confrere with weaker vital forces. However, he is admittedly a better technician, a more highly educated gentleman and perhaps a more sensitive musician.

Charles Frohman, the keenest of theatrical producers, attributed the actor's success to "vitality," In doing this, he merely chose one of the weaker synonyms of magnetism. Vitality, in this sense, does not imply great bodily strength. It is rather soul-strength, mind-strength, and life-strength. Professor John D. Quackenbos, A.M., M.D., formerly of Columbia University, explores the following definition of magnetism in his excellent Hypnotic Therapeutics:

"Magnetism is nothing more than earnestness and sincerity, coupled with insight, sympathy, patience, and tact. These essentials cannot be bought and cannot be taught. They are 'born by nature,' they are dyed with 'the red ripe of the heart.'"

Dr. Quackenbos is a physician and a philosopher. Had he been a lexicographer, he would have found magnetism far more inclusive. He would at least have admitted the phenomenon we witness so often when one possessed with volcanic vitality overwhelms a great audience.

1. which of following is true about magnetism?
   (A) It is one of the usual features of musicians.
   (B) It can be taught or bought.
   (C) It stands for a group of excellent pianists.
   (D) It is an unusual, powerful, and exciting quality which attracts people.
   (E) It is a technique for playing the piano.

2. The passage is primarily about
   (A) the origin of the term "magnetism."
   (B) how pianists exercise their magnetism
   (C) reasons why pianists should have magnetism
   (D) the meaning of magnetism and its characteristics
   (E) Dr. Quackenbos's achievement as a Scholar

3. The author mentioned an example of "Rubinstein" because he wanted
   (A) to introduce a skilled pianist
   (B) to debunk a great musician's hypocrisy
   (C) to elaborate on the meaning of magnetism
   (D) to report on the concert scene
   (E) to discuss the greatness of pianists of the century

4. Which of the following is NOT true about John D. Quackenbos?
   (A) He was a hypnotist.
   (B) He was a professor.
   (C) He was a doctor.
   (D) He was a philosopher.
   (E) He was a lexicographer.

5. The word "blunder" means
   (A) to make a gross mistake
   (B) to enclose in something wound
   (C) to deceive by trickery
   (D) to blend by melting together
   (E) to display tact

6. According to the passage, magnetism
   (A) is one of the usual attributes of successful pianists
   (B) draws larger audiences and arouses more applause
   (C) is more than insincerity and hubris
   (D) could be explained by social phenomena
   (E) is soul-strength, mind-strength, and bodily strength

→ GO ON TO THE NEXT PAGE

In the history of black culture, the Harlem Renaissance in the 1920s was a time when African American culture truly was showcased for the country. Indeed, the world and people started to realize the rich legacy available to all people in black culture. The Harlem Renaissance was more than just a greater exposure to black dance, music, comedy, or theater, even though the chance for all people to appreciate the talents of black artists was indeed worthwhile in their own right.

But the Harlem Renaissance also refers to the cultural and social movements of the time in which black pride was beginning to cause significant changes in how African Americans thought about themselves and, eventually, how all Americans thought of black Americans. Many factors led to black culture's explosion, especially in New York City. The city has been a mecca for artists of every culture for as long as it is today. And during this time, the African American population migrated to the north and the urban industrial areas, mainly to take advantage of the economic opportunities there.

7. This passage is primarily about
   (A) the significance of the Harlem Renaissance to African Americans
   (B) the impact of the Harlem Renaissance in New York
   (C) the meaning of the term "Harlem Renaissance"
   (D) a fundamental change in the concept of black artists
   (E) the Harlem Renaissance details

8. It can be inferred from this passage that all of the following statements about the Harlem Renaissance are correct EXCEPT
   (A) it took place in the 1920s
   (B) it was just a limited cultural movement among black people
   (C) it included dance, music, comedy, and theater
   (D) there were significant changes in the way African Americans thought about themselves
   (E) during this time, African American populations moved to places where they could have better economic opportunities

→ GO ON TO THE NEXT PAGE

9. This passage answers the question
   (A) How did the Harlem Renaissance change the thought of black culture?
   (B) Who was the guru of the Harlem Renaissance?
   (C) Who changed the thought of black culture during the Harlem Renaissance?
   (D) Who assessed the value of the Harlem Renaissance?
   (E) What was the economic advantage of black people?

10. As used in the passage, the word "mecca" means
    (A) a time when something is most powerful, successful, or popular
    (B) a place where many people who are interested in culture go there
    (C) a small building or covered place which is made to protect people
    (D) a group of people who are similar in some way
    (E) an artist's studio or workshop

11. The author's tone is best described as
    (A) ambivalent
    (B) somber
    (C) complacent
    (D) objective
    (E) argumentative

→ GO ON TO THE NEXT PAGE

JULIET:
O Romeo, Romeo! Wherefore art thou Romeo?
Deny thy father and refuse thy name!
Or, if thou wilt not, be but sworn my love,
And I'll no longer be a Capulet.

ROMEO: Aside.
Shall I hear more, or shall I speak at this?

JULIET:
'Tis but thy name that is my enemy.
Thou art thyself, though not a Montague.
What's Montague? It is nor hand, nor foot,
Nor arm, nor face, nor any other part
Belonging to a man. O, be some other name!
What's in a name? That which we call a rose
By any other name would smell as sweet.
So Romeo would, were he not Romeo call'd,
Retain that dear perfection which he owes
Without that title. Romeo, doff thy name;
And for that name, which is no part of thee,
Take all myself.

ROMEO:
I take thee at thy word.
Call me but love, and I'll be new baptiz'd;
Henceforth I never will be Romeo.

JULIET:
What man art thou that, thus bescreeen'd in night,
So stumblest on my counsel?

ROMEO:
By a name
I know not how to tell thee who I am.
My name, dear saint, is hateful to myself,
Because it is an enemy to thee.
Had I it written, I would tear the word.

JULIET:
My ears have yet not drunk a hundred words
Of that tongue's utterance, yet I know the sound.
Art thou not Romeo, and a Montague?

ROMEO:
Neither, fair maid, if either thee dislike.

12. What is the main idea of Juliet's first two speeches?
    (A) Roses smell sweeter than men do.
    (B) A name is not as important as the thing or person it names.
    (C) Romeo should not deny his love for Juliet.
    (D) Juliet no longer wants to be part of the Montague family.
    (E) Romeo is a perfect man.

13. What is the main problem Juliet expresses?
    (A) She cannot leave her place.
    (B) She hates her family.
    (C) She cannot love Romeo because he is a Montague.
    (D) She cannot love Romeo because he is a Capulet.
    (E) Romeo will not come to her.

14. In the context of the passage, the word "doff" means
    (A) to remove
    (B) to speak loudly and clearly
    (C) to write
    (D) to be proud of
    (E) to keep a secret

15. What does Juliet offer to do if Romeo swears his love for her?
    (A) Marry him.
    (B) Deny her family name.
    (C) Give him a rose.
    (D) Become his enemy.
    (E) Send him out into the night.

16. When does the action in this scene take place?

    (A) In the morning
    (B) At lunchtime
    (C) In the afternoon
    (D) At dinnertime
    (E) At night

17. What can readers infer about the relationship between Romeo and Juliet?

    (A) They have been in love for a long time.
    (B) They are an old, married couple.
    (C) They have not known each other long.
    (D) They have hated each other for a long time.
    (E) They see each other for the first time in this scene.

18. What can readers infer about Romeo?

    (A) His love for Juliet is more important to him than his name is.
    (B) Juliet is just one of several women he is interested in.
    (C) He often hides behind trees at night to spy on women.
    (D) He has always hated his name.
    (E) He is very attached to his name.

19. What is Juliet's mood when she thinks she is alone?

    (A) melancholy
    (B) contemplative
    (C) angry
    (D) worried
    (E) frustrated

➜ GO ON TO THE NEXT PAGE

I cannot remember a single instance during my childhood or early boyhood when our entire family sat down at the table together, and God's blessing was asked, and the family ate a meal in a civilized manner.

On the plantation in Virginia, and even later, meals were gotten by the children very
5 much as dumb animals get theirs. It was a piece of bread here and a scrap of meat there. It was a cup of milk at one time and some potatoes at another. Sometimes a portion of our family would eat out of the skillet or pot, while someone else would eat from a tin plate held on the knees, and often using nothing but the hands with which to keep the food. When I had grown to sufficient size, I was required to go to the "big house" at
10 mealtimes to fan the flies from the table by means of a large set of paper fans operated by a pulley.

Naturally, much of the conversation of the white people turned upon the subject of freedom and the war, and I absorbed a good deal of it. I remember that at one time, I saw two of my young mistresses and some lady visitors eating ginger cakes in the yard. At
15 that time, those cakes seemed to me to be the most tempting and desirable things that I had ever seen; and I then and there resolved that if I ever got free, the height of my ambition would be reached if I could get to the point where I could secure and eat ginger-cakes in the way that I saw those ladies doing.

20. It can be inferred that the author is a
    (A) baker
    (B) psychiatrist
    (C) historian
    (D) slave
    (E) rancher

21. The style of this passage is most like that found in a(n)
    (A) almanac
    (B) journal
    (C) autobiography
    (D) novel
    (E) news article

22. What was the author's greatest ambition once he was freed?
    (A) To own a big house.
    (B) To attain a high level of education.
    (C) To achieve financial stability.
    (D) To eat ginger cakes.
    (E) To reunite with his family.

23. The most suitable title for this passage is
    (A) Up from Slavery
    (B) We Wear the Mask
    (C) Remembrance of Things Past
    (D) How to Run a Plantation in Virginia
    (E) Baking Ginger Cakes

→ GO ON TO THE NEXT PAGE

24. The "ginger cakes" in this selection symbolize
	(A) freedom
	(B) qualm
	(C) congregation
	(D) envy
	(E) valiance

In the quiet of twilight's embrace,
Aged knight sits in a solemn space.
His armor worn, his visage weathered,
Time's relentless march, he tethered.

5

With weary hands, he takes his sword,
Its hilt once firm, now touched by Lord.
A blade that gleamed in battles bold,
Now whispers tales of tales untold.

10

Shield beside, adorned with scars,
Witness to triumphs, to many wars.
Its surface etched with memories deep,
A guardian faithful in moments steep.

15

The knight, now gray, his eyes do wander,
Back to days when hearts beat fonder.
A youth adorned in armor bright,
Chasing dreams in the morning light.

25. What is the central theme of the poem?
   (A) he knight's current state of mind
   (B) The knight's reminiscence of youth
   (C) The knight's battle-worn armor
   (D) The knight's weariness with his sword
   (E) The knight's favorite battle victories

26. What do the scars on the shield symbolize?
   (A) The shield's invincibility
   (B) The knight's lack of skill
   (C) Decorative elements
   (D) The shield's weakness
   (E) Past victories in battles

27. In the context of the poem, what does the word "tethered" mean?
    (A) connected
    (B) untouched
    (C) free-spirited
    (D) enthusiastic
    (E) abandoned

28. How would you describe the overall tone of the poem?
    (A) joyful and uplifting
    (B) angry and resentful
    (C) excited and adventurous
    (D) somber and reflective
    (E) playful and carefree

→ GO ON TO THE NEXT PAGE

It's nothing short of a marvel that New York City manages to function. The entire scenario seems improbable. Each time the city's residents go about their daily routine, like brushing their teeth, it requires the extraction of millions of gallons of water from the Catskill Mountains and Westchester hills. When a young man in Manhattan decides to pen a letter to his sweetheart in Brooklyn, the romantic message is swiftly transported to her through a pneumatic tube—just like that. The underground network of telephone cables, power lines, steam pipes, gas mains, and sewer pipes is enough to make one contemplate abandoning the island to the whims of fate and the ever-persistent challenges. Whenever the pavement undergoes the slightest incision, it reveals a complex network of connections that are intricately tangled. By all accounts, New York should have faced its demise ages ago, whether from panic, fires, vital supply line failures in its circulatory system, or some convoluted short circuit. The city should have encountered insurmountable traffic chaos at impossible bottlenecks long ago. It should have succumbed to hunger during days when food supplies faltered. The relentless sea surrounding it should have overwhelmed it from every side. The multitude of workers in its various cells should have given in to nerves due to the pervasive pall of smoke-fog, shrouding everything in darkness by noon and leaving higher-ups in a state of suspension. The August heat should have taken its toll on the city's sanity, pushing it off its equilibrium.

29. According to the passage, what happens when a young man in Manhattan writes a letter to his girl in Brooklyn?
    (A) He uses a carrier pigeon.
    (B) The letter is delivered through a pneumatic tube.
    (C) The letter is sent via traditional mail services.
    (D) He hand-delivers the letter.
    (E) He sends a text message.

30. What does the term "ganglia" refer to in the passage?
    (A) Complex network of connections
    (B) Underground transportation system
    (C) Water extraction process
    (D) Pneumatic tube system
    (E) Traffic congestion

→ GO ON TO THE NEXT PAGE

31. What is the theme of the passage?
    (A) The intricacies of New York City's infrastructure
    (B) The daily routines of New York residents
    (C) The challenges and potential crises faced by the city
    (D) The historical development of New York City
    (E) The geographical features of the Catskill Mountain

32. According to the passage, what is one of the potential reasons for New York City's demise mentioned by the author?
    (A) overpopulation
    (B) lack of cultural opportunities
    (C) traffic snarls
    (D) failure of food supply lines
    (E) excessive rainfall

➜ GO ON TO THE NEXT PAGE

"It may be the kind where, at the age of thirty, you sit in some bar hating everybody who comes in looking as if he might have played football in college. Then again, you may pick up just enough education to hate people who say, 'It's a secret between he and and I.,' Or you may end up in some business office, throwing paper clips at the nearest stenographer. I just don't know. But do you know what I'm driving at, at all?"

"Yes. Sure," I said. I did, too. "But you're wrong about that hating business. I mean about hating football players and all. You really are. I don't hate too many guys. What I may do, I may hate them for a little while, like this guy Stradlater I knew at Pencey, and this other boy, Robert Ackley. I hated them once in a while— admit it— but it doesn't last too long, is what I mean. After a while, if I didn't see them, if they didn't come in the room, or if I didn't see them in the dining room for a couple of meals, I sort of missed them. I mean I sort of missed them."

Mr. Antolini didn't say anything for a while. He got up and got another hunk of ice and put it in his drink, and then he sat down again. You could tell he was thinking. I kept wishing, though, that he'd continue the conversation in the morning, instead of now, but he was hot. People are mostly hot to have a discussion when you're not.

"All right. Listen to me a minute now… I may not word this as memorably as I'd like to, but I'll write you a letter about it in a day or two. Then you can get it all straight. But listen now, anyway." He started concentrating again. Then he said, "This fall I think you're riding for—it's a special kind of fall, a horrible kind. The man falling isn't permitted to feel or hear himself hit bottom. He just keeps falling and falling. The whole arrangement's designed for men who, at some time or other in their lives, were looking for something their own environment couldn't supply them with.

Or they thought their own environment couldn't supply them with. So they gave up looking. They gave it up before they ever really even got started. You follow me?"

33. The tone of Mr. Antolini can be best described as
    (A) inquisitive
    (B) disappointed
    (C) concerned
    (D) fearful
    (E) hysterical

34. In this context, "environment" most closely means
    (A) the Earth's natural environment as a nurturing and life-sustaining force
    (B) the external factors that influence a person's experiences
    (C) the practices, beliefs, and characteristics associated with cults
    (D) unconventional ideas and phenomena outside the societal norm
    (E) the rapid production and quick turnover of inexpensive, trendy clothing

35. What is the primary idea of the passage?
    (A) The protagonist's hatred for certain individuals
    (B) Mr. Antolini's perspective on a specific type of fall
    (C) The protagonist's academic achievements
    (D) The protagonist's experiences with football players
    (E) The challenges of finding fulfillment in one's environment

36. What can be inferred about the protagonist's attitude towards people he initially hates?
    (A) His hatred is short-lived, and he eventually misses them.
    (B) He maintains a lifelong grudge against them.
    (C) He avoids any contact with them at all costs.
    (D) He actively seeks revenge against them.
    (E) He continues to despise them throughout the story.

37. It can be inferred that the speaker views Mr. Antolini with
    (A) deep-seated malice
    (B) relative superiority
    (C) chronic conflict
    (D) sincere respect
    (E) genuine empathy

→ GO ON TO THE NEXT PAGE

In the year 1972, biologist Cynthia Moss embarked on a journey to the Amboseli game reserve in Kenya with the intention of studying elephants whose behavioral patterns remained untouched by external influences. These particular elephants, belonging to the African species, were among the least disturbed, as their counterparts faced threats of being killed for ivory and displacement from lands seized for agricultural purposes in different regions.

Unlike their counterparts, the Amboseli elephants enjoyed a state of tranquility where they were neither stripped of their natural habitat nor pursued for their ivory. Within this serene environment, Moss undertook the task of meticulously documenting the intricate social structure of elephants and unraveling the intricate ways in which environmental shifts influenced their behavior.

Moss's revelations illuminated the dynamic nature of elephant society, challenging the assumption that their social structure remains constant. The elephants exhibited a remarkable ability to swiftly adapt to changes in their surroundings. In times of drought, characterized by the scarcity of food, the typically large herds would fragment into smaller, more manageable groups. Conversely, during periods of plentiful rainfall and abundant vegetation, massive herds would coalesce, and bulls, deviating from their usual behavior, would accompany the cows and calves.

Cynthia Moss's profound conclusion resonated with the idea that elephants, as social beings, exhibit a preference for congregating in sizable groups. However, when faced with the adversity of insufficient food resources, they display a resilience to adapt by dispersing into smaller units. This adaptive behavior showcases the remarkable flexibility and responsiveness of elephants to the challenges presented by their environment.

38. According to the passage, why did Cynthia Moss choose the Amboseli game reserve for her study?
   (A) Due to the availability of modern facilities
   (B) To observe elephants disturbed by outsiders
   (C) Because of the peaceful environment for undisturbed observation
   (D) To investigate the impact of agriculture on elephant behavior
   (E) To witness the effects of drought on animal life

39. What does the term "congregate" mean in the context of the passage?
   (A) disperse
   (B) gather
   (C) split
   (D) displace
   (E) scatter

40. Based on Moss's observations during droughts, what can be inferred about elephant herds?
   (A) They prefer to stay together.
   (B) They become more aggressive.
   (C) They disband entirely.
   (D) They exhibit erratic behavior.
   (E) They migrate to other regions.

IF YOU FINISH BEFORE TIME IS CALLED,
YOU MAY CHECK YOUR WORK ON THIS SECTION ONLY.
DO NOT TURN TO ANY OTHER SECTION IN THE TEST.

SECTION 3

+ Verbal (60 Questions/ 30 Minutes) +

This section consists of two different types of questions: synonyms and analogies. There are directions and a sample question for each type.

Synonyms

Each of the following questions consists of one word followed by five words or phrases. You are to select the one word or phrase whose meaning is closest to the word in capital letters.

Sample Problem:

CHILLY:
(A) lazy
(B) nice
(C) dry
(D) cold
(E) sunny

Ⓐ Ⓑ Ⓒ ● Ⓔ

---

1. DELEGATE:
    (A) foe
    (B) critic
    (C) rabble
    (D) impostor
    (E) representative

2. SUPREME:
    (A) doubtful
    (B) crafty
    (C) revengeful
    (D) paramount
    (E) alert

3. AUDACIOUS:
    (A) discreet
    (B) akin
    (C) daring
    (D) ominous
    (E) disputatious

4. FUTILE:
    (A) slippery
    (B) useless
    (C) ornamental
    (D) garrulous
    (E) possible

➜ GO ON TO THE NEXT PAGE

5. PREVALENT:
   (A) studious
   (B) reclining
   (C) common
   (D) congested
   (E) incumbent

6. CHIDE:
   (A) rebuke
   (B) barter
   (C) mingle
   (D) stifle
   (E) amalgamate

7. ILLEGITIMATE:
   (A) durable
   (B) illicit
   (C) lawful
   (D) subtle
   (E) arid

8. AUTHENTIC:
   (A) dogmatic
   (B) reluctant
   (C) genuine
   (D) belligerent
   (E) contentious

9. MEANTIME:
   (A) forewarning
   (B) interim
   (C) exclusion
   (D) magnitude
   (E) incision

10. BRANDISH:
    (A) wield
    (B) overlook
    (C) perplex
    (D) puzzle
    (E) brink

11. TERSE:
    (A) brusque
    (B) grandiose
    (C) flamboyant
    (D) evasive
    (E) splendid

12. STEADFAST:
    (A) competent
    (B) elastic
    (C) complacent
    (D) austere
    (E) unswerving

13. VALIANT:
    (A) jaunty
    (B) elated
    (C) untold
    (D) gallant
    (E) unwarranted

14. HUMILITY:
    (A) humiliation
    (B) perception
    (C) mortification
    (D) nullification
    (E) humbleness

➜ GO ON TO THE NEXT PAGE

15. MOTIF:

    (A) surf

    (B) boredom

    (C) sequel

    (D) bigot

    (E) theme

16. PREPOSTEROUS:

    (A) unassuming

    (B) perilous

    (C) hazardous

    (D) noisome

    (E) ridiculous

17. HAUGHTY:

    (A) tremendous

    (B) stern

    (C) arrogant

    (D) brief

    (E) conventional

18. HURL:

    (A) purloin

    (B) alienate

    (C) fling

    (D) exclude

    (E) censure

19. FRAIL:

    (A) intolerant

    (B) rotund

    (C) stalwart

    (D) feeble

    (E) concise

20. LAVISH:

    (A) profuse

    (B) obsessive

    (C) colossal

    (D) indolent

    (E) coarse

21. PLACATE:

    (A) appease

    (B) harass

    (C) discern

    (D) constrict

    (E) aggravate

22. PENANCE:

    (A) lore

    (B) inattentiveness

    (C) retaliation

    (D) atonement

    (E) resuscitation

23. LETHARGIC:

    (A) laudable

    (B) dense

    (C) terrified

    (D) singed

    (E) languid

24. CLANDESTINE:

    (A) imprudent

    (B) sluggish

    (C) placid

    (D) inane

    (E) surreptitious

→ GO ON TO THE NEXT PAGE

25. PERPETUATE:
    (A) onslaught
    (B) elude
    (C) maintain
    (D) instigate
    (E) mar

26. RETROSPECT:
    (A) reminisce
    (B) provoke
    (C) officiate
    (D) scorn
    (E) torment

27. REIMBURSE:
    (A) comprise
    (B) meander
    (C) compensate
    (D) jeer
    (E) deplete

28. IMPART:
    (A) dominate
    (B) inform
    (C) hag
    (D) gobble
    (E) detain

29. SOJOURN:
    (A) irrefutable evidence
    (B) temporary stay
    (C) charged meeting
    (D) indelible ink
    (E) unconditional love

30. MOMENTUM:
    (A) impetus
    (B) flotilla
    (C) repartee
    (D) rebuttal
    (E) trek

➜ GO ON TO THE NEXT PAGE

Analogies

The following questions ask you to find relationships between words. For each question, select the answer choice that best completes the meaning of the sentence.

Sample Problem:

Kitten is to cat as
(A) fawn is to colt
(B) puppy is to dog
(C) cow is to bull
(D) wolf is to bear
(E) hen is to rooster

Choice (B) is the best answer because a kitten is a young cat just as a puppy is a young dog. Of all the answer choices, (B) states a relationship that is most like the relationship between kitten and cat.

---

31. Pungent is to odor as
    (A) amble is to ramble
    (B) sleek is to texture
    (C) poignant is to emotion
    (D) lanky is to volume
    (E) disrespectful is to etiquette

32. Armada is to ships as
    (A) church is to congregation
    (B) shoe is to laces
    (C) catalyst is to flasks
    (D) apparel is to robes
    (E) regiment is to soldiers

33. Boring is to experience as
    (A) novel is to time
    (B) chronic is to nostalgia
    (C) bland is to taste
    (D) tart is to pastry
    (E) lukewarm is to beverage

34. Artery is to blood as
    (A) hose is to arm
    (B) kite is to string
    (C) aqueduct is to water
    (D) emerald is to gem
    (E) garlic is to cauliflower

35. Necklace is to clasp as
    (A) door is to latch
    (B) arrow is to quiver
    (C) testimony is to witness
    (D) window is to pane
    (E) knob is to hinge

36. Trivial is to trifling as
    (A) dogged is to amenable
    (B) coach is to referee
    (C) unwilling is to reluctant
    (D) frugal is to prodigal
    (E) irrevocable is to optional

➜ GO ON TO THE NEXT PAGE

37. Innate is to acquired as
    (A) nebulous is to opaque
    (B) substantial is to material
    (C) knotty is to facile
    (D) legible is to literate
    (E) solemn is to sublime

38. Grape is to pulp as
    (A) basalt is to salt
    (B) carrot is to onion
    (C) wine is to paper
    (D) drawstring is to pants
    (E) pony is to colt

39. Dermatologist is to skin as
    (A) vegetarian is to animals
    (B) orthodontist is to spine
    (C) dentist is to drill
    (D) oculist is to throat
    (E) mechanic is to car

40. Headstrong is to stubborn as
    (A) sly is to wily
    (B) furnished is to pertinent
    (C) furtive is to disarming
    (D) meager is to ample
    (E) reasonable is to ludicrous

41. Slat is to salt as
    (A) melon is to felon
    (B) yarn is to cloth
    (C) scallop is to oyster
    (D) inept is to adept
    (E) calm is to clam

42. Mongrel is to pedigree as
    (A) goose is to down
    (B) plateau is to plane
    (C) crater is to moon
    (D) prairie is to meadow
    (E) hybrid is to purebred

43. Famine is to food as
    (A) flood is to mist
    (B) drought is to rain
    (C) sweltering is to heat
    (D) dime is to nickel
    (E) feather is to peacock

44. Ladder is to rung as
    (A) shroud is to mummy
    (B) bracket is to parentheses
    (C) staircase is to step
    (D) innuendo is to implication
    (E) tweezers is to tongs

45. Tonic is to invigorate as
    (A) sedative is to soothe
    (B) amnesia is to paralyze
    (C) placebo is to intoxicate
    (D) antidote is to poison
    (E) antiseptic is to contradict

46. Island is to ocean as
    (A) oasis is to sand
    (B) petal is to pollen
    (C) bough is to twig
    (D) core is to crust
    (E) tree is to bark

→ GO ON TO THE NEXT PAGE

47. Talon is to falcon as
    (A) paw is to cat
    (B) turtle is to tortoise
    (C) panther is to feline
    (D) claw is to tiger
    (E) herd is to stampede

48. Stanza is to line as
    (A) burro is to donkey
    (B) truck is to teamster
    (C) anniversary is to celebration
    (D) siren is to alarm
    (E) paragraph is to sentence

49. Book is to preface as
    (A) gala is to genre
    (B) opera to finale
    (C) play is to intermission
    (D) march is to postlude
    (E) Constitution is to Preamble

50. Medley is to song as
    (A) mosaic is to tile
    (B) calf is to veal
    (C) series is to sequel
    (D) souvenir is to memento
    (E) flower is to bouquet

51. Knack is to skill as
    (A) mural is to city
    (B) query is to question
    (C) vein is to blood
    (D) pump is to pail
    (E) water is to inundation

52. Meritorious is to praise as
    (A) disrespectful is to reverence
    (B) browsing is to sip
    (C) throb is to headache
    (D) despicable is to blame
    (E) sustained is to anguish

53. Doe is to buck as
    (A) warlock is to witch
    (B) hive is to apiary
    (C) ram is to ewe
    (D) elm is to oak
    (E) timepiece is to trailer

54. Budget is to money as
    (A) color is to version
    (B) grandfather is to clock
    (C) plan is to agenda
    (D) schedule is to time
    (E) predator is to prey

55. Sumptuous is to meal as
    (A) whimsical is to fancy
    (B) overdue is to time
    (C) ostentatious is to evening gown
    (D) entertainment is to comedian
    (E) chilly is to complain

56. Telepathy is to mind as
    (A) acoustics is to sound
    (B) residence is to dweller
    (C) telekinesis is to movement
    (D) hymn is to song
    (E) telephone is to letter

→ GO ON TO THE NEXT PAGE

57. Apogee is to orbit as
    (A) trench is to mountain
    (B) surmount is to fresco
    (C) crest is to wave
    (D) mountain is to peak
    (E) star is to constellation

58. Funny is to hilarious as
    (A) bellicose is to combative
    (B) venturesome is to timid
    (C) somnolent is to sleepy
    (D) warm is to torrid
    (E) equivocal is to devious

59. Owl is to wisdom as
    (A) cow is to hide
    (B) bouquet is to flower
    (C) wool is to sheep
    (D) pig is to virtue
    (E) ant is to diligence

60. Tapestry is to wall as
    (A) apprentice is to master
    (B) nobility is to royalty
    (C) carpet is to floor
    (D) lamp is to lampshade
    (E) chandelier is to stage

IF YOU FINISH BEFORE TIME IS CALLED,
YOU MAY CHECK YOUR WORK ON THIS SECTION ONLY.
DO NOT TURN TO ANY OTHER SECTION IN THE TEST.

SECTION 4

+ Quantitative (Math) (25 Questions / 30 Minutes) +

Following each problem in this section, there are five suggested answers. Work each problem in your head or in the blank space provided at the right of the page. Then look at the five suggested answers and decide which one is best.

Note: Figures that accompany problems in this section are drawn as accurately as possible EXCEPT when it is stated in a specific problem that its figure is not drawn to scale.

Sample Problem:

$$5,413 - 4,827$$

(A) 586
(B) 596
(C) 696
(D) 1,586
(E) 1,686

● Ⓑ Ⓒ Ⓓ Ⓔ

USE THIS SPACE FOR FIGURING

1. What is 25% of 32?

    (A) 3
    (B) 6
    (C) 8
    (D) 11
    (E) 15

2. What is the product of 0.03 and $4\frac{1}{5}$?

    (A) 0.126
    (B) 0.135
    (C) 0.246
    (D) 0.643
    (E) 0.792

→ GO ON TO THE NEXT PAGE

3. What is 20% more than 80?
   (A) 64
   (B) 72
   (C) 81
   (D) 96
   (E) 100

4. If $y = 4x - 8$, then what is the value of $y - 4$ in terms of x?
   (A) $2x - 4$
   (B) $2x + 4$
   (C) $4x - 2$
   (D) $4x - 10$
   (E) $4x - 12$

5. In Renee's dance class, the average age of the male dancers is 35, and the average age of the female dancers is 25. If 20% of the members are male, what is the average age of all the dance class members?
   (A) 23
   (B) 24
   (C) 25
   (D) 26
   (E) 27

→ GO ON TO THE NEXT PAGE

6. In triangle ABC, the interior angle at A is 49° and the exterior angle at B is 112°. The interior angle at C measures

   (A) 49°
   (B) 63°
   (C) 68°
   (D) 90°
   (E) 117

7. There are 72 marbles in a pouch containing only red and white marbles. If there are three white marbles for every red marble, how many red marbles are in the bag?

   (A) 3
   (B) 4
   (C) 18
   (D) 35
   (E) 72

8. If Deborah paints houses at the rate x houses per day, how many houses does she paint in y days, in terms of x and y?

   (A) $\dfrac{x}{y}$
   (B) xy
   (C) $y - x$
   (D) $\dfrac{y}{x}$
   (E) $\dfrac{(x+y)}{4}$

→ GO ON TO THE NEXT PAGE

9. The price of an antique couch is reduced by 20%, and then this price is reduced by 10%. If the antique couch originally costs $2,000, what is its final price?
   (A) $1,440
   (B) $1,620
   (C) $1,700
   (D) $1,860
   (E) $2,300

10. Which of the following statements is NOT true?
    (A) $12 < 15$ and $1.2 < 1.25$
    (B) $0.7 < 0.777$ and $71 > 0.711$
    (C) $0.75 = 3 \div 4$ and $3.1 < 30$
    (D) $-19 < 1$ and $-65 > -75$
    (E) None of the above

11. Keith travels 90 miles in 1.5 hours. If he travels at the same rate for another 5 hours, how many more miles will he travel?
    (A) 30 miles
    (B) 120 miles
    (C) 150 miles
    (D) 300 miles
    (E) 390 miles

12. Sandra bought a dress at a 50% discount off the sale price, which was already $20 off the regular price. She paid $35. What was the regular price of the dress?
    (A) $30
    (B) $50
    (C) $70
    (D) $90
    (E) $110

13. A cab driver took between 1.5 and 2 hours and two hours to make a 90-mile trip. The average speed, in miles per hour, must have been between
    (A) 10 and 20
    (B) 20 and 25
    (C) 30 and 40
    (D) 45 and 60
    (E) 50 and 60

14. With pipe A, it takes 6 minutes to fill an aquarium. If you use pipe B, it takes two minutes less. If you use pipe A and B together, how long will it take you to fill the aquarium?
    (A) 0.6 min
    (B) 0.8 min
    (C) 1.2 min
    (D) 1.8 min
    (E) 2.4 min

→ GO ON TO THE NEXT PAGE

15. Of the following, 29% of $9.97 is closest to
    (A) $2.15
    (B) $2.89
    (C) $3.25
    (D) $3.50
    (E) $3.60

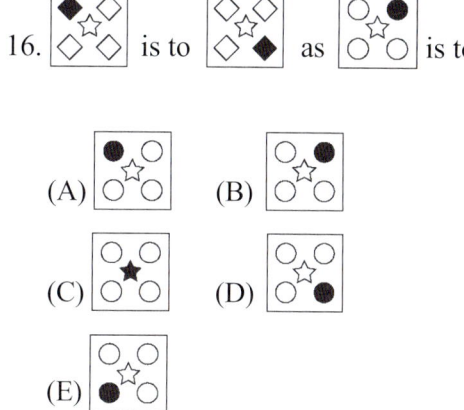

16. [figure] is to [figure] as [figure] is to

    (A) [figure]   (B) [figure]

    (C) [figure]   (D) [figure]

    (E) [figure]

17. Five friends are planning to split the cost of a hotel suite for two nights. Each will pay $180 in total. If one friend cancels at the last minute, and the remaining friends split the cost evenly, how much more would each person spend on the hotel room?
    (A) $45
    (B) $180
    (C) $225
    (D) $270
    (E) $450

18. Ann has $14,600 in savings, on which she receives 6 percent interest per year. How much is half of the interest she earned after a year?

    (A) $438
    (B) $584
    (C) $876
    (D) $4,380
    (E) $87,600

19. From 1990 through 2000, the population of City A increased by 20%. From 2000 through 2010, the population increased by 30%. What was the combined percent increase for the period 1990-2010?

    (A) 10%
    (B) 42%
    (C) 48%
    (D) 56%
    (E) 58%

20. How many distinct digits are in the number 112,345,679?

    (A) 7
    (B) 8
    (C) 9
    (D) 10
    (E) 11

→ GO ON TO THE NEXT PAGE

21. Carrie biked 48 miles uphill at 8 miles per hour and 32 miles downhill at 16 miles per hour. What was Carrie's average mile speed per hour for the entire 80 miles?

   (A) 5.2
   (B) 6.4
   (C) 7.5
   (D) 10
   (E) 12

22. If the lengths of the sides of a right triangle are 5, 12, and 13, what is the area of that triangle?

   (A) 8
   (B) 12
   (C) 15
   (D) 30
   (E) It cannot be determined with the given information.

23. The formula for the lateral surface area S of a right circular cone is $S = \pi r \sqrt{(r^2 + h^2)}$, where r is the radius of the base and h is the altitude. What is the lateral surface area, in square feet, of a right circular cone with a base radius 2 feet and altitude 6 feet?

(A) $2\pi \sqrt{10}$
(B) $4\pi \sqrt{10}$
(C) 15π
(D) $8\pi \sqrt{10}$
(E) $\dfrac{(2\pi + 10)}{4}$

24. 38 x 594 = 22,572

Given the multiplication above, which of the following can be used to find 39 x 594?

(A) 22,572 + 594
(B) 22,572 - 594
(C) 22,572 - 39
(D) 22,572 + 39
(E) 22,572 + 38

→ GO ON TO THE NEXT PAGE

25. If two other black circles are placed on the board so that each column and row has exactly two black circles, what will be the sum of the numbers still showing?

●	6	●	14
3	7	11	●
●	●	12	16
1	●	9	13

(A) 65
(B) 66
(C) 67
(D) 68
(E) 69

IF YOU FINISH BEFORE TIME IS CALLED,
YOU MAY CHECK YOUR WORK ON THIS SECTION ONLY.
DO NOT TURN TO ANY OTHER SECTION IN THE TEST

SSAT Practice Test 4

SSAT
Practice Test 4

UPPER LEVEL (Grade 8–11)

Section	Time Allotted (Number of Questions)
Writing Sample	25 minutes (1Q)
Break	10 minutes
Quantitative (Section 1)	30 minutes (25Q)
Reading (Section 2)	40 minutes (40Q)
Break	10 minutes
Verbal (Section 3)	30 minutes (60Q)
Quantitative (Section 4)	30 minutes (25Q)
Experimental (Section 5)	15 minutes (16Q)
Totals	3 hours, 10 minutes

* Of the 167 items including the writing sample, only 150 questions are scored.

ANSWER SHEET 4

Be sure each mark completely fills the answer space.

Start with number 1 for each new section of the test. You may find more answer spaces than you need. If so, please leave them blank.

Section 1

1 Ⓐ Ⓑ Ⓒ Ⓓ Ⓔ   6 Ⓐ Ⓑ Ⓒ Ⓓ Ⓔ   11 Ⓐ Ⓑ Ⓒ Ⓓ Ⓔ   16 Ⓐ Ⓑ Ⓒ Ⓓ Ⓔ   21 Ⓐ Ⓑ Ⓒ Ⓓ Ⓔ
2 Ⓐ Ⓑ Ⓒ Ⓓ Ⓔ   7 Ⓐ Ⓑ Ⓒ Ⓓ Ⓔ   12 Ⓐ Ⓑ Ⓒ Ⓓ Ⓔ   17 Ⓐ Ⓑ Ⓒ Ⓓ Ⓔ   22 Ⓐ Ⓑ Ⓒ Ⓓ Ⓔ
3 Ⓐ Ⓑ Ⓒ Ⓓ Ⓔ   8 Ⓐ Ⓑ Ⓒ Ⓓ Ⓔ   13 Ⓐ Ⓑ Ⓒ Ⓓ Ⓔ   18 Ⓐ Ⓑ Ⓒ Ⓓ Ⓔ   23 Ⓐ Ⓑ Ⓒ Ⓓ Ⓔ
4 Ⓐ Ⓑ Ⓒ Ⓓ Ⓔ   9 Ⓐ Ⓑ Ⓒ Ⓓ Ⓔ   14 Ⓐ Ⓑ Ⓒ Ⓓ Ⓔ   19 Ⓐ Ⓑ Ⓒ Ⓓ Ⓔ   24 Ⓐ Ⓑ Ⓒ Ⓓ Ⓔ
5 Ⓐ Ⓑ Ⓒ Ⓓ Ⓔ   10 Ⓐ Ⓑ Ⓒ Ⓓ Ⓔ   15 Ⓐ Ⓑ Ⓒ Ⓓ Ⓔ   20 Ⓐ Ⓑ Ⓒ Ⓓ Ⓔ   25 Ⓐ Ⓑ Ⓒ Ⓓ Ⓔ

Section 2

1 Ⓐ Ⓑ Ⓒ Ⓓ Ⓔ   9 Ⓐ Ⓑ Ⓒ Ⓓ Ⓔ   17 Ⓐ Ⓑ Ⓒ Ⓓ Ⓔ   25 Ⓐ Ⓑ Ⓒ Ⓓ Ⓔ   33 Ⓐ Ⓑ Ⓒ Ⓓ Ⓔ
2 Ⓐ Ⓑ Ⓒ Ⓓ Ⓔ   10 Ⓐ Ⓑ Ⓒ Ⓓ Ⓔ   18 Ⓐ Ⓑ Ⓒ Ⓓ Ⓔ   26 Ⓐ Ⓑ Ⓒ Ⓓ Ⓔ   34 Ⓐ Ⓑ Ⓒ Ⓓ Ⓔ
3 Ⓐ Ⓑ Ⓒ Ⓓ Ⓔ   11 Ⓐ Ⓑ Ⓒ Ⓓ Ⓔ   19 Ⓐ Ⓑ Ⓒ Ⓓ Ⓔ   27 Ⓐ Ⓑ Ⓒ Ⓓ Ⓔ   35 Ⓐ Ⓑ Ⓒ Ⓓ Ⓔ
4 Ⓐ Ⓑ Ⓒ Ⓓ Ⓔ   12 Ⓐ Ⓑ Ⓒ Ⓓ Ⓔ   20 Ⓐ Ⓑ Ⓒ Ⓓ Ⓔ   28 Ⓐ Ⓑ Ⓒ Ⓓ Ⓔ   36 Ⓐ Ⓑ Ⓒ Ⓓ Ⓔ
5 Ⓐ Ⓑ Ⓒ Ⓓ Ⓔ   13 Ⓐ Ⓑ Ⓒ Ⓓ Ⓔ   21 Ⓐ Ⓑ Ⓒ Ⓓ Ⓔ   29 Ⓐ Ⓑ Ⓒ Ⓓ Ⓔ   37 Ⓐ Ⓑ Ⓒ Ⓓ Ⓔ
6 Ⓐ Ⓑ Ⓒ Ⓓ Ⓔ   14 Ⓐ Ⓑ Ⓒ Ⓓ Ⓔ   22 Ⓐ Ⓑ Ⓒ Ⓓ Ⓔ   30 Ⓐ Ⓑ Ⓒ Ⓓ Ⓔ   38 Ⓐ Ⓑ Ⓒ Ⓓ Ⓔ
7 Ⓐ Ⓑ Ⓒ Ⓓ Ⓔ   15 Ⓐ Ⓑ Ⓒ Ⓓ Ⓔ   23 Ⓐ Ⓑ Ⓒ Ⓓ Ⓔ   31 Ⓐ Ⓑ Ⓒ Ⓓ Ⓔ   39 Ⓐ Ⓑ Ⓒ Ⓓ Ⓔ
8 Ⓐ Ⓑ Ⓒ Ⓓ Ⓔ   16 Ⓐ Ⓑ Ⓒ Ⓓ Ⓔ   24 Ⓐ Ⓑ Ⓒ Ⓓ Ⓔ   32 Ⓐ Ⓑ Ⓒ Ⓓ Ⓔ   40 Ⓐ Ⓑ Ⓒ Ⓓ Ⓔ

Section 3

1 Ⓐ Ⓑ Ⓒ Ⓓ Ⓔ   13 Ⓐ Ⓑ Ⓒ Ⓓ Ⓔ   25 Ⓐ Ⓑ Ⓒ Ⓓ Ⓔ   37 Ⓐ Ⓑ Ⓒ Ⓓ Ⓔ   49 Ⓐ Ⓑ Ⓒ Ⓓ Ⓔ
2 Ⓐ Ⓑ Ⓒ Ⓓ Ⓔ   14 Ⓐ Ⓑ Ⓒ Ⓓ Ⓔ   26 Ⓐ Ⓑ Ⓒ Ⓓ Ⓔ   38 Ⓐ Ⓑ Ⓒ Ⓓ Ⓔ   50 Ⓐ Ⓑ Ⓒ Ⓓ Ⓔ
3 Ⓐ Ⓑ Ⓒ Ⓓ Ⓔ   15 Ⓐ Ⓑ Ⓒ Ⓓ Ⓔ   27 Ⓐ Ⓑ Ⓒ Ⓓ Ⓔ   39 Ⓐ Ⓑ Ⓒ Ⓓ Ⓔ   51 Ⓐ Ⓑ Ⓒ Ⓓ Ⓔ
4 Ⓐ Ⓑ Ⓒ Ⓓ Ⓔ   16 Ⓐ Ⓑ Ⓒ Ⓓ Ⓔ   28 Ⓐ Ⓑ Ⓒ Ⓓ Ⓔ   40 Ⓐ Ⓑ Ⓒ Ⓓ Ⓔ   52 Ⓐ Ⓑ Ⓒ Ⓓ Ⓔ
5 Ⓐ Ⓑ Ⓒ Ⓓ Ⓔ   17 Ⓐ Ⓑ Ⓒ Ⓓ Ⓔ   29 Ⓐ Ⓑ Ⓒ Ⓓ Ⓔ   41 Ⓐ Ⓑ Ⓒ Ⓓ Ⓔ   53 Ⓐ Ⓑ Ⓒ Ⓓ Ⓔ
6 Ⓐ Ⓑ Ⓒ Ⓓ Ⓔ   18 Ⓐ Ⓑ Ⓒ Ⓓ Ⓔ   30 Ⓐ Ⓑ Ⓒ Ⓓ Ⓔ   42 Ⓐ Ⓑ Ⓒ Ⓓ Ⓔ   54 Ⓐ Ⓑ Ⓒ Ⓓ Ⓔ
7 Ⓐ Ⓑ Ⓒ Ⓓ Ⓔ   19 Ⓐ Ⓑ Ⓒ Ⓓ Ⓔ   31 Ⓐ Ⓑ Ⓒ Ⓓ Ⓔ   43 Ⓐ Ⓑ Ⓒ Ⓓ Ⓔ   55 Ⓐ Ⓑ Ⓒ Ⓓ Ⓔ
8 Ⓐ Ⓑ Ⓒ Ⓓ Ⓔ   20 Ⓐ Ⓑ Ⓒ Ⓓ Ⓔ   32 Ⓐ Ⓑ Ⓒ Ⓓ Ⓔ   44 Ⓐ Ⓑ Ⓒ Ⓓ Ⓔ   56 Ⓐ Ⓑ Ⓒ Ⓓ Ⓔ
9 Ⓐ Ⓑ Ⓒ Ⓓ Ⓔ   21 Ⓐ Ⓑ Ⓒ Ⓓ Ⓔ   33 Ⓐ Ⓑ Ⓒ Ⓓ Ⓔ   45 Ⓐ Ⓑ Ⓒ Ⓓ Ⓔ   57 Ⓐ Ⓑ Ⓒ Ⓓ Ⓔ
10 Ⓐ Ⓑ Ⓒ Ⓓ Ⓔ   22 Ⓐ Ⓑ Ⓒ Ⓓ Ⓔ   34 Ⓐ Ⓑ Ⓒ Ⓓ Ⓔ   46 Ⓐ Ⓑ Ⓒ Ⓓ Ⓔ   58 Ⓐ Ⓑ Ⓒ Ⓓ Ⓔ
11 Ⓐ Ⓑ Ⓒ Ⓓ Ⓔ   23 Ⓐ Ⓑ Ⓒ Ⓓ Ⓔ   35 Ⓐ Ⓑ Ⓒ Ⓓ Ⓔ   47 Ⓐ Ⓑ Ⓒ Ⓓ Ⓔ   59 Ⓐ Ⓑ Ⓒ Ⓓ Ⓔ
12 Ⓐ Ⓑ Ⓒ Ⓓ Ⓔ   24 Ⓐ Ⓑ Ⓒ Ⓓ Ⓔ   36 Ⓐ Ⓑ Ⓒ Ⓓ Ⓔ   48 Ⓐ Ⓑ Ⓒ Ⓓ Ⓔ   60 Ⓐ Ⓑ Ⓒ Ⓓ Ⓔ

Section 4

1 Ⓐ Ⓑ Ⓒ Ⓓ Ⓔ   6 Ⓐ Ⓑ Ⓒ Ⓓ Ⓔ   11 Ⓐ Ⓑ Ⓒ Ⓓ Ⓔ   16 Ⓐ Ⓑ Ⓒ Ⓓ Ⓔ   21 Ⓐ Ⓑ Ⓒ Ⓓ Ⓔ
2 Ⓐ Ⓑ Ⓒ Ⓓ Ⓔ   7 Ⓐ Ⓑ Ⓒ Ⓓ Ⓔ   12 Ⓐ Ⓑ Ⓒ Ⓓ Ⓔ   17 Ⓐ Ⓑ Ⓒ Ⓓ Ⓔ   22 Ⓐ Ⓑ Ⓒ Ⓓ Ⓔ
3 Ⓐ Ⓑ Ⓒ Ⓓ Ⓔ   8 Ⓐ Ⓑ Ⓒ Ⓓ Ⓔ   13 Ⓐ Ⓑ Ⓒ Ⓓ Ⓔ   18 Ⓐ Ⓑ Ⓒ Ⓓ Ⓔ   23 Ⓐ Ⓑ Ⓒ Ⓓ Ⓔ
4 Ⓐ Ⓑ Ⓒ Ⓓ Ⓔ   9 Ⓐ Ⓑ Ⓒ Ⓓ Ⓔ   14 Ⓐ Ⓑ Ⓒ Ⓓ Ⓔ   19 Ⓐ Ⓑ Ⓒ Ⓓ Ⓔ   24 Ⓐ Ⓑ Ⓒ Ⓓ Ⓔ
5 Ⓐ Ⓑ Ⓒ Ⓓ Ⓔ   10 Ⓐ Ⓑ Ⓒ Ⓓ Ⓔ   15 Ⓐ Ⓑ Ⓒ Ⓓ Ⓔ   20 Ⓐ Ⓑ Ⓒ Ⓓ Ⓔ   25 Ⓐ Ⓑ Ⓒ Ⓓ Ⓔ

점선을 따라 오려서 사용하세요

Writing Sample

Schools would like to get to know you better through an essay you write. If you choose to write a personal essay, base your essay on the topic presented in A. If you choose to write a general essay, base your essay on the topic presented in B.

> A. Do you think altering your stance in response to new information is a display of strength or weakness? Justify your response with explanations and examples.

> B. Habits like bicycle riding can be membered for a long time without practicing. What other habits share this trait, and why do you think this occurs?

Use this page and the next page to complete your writing sample.

Continue on the next page

SECTION 1

+ Quantitative (Math) (25 Questions / 30 Minutes) +

Following each problem in this section, there are five suggested answers. Work each problem in your head or in the blank space provided at the right of the page. Then look at the five suggested answers and decide which one is best.

Note: Figures that accompany problems in this section are drawn as accurately as possible EXCEPT when it is stated in a specific problem that its figure is not drawn to scale.

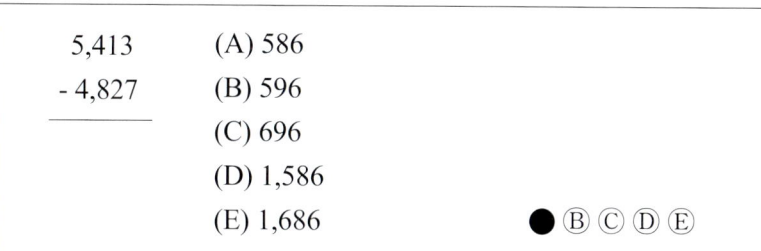

USE THIS SPACE FOR FIGURING

1. Find the missing number in the sequence:

    ____ , 28, 34, 40, 46

    (A) 22
    (B) 24
    (C) 19
    (D) 16
    (E) 14

2. Of the following, 102.29 × (270.58 − 193.79) is closest to

    (A) 70,000
    (B) 8,000
    (C) 7,000
    (D) 5,500
    (E) 5,000

→ GO ON TO THE NEXT PAGE

3. If $x+y=9$ and $x=8$, what value does x^2+y^2 have?

   (A) 30
   (B) 41
   (C) 53
   (D) 65
   (E) It cannot be determined from the information given.

4. Let h represent the height of a rectangle. Which expression would represent the perimeter of this rectangle if the base is five less than the height?

   (A) $h^2 + 5h$
   (B) $4h - 10$
   (C) $2h - 5$
   (D) $h^2 + 5$
   (E) $4h + 10$

5. What is the value of the underlined digit?

   358.7<u>2</u>7

   (A) 2 thousandths
   (B) 2 hundredths
   (C) 2 tenths
   (D) 2 ones
   (E) 2 oneths

➜ GO ON TO THE NEXT PAGE

6. In the multiplication problem 2 x □3, where □ represents an unknown digit. Which of the following could be the product?

   (A) 406
   (B) 546
   (C) 716
   (D) 1,366
   (E) 1,816

7. How many yards of fencing is needed to enclose a 12-yard-long by 24-foot-wide patio?

   (A) 8 yd.
   (B) 24 yd.
   (C) 40 yd.
   (D) 120 yd.
   (E) 384 yd.

8. The average time for each leg of a three-leg bus journey took Carl four hours and twenty minutes. How long did it take Carl to complete the journey?

   (A) 6 hours 20 minutes
   (B) 7 hours
   (C) 9 hours 30 minutes
   (D) 13 hours
   (E) 13 hours 10 minutes

USE THIS SPACE FOR FIGURING

→ GO ON TO THE NEXT PAGE

9. Each person contributed the same whole number of dollars toward a gift. If $80 was collected, which cannot be the amount each person gave?

   (A) $ 0.50
   (B) $ 3.00
   (C) $ 5.00
   (D) $ 20.00
   (E) $ 40.00

10. 28 is 25 percent of

    (A) 14
    (B) 84
    (C) 100
    (D) 112
    (E) 700

11. If W is a number between 0.9 and 1, which of the following is the greatest?

    (A) $\dfrac{1}{W}$
    (B) $\dfrac{W}{1}$
    (C) $W \times W$
    (D) 1
    (E) It cannot be determined from the information given.

➜ GO ON TO THE NEXT PAGE

12. Ms. Han purchased 873 square yards of carpet for $23,571. What was her cost per square foot?

   (A) $0.037
   (B) $3
   (C) $9
   (D) $27
   (E) $23,571

13. A taxi charges $30.00 for the first $\frac{1}{2}$ mile and $7.50 for each additional $\frac{1}{2}$ mile. How many miles can a passenger ride for $60.00?

   (A) 2.5
   (B) 3
   (C) 3.5
   (D) 4
   (E) 7

14. Find the equation of the line through the points (-3, 5) and (2, 1)

   (A) $y = -3x + 3$
   (B) $y = -\frac{12}{5}x + \frac{2}{5}$
   (C) $y = -\frac{13}{5}x + \frac{4}{5}$
   (D) $y = -\frac{2}{5}x + \frac{12}{5}$
   (E) $y = -\frac{4}{5}x + \frac{13}{5}$

15. Tony plans to place a balloon on the chair of each one of his 25 grandchildren attending the family banquet. There are three balloons in each package. How many packages must he buy?

    (A) 5
    (B) 6
    (C) 7
    (D) 8
    (E) 9

16. In a survey, each of 530 bakers was found to own either a spatula, a whisk, or both. If 253 bakers have a spatula and 351 bakers have a whisk, how many bakers have both?

    (A) 74
    (B) 98
    (C) 179
    (D) 277
    (E) 604

17. If $n > 2$, which of the following is greatest?

    (A) $2n + 2$
    (B) $n + 2$
    (C) $n - 2$
    (D) $\dfrac{n}{n+2}$
    (E) $\dfrac{n+3}{n}$

➜ GO ON TO THE NEXT PAGE

18. The teddy bear sales increased from fifty thousand units sold in 2011 to two million units sold in 2015. The number of units sold in 2015 was how many times the number sold in 2011?

   (A) 4
   (B) 40
   (C) 439
   (D) 1,950
   (E) 3,900

19. To which of the following is 7.07 closest?

   (A) 7
   (B) 7.1
   (C) 7.7
   (D) 8
   (E) 71

20. According to a demographic survey, City A has 1.25 millionaires per 1,000 people. If there are 9 million people in City A, how many millionaires are there?

   (A) 11,000
   (B) 1,125
   (C) 1,250
   (D) 11,250
   (E) 12,500

→ GO ON TO THE NEXT PAGE

21. A garden has r parallel rows of plants, with seven plants in each row. If x plants are added to each row, how many plants will then be in the garden, in terms of r and x?

(A) $r + x$
(B) $7r + x$
(C) rx
(D) $r + x + 7$
(E) $7r + rx$

22. In the triangle ABC, the length of AB is 3, and D is the midpoint of AC. What is the length of BC?

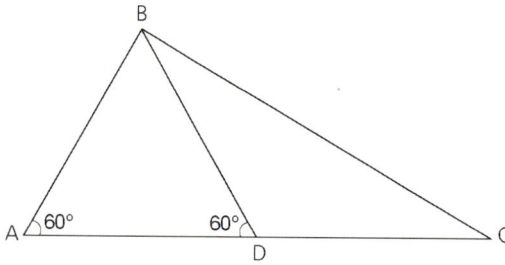

Figure 1

(A) $4\sqrt{2}$
(B) $3\sqrt{3}$
(C) $4\sqrt{3}$
(D) $6\sqrt{2}$
(E) $5\sqrt{3}$

➜ GO ON TO THE NEXT PAGE

23. Michelle would like to buy a school jacket priced at $73, but the price of the jacket is $34 more than she has. Which of the following equations represents the number of dollars Michelle has?

   (A) $x + 73 = 34$
   (B) $x - 73 = 34$
   (C) $x - 34 = {^-}73$
   (D) $x + 34 = 73$
   (E) $x - 34 = 73$

24. Two lines are parallel. If the slope of the first line is $-\dfrac{4}{3}$, which of the following sets of points could lie on the second line?

   (A) (3, 6) and (-3, 10)
   (B) (7, 5) and (4, 9)
   (C) (3, 6) and (-6, -10)
   (D) (-5, 5) and (2, -9)
   (E) (10, 4) and (3, 7)

25. Jessie noted that she is both the 12th tallest and the 12th shortest in the class. How many students are there if everyone in the class is of a different height?

(A) 21
(B) 22
(C) 23
(D) 24
(E) 25

IF YOU FINISH BEFORE TIME IS CALLED,
YOU MAY CHECK YOUR WORK ON THIS SECTION ONLY.
DO NOT TURN TO ANY OTHER SECTION IN THE TEST.

SECTION 2

+ Reading (40 Questions / 40 Minutes) +

Read each passage carefully and then answer the questions about it. For each question, decide on the basis of the passage which one of the choices best answers the question.

    Dr. Sophie Anderson insisted that her father, surgeon Derrick Anderson, never pressured her to study medicine; indeed, he warned her how hard becoming a doctor would be. Her father's fame made her training harder in some ways. "His being so good makes it very difficult," Anderson told a newspaper interviewer soon after she
5   graduated from medical school in 1974. "Everyone knows who Papa is."
    She came by a necessarily tortuous route because the last thing she had wanted as a youth was to follow in her father's footsteps and take medicine. The sight of blood, she said, had always made her knees weak. From age 17, she yearned to teach classics, preferably at Yale, where she eventually went to college. However, no job awaited her
10   after graduation, and, at a loss for what else to do, she enrolled at the College of Physicians and Surgeons in New York. The New York College was then considered one of the best medical schools in the country.

1. The passage suggests Sophie Anderson's medical training was made more difficult because
   (A) her father flaunted his success
   (B) her father warned her not to study medicine
   (C) she was inevitably compared to her father
   (D) she had the benefit of her father's fame
   (E) she did not spend adequate time studying

2. The passage is primarily concerned with Sophie Anderson's
   (A) childhood recollections
   (B) reluctance to collaborate with her father
   (C) route to becoming a doctor
   (D) views of the medical profession
   (E) gratitude for her father's admonishment

3. The type of passage is most likely a
   (A) news article
   (B) narrative
   (C) obituary
   (D) script
   (E) biography

4. As used in the passage, the word "tortuous" means
   (A) twisting or complicated
   (B) easy or ordinary
   (C) beautiful or delicate
   (D) graceful or skillful
   (E) promising or auspicious

5. The attitude of Dr. Sophie Anderson appears to be
   (A) optimistic
   (B) determined
   (C) nostalgic
   (D) tedious
   (E) reluctant

In our fantasies, we become heroes. In the practical world, we must invent them.

Unable to recreate the universe according to our desires, we require heroes in the real world to redeem a fallen world. These seductive figures, bold and daring, promise power to the weak, glamour to the dull, and liberty to the oppressed. They cross borders and advance into new territory. We create real heroes to fit our dreams. In exchange, our heroes alter our lives.

Heroism needs an initial instability; it feeds on the energy released when consensus dissipates and expectations fail. "Unhappy is the land that needs a hero," remarks a character in a play-unmasking misery and risking present pain for the sake of a future ideal. Heroes always rise from uncertainty. And who they are is, initially, unknown.

Villain and hero are each other's shadows. Only at the quest's end, when the whole picture can be retrospectively seen, is success or failure measurable. Only then is the hero distinguished clearly from the fraud.

Ambiguity disappears in retrospect. But then, of course, it is too late. When the hero stands adored at society's center, the hero's life as a hero is effectively finished.

The quest over, the hero rests and rusts and becomes a statue. When this order is, in its turn, threatened, a new hero begins slowly to emerge. Nostalgia replaces the dangerous uncertainty of action.

6. The primary purpose of the passage is to
   (A) identify the characteristics of true and false heroes
   (B) point to conflicting examples of heroism
   (C) consider the relationship between heroes and society
   (D) dismiss the notion of recurrent patterns of heroic action
   (E) question the importance of heroism in daily life

7. In the passage, the author implies the emergence of heroes in society is
   (A) unforeseen
   (B) cyclical
   (C) a necessary evil
   (D) beneficial
   (E) detrimental

8. According to the passage, which statements would characterize a hero?

   I. A hero initially may not be distinguishable from a villain.
   II. A hero is willing to suffer for a cause.
   III. A hero spurs their admirers to become actual heroes themselves.

   (A) I only
   (B) II only
   (C) I and II only
   (D) II and III only
   (E) I II, and III

9. Which of the following statements concerning heroism would the author most likely agree with?

   (A) A hero must be an average individual.
   (B) Individuals who initially appear heroic are, in fact, frauds.
   (C) Societies destroy their heroes with disdain.
   (D) Chance determines who will be regarded as a hero or a villain.
   (E) Periods of unity and peace are not conducive to acts of heroism.

➜ GO ON TO THE NEXT PAGE

Ralph Waldo Emerson is one of the most influential figures in American culture as a speculative thinker and essayist. He was renowned for personal integrity, humanitarian sympathy, persistent curiosity, and broad intellectual interests.

When he was twenty, he converted to the abolitionist cause; his journal for the year 1822 records his conviction that slavery was morally wrong, and Southerners who defended it did so with ingenious sophistry rather than logical reason. Their vested interest in the institution naturally prejudiced them in its favor. Gradually, his opinion of the South's peculiar institution hardened into the mold fashioned by the abolitionists, and as slavery became a national issue and one cause of the Civil War, his antipathy toward slavery came to include the whole region that practiced it.

10. This passage is primarily about
(A) Emerson's response to slavery
(B) Emerson's significant role as a speculative thinker
(C) the abolitionist movements of the nineteenth century
(D) Emerson's analysis of slavery.
(E) the political actions of philosophy student

11. According to the passage, Emerson was famous for all of the following EXCEPT
(A) humanitarian sympathy
(B) personal integrity
(C) faithful fidelity
(D) persistent curiosity
(E) intellectual interests

12. What does the phrase "peculiar institution" refer to in the passage?
(A) Emerson's abolitionist cause
(B) Slavery in the South
(C) Southerners' ingenious sophistry
(D) Logical reasoning
(E) Broad intellectual interests

13. What term is used in the passage to describe the Southerners' defense of slavery?
(A) ingenious sophistry
(B) logical reasoning
(C) personal integrity
(D) broad intellectual interests
(E) humanitarian sympathy

14. How does the tone shift in the latter part of the passage?
    (A) From positive to neutral
    (B) From critical to admiring
    (C) From neutral to approving
    (D) From confused to clear
    (E) From admiring to critical

15. In the context of the passage, the word "vested" means
    (A) fixed and absolute
    (B) holistic and realistic
    (C) variable and multifaceted
    (D) extensive and profound
    (E) fanciful and unrealistic

→ GO ON TO THE NEXT PAGE

Whenever I see a penny on the ground and stoop to pick it up, I can hear my mother saying, "If you're not too proud to pick up a penny, you'll never be poor." When I was a child, I did not understand what she meant; even then, a penny was not worth a great deal. I chalked it up to her having grown up in the Great Depression when a penny did carry some clout. I also remember one day when a friend and I were taking denigrating the job that someone had. She overheard our comments and let us know in no uncertain terms that there is no shame in any honest labor. That lesson too has stayed with me.

As a child, I often wished that my parents were like the ones I saw on television, dispensing wisdom and solving all problems thrown their way in half-hour segments, including time for commercials. And I was stuck with two people who told me what to do when I did not have to be told, or so I thought. I knew what to wear, when to go to bed, or what dangers lurked around me. They did not have to tell me.

Only with age have I realized how much that early advice has formed me. If I find money on the ground, I will pick it up, no matter how minuscule the amount, and put the coin in my pocket. A larger amount requires trying to find the person who lost it if at all possible. If undercharged or given too much change by a cashier, I will point out the mistake and pay the proper amount. In my father's words, "You have to live with yourself." I have tried to make this statement of basic integrity a guiding principle, not because it makes me superior to others but because it allows me to interact with them with greater ease.

16. The narrator's primary purpose in the passage is to
   (A) introduce a setting
   (B) create a mystery
   (C) impart a lesson
   (D) resolve a question
   (E) introduce a character

17. The first sentence of the second paragraph provides a literay device example of
   (A) simile
   (B) metaphor
   (C) alliteration
   (D) hyperbole
   (E) pun

18. In line 4, "chalked" most nearly means
    (A) rubbed
    (B) credited
    (C) wrote
    (D) thought
    (E) clued

19. The narrator's overall tone in this passage is primarily one of
    (A) disgruntlement
    (B) entitlement
    (C) unbelief
    (D) nostalgia
    (E) justice

20. As it is used in the fourth line of the first paragraph, "clout" most nearly means
    (A) nuance
    (B) heaviness
    (C) nuisance
    (D) power
    (E) punch

> This rose-tree is not made to bear
> The violet blue, nor lily fair,
> Nor the sweet mignionet:
> And if this tree were discontent,
> 5   Or wished to change its natural bent,
> It all in vain would fret.
>
> And should it fret, you would suppose
> It ne'er had seen its own red rose,
> 10 Nor after gentle shower
> Had ever smelled its rose's scent,
> Or it could ne'er be discontent
> With its own pretty flower.
>
> 15 Like such a blind and senseless tree
> As I've imagined this to be,
> All envious persons are:
> With care and culture all may find
> Some pretty flower in their own mind,
> 20 Some talent that is rare.

21. What does the rose-tree's discontent or wish to change its natural bent result in?

    (A) Bearing more flowers
    (B) Fretting in vain
    (C) A change in its natural characteristics
    (D) Smelling its own scent
    (E) Producing rare talents

22. In the second stanza, what is the consequence mentioned if the tree were to fret?

    (A) Losing its flowers
    (B) Discontentment with its own flower
    (C) Forgetting its natural bent
    (D) Never seeing its own red rose
    (E) Withstanding a gentle shower

23. Lines four, five, and six provide an example of which literary device?
    (A) onomatopoeia
    (B) alliteration
    (C) personification
    (D) simile
    (E) pun

24. As it is used in the first stanza, the word "mignionet" most nearly means
    (A) a dessert
    (B) an instrument
    (C) an eloquent dancer
    (D) a song
    (E) a flower

25. What literary device is used in the line "And should it fret, you would suppose"?
    (A) Simile
    (B) Personification
    (C) Oxymoron
    (D) Alliteration
    (E) Onomatopoeia

26. As it is used in line 1, the word "bear" most nearly means
    (A) support
    (B) accept
    (C) take
    (D) produce
    (E) allow

27. In depicting the poet's sentiment toward the rose tree in the second stanza, the poet adopts a tone of
    (A) exhilaration
    (B) assertiveness
    (C) contemplation
    (D) premonition
    (E) contempt

→ GO ON TO THE NEXT PAGE

From 1958 through 1963, Project Mercury was the nation's first manned spaceflight initiative. Its objective was to launch a man into Earth orbit and safely return him, ideally before the Soviet Union. It was an early high point of the Space Race. The newly established private space agency NASA took over the US Air Force and carried out 20 unmanned developmental flights (some employing animals) as well as six successful astronaut trips. The crew was referred to as the "Mercury Seven," and each spacecraft's pilot gave it a moniker that ended in "7."

The Soviet satellite Sputnik 1 was launched in 1957, sparking the start of the Space Race. The American public was shocked by this, which prompted the establishment of NASA to quicken already-existing US space exploration operations and turn most of them over to civilian management. The next objective after the successful launch of the Explorer 1 satellite in 1958 was crewed spaceflight. On April 12, 1961, the Soviet Union launched astronaut Yuri Gagarin into space aboard Vostok 1. Soon later, on May 5, the US sent Alan Shepard, its first astronaut, on a suborbital journey. In August 1961, Soviet Gherman Titov made an orbital trip that lasted one entire day. On February 20, 1962, John Glenn announced that the US had achieved its orbital aim. When John Glenn completed three circles of the Earth on February 20, 1962, the US had accomplished its orbital objective. Both countries had sent six astronauts into space by the time Mercury concluded in May 1963, but the Soviet Union had spent more time in orbit than the US overall.

The Manned Space Flight Network, a system of tracking and communications stations, was intended to be used to direct the flight from the ground; backup controls were installed on board. The spacecraft was launched from its orbit using tiny retrorockets, and then an ablative heat shield shielded it from the heat of atmospheric reentry. Finally, a parachute slowed the drone so that it could land on water. Helicopters sent from a US Navy ship rescued the astronaut along with the capsule.

As the Project Mercury acquired popularity, millions of people worldwide listened to and watched its missions on radio and television. Because of its success, Project Gemini was able to develop the space docking techniques necessary for crewed lunar landings in the future.

28. As it is used in the first paragraph, the word "moniker" most nearly means
    (A) tracker
    (B) number
    (C) alias
    (D) alms
    (E) age

29. The most suitable title for this passage would be
    (A) The Importance of Project Mercury
    (B) The Fiasco of the Sputnik Project
    (C) A Brief History of Space
    (D) The Race to Space
    (E) NASA

30. As it is used in the first paragraph, the word "employing" most nearly means
    (A) hiring
    (B) signing
    (C) appointing
    (D) applying
    (E) using

31. According to the passage, what was used in order to control the missions from the ground
    (A) US Navy ship
    (B) Mercury Seven
    (C) NASA
    (D) Manned Space Flight Network
    (E) Vostok 1

32. Which of following is the text type of this passage?
    (A) narrative
    (B) descriptive
    (C) persuasive
    (D) argumentative
    (E) expository

33. According to this passage, NASA's establishment is because of
    (A) the U.S. Air Force's failures
    (B) the Project Mercury
    (C) the competition between the United States and the Soviet Union
    (D) the American Public
    (E) the launching of Project Gemini

➜ GO ON TO THE NEXT PAGE

The Pony Express was a mail service delivering messages, newspapers, mail, and small packages from St. Joseph, Missouri, to Sacramento, California. The mail was delivered on horseback. The riders use a series of relay stations spread across the Great Plains and through the Rocky Mountains and the Sierra Nevada. During its 19 months
5   of operation, the Pony Express reduced the time for messages to travel between the Atlantic and Pacific coasts to about ten days. From April 3, 1860, to October 1861, it became the West's most direct means of east-west communication and was vital for tying the new state of California to the rest of the United States.

In 1860, riding for the Pony Express was challenging; riders had to be rugged and
10   lightweight. A famous advertisement allegedly read:

Wanted: Young, skinny, wiry fellows not over eighteen. They must be expert riders, willing to risk death daily. Orphans preferred.

15   The development of the Pony Express looms taller than truth, a stew of fact and legend. Many young men applied for jobs with the Pony Express, all eager to face the dangers and the challenges that sometimes lay along the delivery route. Despite the legendary full-tilt gallop, the fact is that the rider had to average only ten miles an hour, that in darkness or going uphill, he slowed for safety or to spare the horse, and that he
20   usually arrived on time. Even facts have a legendary flavor.

34. According to the passage, the original purpose of the Pony Express was to
    (A) enable gold prospectors to communicate with one another
    (B) provide entertainment and sports events
    (C) aid new settlers in finding home sites in a foreign region
    (D) inform news of recruitment to new settlers
    (E) help Californian communicate with the rest of the United States

35. The passage implies that a Pony Express rider must be
    (A) feeble
    (B) audacious
    (C) timid
    (D) generous
    (E) frail

→ GO ON TO THE NEXT PAGE

36. As used in the passage, "stew" most nearly means
   (A) commerce
   (B) continuity
   (C) discombobulation
   (D) irony
   (E) blend

37. During its 19 months of operation, what was the Pony Express's significant achievement in terms of message delivery time?
   (A) Reduced time to one day
   (B) Eliminated delivery time
   (C) Increased time to a month
   (D) Maintained the same time
   (E) Reduced time to about ten days

38. Which of the following is the closest in meaning to "looms"?
   (A) weaves
   (B) conveys
   (C) mixes
   (D) appears
   (E) debunks

39. The tone of the passage can best be described as
   (A) incredulous
   (B) prophetic
   (C) illuminative
   (D) querulous
   (E) revealing

40. In the context of the passage's advertisement, the jobs of Pony Express riders were most likely
   (A) sensational
   (B) hazardous
   (C) pleasant
   (D) trivial
   (E) secure

IF YOU FINISH BEFORE TIME IS CALLED,
YOU MAY CHECK YOUR WORK ON THIS SECTION ONLY.
DO NOT TURN TO ANY OTHER SECTION IN THE TEST.

SECTION 3

+ Verbal (60 Questions/ 30 Minutes) +

This section consists of two different types of questions: synonyms and analogies. There are directions and a sample question for each type.

Synonyms

Each of the following questions consists of one word followed by five words or phrases. You are to select the one word or phrase whose meaning is closest to the word in capital letters.

Sample Problem:

> CHILLY:
> (A) lazy
> (B) nice
> (C) dry
> (D) cold
> (E) sunny   Ⓐ Ⓑ Ⓒ ● Ⓔ

1. INQUIRE:
    (A) ask
    (B) load
    (C) demand
    (D) get
    (E) pardon

2. MURKY:
    (A) smooth
    (B) blooming
    (C) sensational
    (D) immortal
    (E) gloomy

3. IMPLICATE:
    (A) imply
    (B) involve
    (C) mislead
    (D) induce
    (E) intricate

4. INFALLIBLE:
    (A) substantial
    (B) omnivorous
    (C) absurd
    (D) unerring
    (E) furious

→ GO ON TO THE NEXT PAGE

5. MERELY:
   (A) lovely
   (B) slightly
   (C) positively
   (D) deadly
   (E) immediately

6. HIDEOUS:
   (A) innocuous
   (B) unsightly
   (C) precocious
   (D) insipid
   (E) gorgeous

7. TEMPORAL:
   (A) earthly
   (B) immaterial
   (C) wasting
   (D) extravagant
   (E) convenient

8. IMPLAUSIBLE:
   (A) dubious
   (B) latent
   (C) fractious
   (D) demure
   (E) frolicsome

9. POLISH:
   (A) revoke
   (B) protect
   (C) retain
   (D) burnish
   (E) conserve

10. TRICKERY:
    (A) deception
    (B) authority
    (C) maneuver
    (D) accuracy
    (E) ecumenical

11. MUNDANE:
    (A) competent
    (B) intransigent
    (C) conclusive
    (D) ordinary
    (E) mandate

12. AFFIX:
    (A) disjoin
    (B) attach
    (C) decode
    (D) manipulate
    (E) relinquish

13. DECREE:
    (A) verdict
    (B) mandate
    (C) imitation
    (D) oracle
    (E) character

14. AUSPICIOUS:
    (A) obsolete
    (B) dogmatic
    (C) mythical
    (D) lugubrious
    (E) favorable

→ GO ON TO THE NEXT PAGE

15. SELF-RELIANT:
    (A) autonomous
    (B) sensitive
    (C) advantageous
    (D) baffled
    (E) venturesome

16. GRATITUDE:
    (A) handicap
    (B) aptitude
    (C) bulletin
    (D) permission
    (E) thankfulness

17. BOURGEOIS:
    (A) daunting task
    (B) middle class
    (C) compelling conundrum
    (D) serious obstacle
    (E) profound mystery

18. BRAZEN:
    (A) humble
    (B) timid
    (C) scarce
    (D) perpetual
    (E) unabashed

19. ELUSIVE:
    (A) agile
    (B) acute
    (C) substantial
    (D) chronic
    (E) ambiguous

20. SIGNATURE:
    (A) maverick
    (B) boycott
    (C) trademark
    (D) brand
    (E) promenade

21. UNCHARTED:
    (A) wimpy
    (B) effective
    (C) unknown
    (D) firm
    (E) unwarranted

22. NEFARIOUS:
    (A) uproarious
    (B) aesthetic
    (C) pragmatic
    (D) amorphous
    (E) egregious

23. BALEFUL:
    (A) threatening
    (B) artless
    (C) exacting
    (D) punctilious
    (E) benign

24. RELAPSE:
    (A) transformation
    (B) organization
    (C) precipitation
    (D) orientation
    (E) deterioration

→ GO ON TO THE NEXT PAGE

25. SWIVEL:
    (A) submerge
    (B) rotate
    (C) adorn
    (D) spurn
    (E) flinch

26. RUSE:
    (A) stigma
    (B) prejudice
    (C) rampart
    (D) blockade
    (E) stratagem

27. QUIXOTIC:
    (A) ribald
    (B) acrimonious
    (C) idealistic
    (D) luminary
    (E) copious

28. REVULSION:
    (A) disgust
    (B) rendezvous
    (C) admiration
    (D) pretension
    (E) grimace

29. INFAMY:
    (A) bedlam
    (B) remission
    (C) notoriety
    (D) amity
    (E) nomination

30. METICULOUS:
    (A) reverent
    (B) limpid
    (C) contrite
    (D) tyrannical
    (E) fastidious

→ GO ON TO THE NEXT PAGE

Analogies

The following questions ask you to find relationships between words. For each question, select the answer choice that best completes the meaning of the sentence.

Sample Problem:

> Kitten is to cat as
> (A) fawn is to colt
> (B) puppy is to dog
> (C) cow is to bull
> (D) wolf is to bear
> (E) hen is to rooster

Choice (B) is the best answer because a kitten is a young cat just as a puppy is a young dog. Of all the answer choices, (B) states a relationship that is most like the relationship between <u>kitten</u> and <u>cat</u>.

---

31. Head is to hammer as
    (A) knight is to armor
    (B) bit is to drill
    (C) sheath is to sword
    (D) hatchet is to axe
    (E) assassin is to rifle

32. Terrestrial is to earth as
    (A) celestial is to sky
    (B) aquatic is to fish
    (C) papal is to city
    (D) municipal is to region
    (E) lunar is to constellation

33. Needle is to sew as
    (A) cane is to walk
    (B) tweezers is to hold
    (C) loom is to weave
    (D) tongs is to pluck
    (E) pliers is to snip

34. Bee is to apiary as
    (A) snake is to hiss
    (B) bird is to aviary
    (C) camel is to stream
    (D) parrot is to jungle
    (E) elephant is to tusk

35. Trucker is to cab as
    (A) balloonist is to parachute
    (B) burro is to wagon
    (C) pilot is to cockpit
    (D) driver is to mill
    (E) taxi is to commuter

36. Pedestrian is to sidewalk as
    (A) orbit is to planet
    (B) train is to caboose
    (C) caravan is to route
    (D) sprinter is to marathon
    (E) spectator is to arena

➜ GO ON TO THE NEXT PAGE

37. Sluggishness is to snail as
    (A) sharpness is to teeth
    (B) softness is to fur
    (C) barking is to dog
    (D) agility is to cat
    (E) pond is to fish

38. Coat is to warmth as
    (A) sandal is to toe
    (B) fan is to breeze
    (C) umbrella is to rain
    (D) sunglasses is to glare
    (E) mitten is to hand

39. Hunger is to eat as
    (A) fumble is to finger
    (B) nose is to sniff
    (C) itch is to scratch
    (D) nap is to sleep
    (E) pain is to injure

40. Ton is to weight as
    (A) ladder is to height
    (B) infinity is to boundary
    (C) sprint is to distance
    (D) millennium is to time
    (E) latitude is to equator

41. Curtain is to privacy as
    (A) crutches is to movement
    (B) knob is to door
    (C) lantern is to illumination
    (D) stethoscope is to surgery
    (E) pane is to sound

42. Gasp is to surprise as
    (A) lie is to honesty
    (B) dishonesty is to distrust
    (C) wheeze is to breathing
    (D) blush is to embarrassment
    (E) squint is to clarity

43. Biography is to life as
    (A) departure is to flight
    (B) envelope is to letter
    (C) epilogue is to end
    (D) memoir is to experience
    (E) catalog is to gift

44. Eclair is to pastry as
    (A) diamond is to gemstone
    (B) thermometer is to temperature
    (C) conductor is to orchestra
    (D) chef is to spatula
    (E) teacher is to classroom

45. Hermit is to reclusive as
    (A) innovator is to imitated
    (B) seer is to intimidating
    (C) extrovert is to sociable
    (D) composer is to harmonic
    (E) narrator is to omniscient

46. Mogul is to power as
    (A) explorer is to tenacity
    (B) sentinel is to danger
    (C) disciple is to magnitude
    (D) sage is to wisdom
    (E) pilot is to direction

→ GO ON TO THE NEXT PAGE

47. Thirst is to quench as
    (A) picturesque is to scenic
    (B) flexibility is to lithe
    (C) uprising is to quell
    (D) chisel is to etch
    (E) ignite is to fire

48. Metal is to weld as
    (A) blowtorch is to lantern
    (B) paper is to glue
    (C) lawn is to mow
    (D) crochet is to yarn
    (E) gold is to ore

49. Singed is to charred as
    (A) meritorious is to detestable
    (B) scald is to fuzzy
    (C) flabbergasted is to humiliated
    (D) dumbfounded is to baffled
    (E) obvious is to conspicuous

50. Anthology is to work as
    (A) thesaurus is word
    (B) semantics is to sound
    (C) lexicon is to origin
    (D) phonetics is meaning
    (E) inventory is to index

51. Wince is to discomfort as
    (A) nod is to disapproval
    (B) salute is to respect
    (C) slur is to articulation
    (D) yawn is to fascination
    (E) sneer is to delight

52. Bow is to arrow as
    (A) pistol is to trigger
    (B) missile is to rocket
    (C) slingshot is to stone
    (D) knife is to blade
    (E) firecracker is to fuse

53. Municipal is to city as
    (A) judicial is to recreation
    (B) interstellar is to moon
    (C) administrative is to park
    (D) maritime is to seafaring
    (E) corporate is to federation

54. Euphemism is to circumlocution as
    (A) simile is to metaphor
    (B) alliteration is to connotation
    (C) caricature is to hyperbole
    (D) annotation is to connotation
    (E) pun is to wordplay

55. Submarine is to porthole as
    (A) rope is to pulley
    (B) camera is to aperture
    (C) piston is to engine
    (D) ceiling is to chandelier
    (E) wire is to electricity

56. Reprehensible is to blame as
    (A) virtuous is to isolation
    (B) enviable is to restriction
    (C) laudable is to praise
    (D) trustworthy is to confidence
    (E) questionable is to ignorance

→ GO ON TO THE NEXT PAGE

57. Contentment is to complacency as
    (A) obedience is to subservience
    (B) vicinity is to province
    (C) threat is to brandish
    (D) prowess is to skill
    (E) substitute is to surrogate

58. Indistinct is to discern as
    (A) quaint is to renovate
    (B) authentic is to real
    (C) practical is to utilize
    (D) abstruse is to comprehend
    (E) valid is to authenticate

59. Skulk is to move as
    (A) eavesdrop is to leave
    (B) abscond is to listen
    (C) lurk is to wait
    (D) hoard is to quiver
    (E) spy is to store

60. Bustle is to hurried as
    (A) fidget is to restless
    (B) suffocate is to humid
    (C) reckon is to unnerving
    (D) comply is to impudent
    (E) soar is to air

IF YOU FINISH BEFORE TIME IS CALLED,
YOU MAY CHECK YOUR WORK ON THIS SECTION ONLY.
DO NOT TURN TO ANY OTHER SECTION IN THE TEST.

SECTION 4

+ Quantitative (Math) (25 Questions / 30 Minutes) +

Following each problem in this section, there are five suggested answers. Work each problem in your head or in the blank space provided at the right of the page. Then look at the five suggested answers and decide which one is best.

Note: Figures that accompany problems in this section are drawn as accurately as possible EXCEPT when it is stated in a specific problem that its figure is not drawn to scale.

Sample Problem:

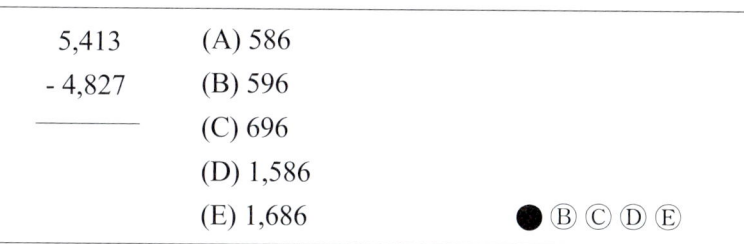

USE THIS SPACE FOR FIGURING

1. $-\left(\dfrac{1}{16}\right)^{\frac{-1}{2}} =$

   (A) 4

   (B) $-\dfrac{1}{8}$

   (C) $-\dfrac{1}{4}$

   (D) $\dfrac{1}{8}$

   (E) 8

→ GO ON TO THE NEXT PAGE

2. If N is an odd number, which of the following is an even number?

   (A) $N + 2$
   (B) $N + 3$
   (C) $(3 \times N) + 2$
   (D) $(2 \times N) + 3$
   (E) $(2 \times N) + 1$

3. A cloth strip $3\frac{1}{4}$ feet long can be cut into how many strips, each 13 inches long?

   (A) 3
   (B) 4
   (C) 26
   (D) 39
   (E) 42.25

4. The average weight of 5 boys is 120 pounds, and the average weight of 3 girls is 100 pounds. What is the average weight in pounds of all 8 children?

   (A) 112.5
   (B) 122.8
   (C) 600
   (D) 720.5
   (E) 900

USE THIS SPACE FOR FIGURING

5. If each of the following numbers is divided by 10, which will have the greatest remainders?
    (A) 11
    (B) 22
    (C) 35
    (D) 44
    (E) 53

6. 23 passengers are waiting in line for a shuttle bus. If at least 1 but no more than 8 passengers must go in each shuttle and no two shuttles have the same number of passengers, what is the smallest number of shuttle buses required to accommodate the 23 passengers?
    (A) 3
    (B) 4
    (C) 5
    (D) 8
    (E) 184

7. If one-half of the weight of a given ship is 302 tons, the weight of four ships of the same weight as the given ship can be determined by multiplying 302 by
    (A) one half
    (B) one and a half
    (C) four
    (D) six
    (E) eight

➜ GO ON TO THE NEXT PAGE

8. Lisa correctly answered 48 questions on her math exam. If she answered 60% of the questions correctly, how many did she get wrong?

   (A) 17
   (B) 27
   (C) 32
   (D) 44
   (E) 58

9. An irregularly shaped field has a perimeter of 936 feet. If each fence segment is 12 yards long, how many segments are required to enclose the field?

   (A) 13
   (B) 26
   (C) 39
   (D) 78
   (E) 11,232

10. The answer to a problem is 48 when the last step is to divide by 2. What would the answer be if the last step had been dividing 4 instead of dividing by 2?

    (A) 48
    (B) 2
    (C) 11
    (D) 16
    (E) 24

→ GO ON TO THE NEXT PAGE

11. Solve for x: -|4x| - 2 = -6

    (A) x = 1 or x = -1
    (B) x = 1
    (C) x = 2 or x = -2
    (D) x = 2
    (E) No real solutions exist

12. In addition to the two 3-digit numbers below, A and B represent two different digits, and the units digit of the answer is zero. What digit does B represent?

    ```
      A 2 A
    + 6 B 9
    -------
      B A 0
    ```

    (A) 1
    (B) 6
    (C) 7
    (D) 8
    (E) 9

13. If the average of the 3 numbers including x, $2x$, and y is $2x$, what is y in terms of x?

    (A) x
    (B) $\frac{2}{3}x$
    (C) $2x$
    (D) $\frac{5}{2}x$
    (E) $3x$

→ GO ON TO THE NEXT PAGE

14. Write 13.2×10^0 as a decimal numeral.

    (A) 0
    (B) 1.32
    (C) 13.2
    (D) 132
    (E) None of the above

15. Five points are placed on a circle. What is the greatest number of different lines that can be drawn so that each line passes through two of these points?

    (A) 6
    (B) 10
    (C) 15
    (D) 21
    (E) 28

16. If a is the greatest prime factor of 38 and b is the greatest prime factor of 10, what is the value of $a+b$?

    (A) 2
    (B) 19
    (C) 21
    (D) 24
    (E) 48

→ GO ON TO THE NEXT PAGE

17. What number, when used in place of a, makes the statement true?

$$\frac{5+a}{3} = 8\frac{1}{3}$$

(A) 3
(B) 4
(C) 15
(D) 20
(E) 25

18. There is the same number of men and women on a bus when it departs from the station. At the first stop, 4 men get off the bus, and nobody gets on. If there are now twice as many women as men on the bus, how many women are on the bus?

(A) 6
(B) 8
(C) 12
(D) 16
(E) 18

19. A family's three children started summer camp on the same day. If the oldest child calls home once every 18 days, the middle child once every 6 days, and the youngest child once every 2 days, what is the least number of days before all would call home on the same day?

    (A) 12
    (B) 18
    (C) 26
    (D) 36
    (E) 40

20. The decimal number consists of only 1's and 2's to the right of the decimal point. The first 1 is followed by one 2, the second 1 is followed by two 2's, the third 1 is followed by three 2's, and so on. What is the total number of 2's between the 98th and the 101st 1 in this decimal?

    7.121221222122221222220⋯⋯⋯⋯

    (A) 281
    (B) 297
    (C) 289
    (D) 300
    (E) 312

→ GO ON TO THE NEXT PAGE

21. David's weight first increased by 10 percent, and then his new weight decreased by 25 percent. His final weight was what percent of his initial weight?

   (A) 62.5%
   (B) 70%
   (C) 72.5%
   (D) 80%
   (E) 82.5%

22. The library has books on Music, Psychology, Communications, Autobiography, and Biology. Of these books, 30 percent are on Music, 30 percent on Psychology, 25 percent on Communications, 10 percent on Autobiography, and 75 books on Biology. If this library has no other books, how many Psychology books are there?

   (A) 150
   (B) 450
   (C) 700
   (D) 1,500
   (E) 7,500

→ GO ON TO THE NEXT PAGE

23. Three lines are drawn in a plane so that there are exactly three different intersection points. Into how many nonoverlapping regions do these lines divide the plane?

    (A) 3
    (B) 4
    (C) 5
    (D) 6
    (E) 7

24. If a and b are odd integers, which of the following must also be an odd integer?

    I. $(a+1)b$
    II. $(a+1)+b$
    III. $(a+1)-b$

    (A) I only
    (B) II only
    (C) III only
    (D) I and II
    (E) II and III

➜ GO ON TO THE NEXT PAGE

25. In the semicircle below, the center is at (3.0). Which of the following are x-coordinates of two points on this semicircle whose y-coordinates are equal?

Figure 1

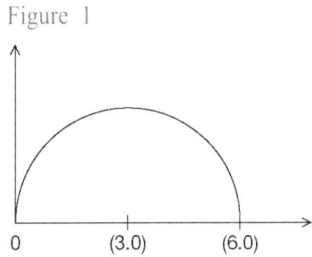

(A) 1 and 4
(B) 1 and 2
(C) 2 and 4
(D) 2 and 5
(E) 3 and 5

SSAT
Practice Test

SSAT
Answers & Explanations

Practice Test 1   229p
Practice Test 2   254p
Practice Test 3   277p
Practice Test 4   299p

TEST ANSWERS

Practice 1

Section 1, 4: Quantitative (MATH) Answer

*Quantitative (Math) scores should be calculated based on the total of 50 questions from Section 1 and Section 4.

pp.27 – 36

TEST 1 SECTION 1 MATH 1

1. A	6. D	11. C	16. D	21. B
2. E	7. B	12. D	17. D	22. E
3. C	8. B	13. C	18. A	23. B
4. B	9. E	14. E	19. A	24. D
5. D	10. E	15. C	20. B	25. C

pp.60 – 71

TEST 1 SECTION 4 MATH 2

1. E	6. D	11. B	16. D	21. E
2. C	7. D	12. D	17. D	22. B
3. B	8. D	13. C	18. D	23. E
4. E	9. E	14. E	19. B	24. D
5. C	10. A	15. C	20. D	25. A

My Quantitative(Math) Score (Section 1 ＋ Section 4)

Right	Wrong	Omitted	Raw Score ($=\text{right}-\dfrac{\text{wrong}}{4}$)	Scaled Score	Percentile
					%

Please consult the Scaled Score & Percentile Chart on the back of this book for the calculation of your Scaled Score and Percentile.

Section 2: Reading Answer

pp.37–51

TEST 1 SECTION 2 READING

1. A	9. B	17. C	25. B	33. D
2. A	10. E	18. E	26. D	34. D
3. C	11. C	19. A	27. B	35. A
4. B	12. E	20. E	28. A	36. B
5. A	13. B	21. B	29. B	37. B
6. D	14. E	22. C	30. D	38. D
7. E	15. C	23. A	31. E	39. C
8. A	16. A	24. B	32. D	40. A

My Reading Score

Right	Wrong	Omitted	Raw Score ($=\text{right}-\dfrac{\text{wrong}}{4}$)	Scaled Score	Percentile
					%

Please consult the Scaled Score & Percentile Chart on the back of this book for the calculation of your Scaled Score and Percentile.

Section 3: Verbal Answer

pp.52–59

TEST 1 SECTION 3 VERBAL

1. A	13. C	25. C	37. D	49. C
2. D	14. C	26. A	38. D	50. A
3. C	15. D	27. D	39. A	51. B
4. A	16. A	28. E	40. E	52. C
5. B	17. C	29. A	41. C	53. B
6. E	18. A	30. D	42. D	54. E
7. E	19. B	31. D	43. B	55. C
8. D	20. E	32. B	44. A	56. D
9. D	21. A	33. A	45. B	57. B
10. E	22. D	34. B	46. E	58. E
11. E	23. C	35. E	47. A	59. A
12. A	24. A	36. C	48. D	60. C

My Reading Score

Right	Wrong	Omitted	Raw Score ($= \text{right} - \dfrac{\text{wrong}}{4}$)	Scaled Score	Percentile
					%

Please consult the Scaled Score & Percentile Chart on the back of this book for the calculation of your Scaled Score and Percentile.

Practice Test 1

SECTION 1

1 A

Given the equation:

$(0.0003)x = 0.0003$

To solve for x, we can divide both sides by 0.0003, which gives:

$(0.0003)x \,/\, 0.0003 = 0.0003 \,/\, 0.0003$

Simplifying the left side, we get:

$x = 1$

Therefore, the answer is (A) 1.

2 E

Given that n is a positive integer divisible by 3, and $n < 60$. We can find the greatest possible value of n by looking for the largest multiple of 3 that is less than 60. The largest multiple of 3 less than 60 is 57.

Therefore, the answer is (E) 57.

3 C

To find the number of books not on sale, we can first find the number of books that are on sale. Since 30 percent of the 330 books are on sale, we can multiply 330 by 0.3 to get:

$330 \times 0.3 = 99$

Therefore, 99 books are on sale. To find the number of books that are not on sale, we can subtract 99 from the total number of books:

$330 - 99 = 231$

Therefore, the answer is (C) 231.

4 B

Alex was paid $9 per hour for the first 10 hours, so he earned:

$10 \times \$9 = \$90$

For the remaining 6 hours, he was paid $12 per hour, so he earned:

$6 \times \$12 = \$72$

Adding these amounts together, we get:

$\$90 + \$72 = \$162$

Therefore, the answer is (B) $162.

5 D

We can solve this problem by testing each option and seeing if we can find an integer value of ✕ that satisfies $x^2 = $ n.

(A) If n = 2, there is no integer value of x that satisfies $x^2 = 2$ (since the square of any integer is positive).
(B) If n = 3, there is no integer value of x that satisfies $x^2 = 3$
(C) If n = 6, we can find that ✕ = 2 is an integer solution to $x^2 = 6$ (since $2^2 = 4 < 6$ and $3^2 = 9 > 6$).
(D) If n = 9, we can find that ✕ = 3 is an integer solution to $x^2 = 9$.
(E) If n = 12, there is no integer value of x that satisfies $x^2 = 12$

Therefore, the answer is (D) 9.

6   D

The equation we can use to solve this problem is:

40% of $n = 60$

We can start by multiplying both sides by $\frac{10}{4}$ to get rid of the percentage:

$(\frac{10}{4}) \times (40\%$ of $n) = (\frac{10}{4}) \times 60$

Simplifying this, we get:

10% of $n = 15$

Finally, we can multiply both sides by 3 to find 30% of n:

$3 \times (10\%$ of $n) = 3 \times 15$

30% of $n = 45$

Therefore, the answer is (D) 45.

7   B

Since 6 out of 10 beds are bunk beds, the probability of randomly selecting a bunk bed is:

$\frac{6}{10} = \frac{3}{5}$

Therefore, the answer is (B) $\frac{3}{5}$.

8   B

The equation we can use to solve this problem is:

$(24 - x) / x = 2$

We can start by multiplying both sides by x to get rid of the denominator:

$24 - x = 2x$

Next, we can add x to both sides:

$24 = 3x$

Finally, we can divide both sides by 3 to find the value of x:

$x = 8$

Therefore, the answer is (B) 8.

9   E

Starting from the A note, let's calculate the pitch differences. Moving up three whole steps would take us to D, as each whole step consists of two half steps (A → A# → B → C → C# → D). Next, we need to move up one half step from D. Since D itself is a white key, moving up one half step would take us to the adjacent black key, D#. Therefore, the musician will end up playing the D# note. The answer is (E) D#.

10   E

If n is a negative number, then dividing it by a positive number (3) will give a negative result. Therefore, option (A) is not necessarily positive. Multiplying a negative number by a positive number (3) will also give a negative result. Therefore, option (B) is not necessarily positive.

Adding a negative number (n) to a positive number (3) can result in either a positive or negative number, depending on the magnitude of n. Therefore, option (C) is not necessarily positive.

Subtracting a negative number (3) from a negative number (n) can result in either a positive or negative number, depending on the magnitude of n. Therefore, option (D) is not necessarily positive.

Subtracting a negative number ($-n$) from a positive number (3) will always give a positive result. Therefore, option (E) must be positive.

Answer: (E) $3-n$

11   C

- Ted uses 4 pieces of tape for each poster, and each piece of tape is 6 inches long. Therefore, he uses 24 inches of tape for each poster.
- There are 12 inches in a foot, so Ted uses 2 feet of tape for each poster.
- If Ted puts up 'n' posters, then he will use $2n$ feet of tape in total.
- If he started with a 200-foot roll of tape and used $2n$ feet, then he will have $200-2n$ feet of tape left.

Answer: (C) $200-2n$

12   D

Let's call the number of chocolates Josephine bought x. According to the problem, Megan bought 39 more pieces of chocolate than Josephine did, which means she bought $x+39$ chocolates.

Together, they bought a total of 173 chocolates, so we can set up an equation:

$x+(x+39)=173$

Simplifying and solving for x, we get:

$2x+39=173$
$2x=134$
$x=67$

So Josephine bought 67 chocolates, and Megan bought $x+39=67+39=106$ chocolates.

Therefore, (D) 106 could be the number of chocolates that Megan bought.

13   C

The probability of Leonardo drawing a boy's name is given by the number of boys in the class divided by the total number of students in the class. Therefore, the probability is:

17 boys / (17 boys + 16 girls) = 17/33

So the answer is (C) 17 in 33.

14   E

- Monica reads 4 pages in 10 minutes, which means she reads 0.4 pages per minute (4/10 = 0.4).
- To read a 128-page book, she needs to read 128 pages / 0.4 pages per minute = 320 minutes.
- 320 minutes is equal to 5 hours and 20 minutes.

Answer: (E) 5 hours 20 minutes

15   C

Let r be the radius of the larger circle.
The shaded area is the difference between the area of the larger circle and the area of the smaller circle:

$32\pi = \pi r^2 - \pi 2^2$
$32\pi = \pi r^2 - 4\pi$
$36\pi = \pi r^2$
$r^2 = 36$
$r = 6$

Therefore, the radius of the larger circle is (C) 6 inches.

16   D

Ratios
- To compare two ratios, we need to make sure they have the same units. We can do this by multiplying or dividing both parts of one or both ratios by the same number.
- In this case, we can multiply the first ratio by 0.5 to get: 0.75 to 0.5.
- This is the same as the ratio 3 to 2.

Answer: (D) 3 to 2

17   D

Since one number is even and one number is a multiple of 5, the third number must be the day in the month of Josh's birthday. The largest number that satisfies this condition is 31.

Therefore, the smallest possible combination would be the even number, the multiple of 5, and 31. The only option that fits this criteria is (D) 20-11-15, where 20 is even, 15 is a multiple of 5, and 11 is the day in the month.

Answer: (D) 20-11-15

18   A

To find the number of erasers per student, we need to divide the total number of erasers by the total number of students. The total number of students is n times k, so the answer is p divided by nk. Therefore, the answer is (A) $\frac{p}{kn}$.

19   A

We can derive the following equation because the sum of interior angles in a triangle is 90 degrees.

$60 + x = 90$
$40 + y = 90$

To find $x + y$, we need to solve for x and y separately and then add them.

From the first equation, we have:
$y = 90 - 40 = 50$

From the second equation, we have:
$x = 90 - 60 = 30$

Therefore, $x + y = 30 + 50 =$ (A) 80.

20   B

Let's call the total number of students in the class 'x'. By 8:00 P.M., 1/4 of the class had arrived, so the number of students who had arrived is $x/4$. By 9:00 P.M., 20 more students had arrived, raising attendance to 1/2 of the class. This means that the number of students who had arrived by 9:00 P.M. is $(x/2) - 20$. We can set up an equation to solve for x:

$(x/4) + 20 = (x/2)$

Solving for x, we get: $x = 80$. Therefore, there are (B) 80 people in the class.

21   B

The perimeter of a circle is equal to the product of its diameter and pi. The diameter of the semicircular piece is 6 inches, so its perimeter is $(\frac{6}{2})\pi + 6 =$ (B) $3\pi + 6$ inches.

22   E

Since 1 liter is equal to 1,000 milliliters, we can convert 28 liters to milliliters by multiplying by 1,000:

28 liters × 1000 milliliters/liter = 28,000 milliliters

Now we can use the information given in the problem to set up a proportion to find the mass of 28 liters of this liquid:

14 milliliters : 16 grams = 28,000 milliliters : x grams

To solve for x, we can cross-multiply:

$14 \times x = 16 \times 28,000$
$x = 16 \times 28,000 / 14$
$x = 32,000$

Therefore, the mass of 28 liters of this liquid is (E) 32,000 grams.

23   B

The distance that Mr. Emerson travels is equal to his rate multiplied by the time he spends traveling. Therefore, the distance he travels in the first t hours is $60t$. Since he has 300 miles to travel in total, the number of miles remaining after t hours is $300 - 60t$. Therefore, the answer is (B) $300 - 60t$.

24 D

Let's start by finding the fraction of marbles that are neither yellow, green, nor blue:

$1 - \dfrac{1}{2} - \dfrac{1}{4} - \dfrac{1}{5} = \dfrac{1}{20}$

This means that $\dfrac{1}{20}$ of the marbles in the bag are red. We also know that there are 2 red marbles, so there must be:

$20 \times 2 = 40$ total marbles

Now we can find the number of green marbles:

$\dfrac{1}{4}$ of the marbles are green, so

$(\dfrac{1}{4}) \times 40 = 10$

So there are 10 green marbles in the bag. The answer is (D) 10.

25 C

The sum of the integers from -25 to x can be found using the formula:

sum $= (n/2) \times$ (first + last)

where n is the number of integers in the sequence, and first and last are the first and last integers in the sequence, respectively.

The number of integers from -25 to x is $(x - (-25) + 1) = (x + 26)$, so we can set up an equation to solve for x:

$81 = ((x + 26) / 2) \ (-25 + x)$

Multiplying both sides by 2 and simplifying, we get:

$162 = (x + 26)(x - 25)$

Expanding and simplifying, we get:

$x^2 + x - 662 = 0$

The negative root is extraneous, so we take the positive root and get:

$x =$ (C) 28

SECTION 2

Questions 1-5

Excerpt from "Treasure Island" by Robert Louis Stevenson (1883)

The man in the story is a quiet, solitary figure who spends his days watching the cove with a telescope and drinking rum at night. He frequently asks if any seafaring men have passed by but seems to be avoiding them when they do. He hires the narrator to keep an eye out for a seafaring man with one leg and pays him a silver fourpenny each month. The narrator becomes frightened by the idea of this man and has nightmares about him.

1   A

In line 7, "At first we thought it was the want of company of his own kind that made him ask this question, but at last, we began to see he was desirous to avoid them," we can find the man asks every day if any seafaring men have passed by because he wants to avoid encountering them.

2   A

The author continues to think about this seafaring one legged man with great fear. He is all consumed by his fear, he even sees it in his nightmares. Therefore, he has an obsessive tone as he describes his thoughts.

3   C

Fancies are imaginative thoughts. We know this because of the context. Previously in this paragraph, the speaker tells the reader of his nightmares and dreams for his imagination.

4   B

The watchman paid for receiving the monthly fourpenny piece by his lack of peace. The reader will know this because he ends the sentence with "in the shape of abominable fancies." These fancies caused him unrest.

5   A

The words "put up at" shows the reader Admiral Benbow is most likely a place where one stays during their travels. While Admiral Benbow could be a person, in the context, it is referring to a place that is quite possibly named after a person.

Questions 6-10

The author discusses the meaning of certain phrases in the English language, noting that some are self-evident while others are not. The author mentions that explanations for the origin of such phrases are often suggested, but are often not convincing. The author gives an example of a popular dictionary linking the word "pundit" to "pun," but explains that they actually have different origins and meanings.

Here are some more examples of idioms or phrases with unclear origins:

- **Barking up the wrong tree**: "barking up the wrong tree" is an idiomatic expression used to describe a situation where someone is making a wrong assumption or pursuing a mistaken or misguided course of action. It can also refer to someone who is blaming or accusing the wrong person or thing. For example, if someone is blaming their co-worker for a mistake that they did not actually make, they could be said to be "barking up the wrong tree."

- **Bite the bullet** : "Bite the bullet" is an idiomatic expression that means to face a difficult or unpleasant situation with courage and determination. The phrase originally referred to soldiers who were instructed to bite on a bullet during surgery to help manage the pain. The phrase is now used more generally to refer to facing any situation that requires a great deal of courage and fortitude.

- **Cry over spilled milk** : "Cry over spilled milk" is an idiomatic expression that means to mourn or complain about something that has already happened and cannot be changed. It's used to encourage someone to accept a difficult situation and move on instead of dwelling on it.
- **Cut the mustard** : "Cut the mustard" is an idiomatic expression that means to meet or exceed expectations, to perform adequately or satisfactorily. It can also refer to the ability to measure up to a standard or requirement.
- **Full of beans** : "Full of beans" means energetic and lively. It's used to describe someone who is feeling enthusiastic and ready to tackle anything that comes their way. The phrase typically implies that the person is full of energy, like they have a lot of "beans" inside of them.
- **Get up on the wrong side of bed** : To be in a bad mood or grumpy from the start of the day, as if one woke up on the "wrong side" of the bed.
- **Hang in there** : "Hang in there" means to persist, endure, and remain strong or steadfast in the face of difficulties or challenges. It is a phrase of encouragement to someone who may be struggling or facing a difficult situation, implying that they should maintain their resolve and keep going.
- **Jump the gun** : "Jump the gun" means to act prematurely or impulsively, especially in starting an action or process before the appropriate or opportune moment.
- **Kick the bucket** : "Kick the bucket" is an idiomatic expression that means to die or pass away.

- **Let the cat out of the bag** : "Let the cat out of the bag" is an idiom that means to reveal a secret or surprise unintentionally or carelessly.
- **Pull someone's leg** : "Pull someone's leg" means to tease or play a practical joke on someone, often in a good-natured way.
- **Rain on someone's parade** : "Rain on someone's parade" means to spoil or ruin someone's plans or to dampen someone's enthusiasm or excitement.
- **Sleep like a baby** : "Sleep like a baby" means To sleep soundly and peacefully.
- **Take the bull by the horns** : "Take the bull by the horns" is an idiomatic expression meaning to take decisive and immediate action to deal with a difficult or challenging situation. It comes from bullfighting, where a bullfighter would grab the bull by its horns to control it. In a metaphorical sense, the expression means to confront a problem head-on and handle it with determination and courage.
- **Turn over a new leaf** : To "turn over a new leaf" means to change one's behavior or habits for the better and start anew. It is often used to describe someone who has made a resolution to improve their life or overcome a negative aspect of their behavior.

These phrases are often used in conversation and carry figurative meanings that can be quite different from their literal meanings.

6　　　　　　　　　　　　　　　　　　**D**

The author is looking for a phrase that does not have a self-evident meaning, and "apple of my eye" fits this description as its origin is unclear.

7　　　　　　　　　　　　　　　　　　**E**

The last sentence explains the origin and meaning of the word "pundit" in contrast to the incorrect suggestion that it is related to "pun."

8   **A**

"Self-evident" means that something is clear and obvious without needing to be explained.

9   **B**

"Out of the blue" means that something happens suddenly and unexpectedly, without any warning.

10   **E**

The main idea of the passage is that some phrases have unclear or unexpected origins and meanings, despite being commonly used in language.

Questions 11-15

The article discusses recent experiments at the University of Iowa that challenge the belief that only humans have the ability to recognize human facial expressions. The experiments showed that pigeons can learn to recognize emotions in photographs of human faces, even those of unfamiliar faces. This challenges the theory that only humans have specialized nervous systems for recognizing emotions, and suggests that the ability to recognize expressions may have to be learned, like how pigeons learned in the experiments. The findings align with Charles Darwin's theory of the continuity of mental development from animals to humans.

11   **C**

The passage discusses the ability of pigeons to recognize human facial expressions, and how this ability challenges previous beliefs about the uniqueness of the human nervous system. The passage also discusses the continuity of mental development from animals to humans, which supports the idea that there is a mental continuity between animals and humans.

12   **E**

The passage challenges the idea that humans are superior to animals in terms of their ability to recognize facial expressions. The author presents evidence that pigeons can also recognize facial expressions and suggests that the ability to recognize facial expressions may not be inherent even in human babies but may have to be learned in much the same way as pigeons learn.

13   **B**

The author suggests that the ability to recognize facial expressions may not be inherent even in human babies, which implies that it is not instinctive.

14   **E**

The author presents the findings of the experiments in a straightforward manner, without expressing a particularly positive or negative attitude toward them.

15   **C**

The experiments with pigeons further confirm Darwin's evolutionary theories. The author notes that the findings of the experiments would not surprise Charles Darwin, who long ago wrote about the continuity of mental development from animals to humans. This suggests that the experiments with pigeons support Darwin's theories about the evolution of mental capabilities in animals.

Questions 16-21

The excerpt describes a writer who becomes consumed by the process of writing a book, to the point where her behavior becomes erratic and she becomes increasingly anxious. The writer has a particular interest in historical fiction and believes that great characters can only exist in great times, and that understanding violence, the differences between past and present people, and the power of the dead over the living is necessary for writing historical fiction. The writer also wants to reflect on the motivations and mindset of a person who writes about the past.

16   A

The narrator is describing a writer who is deeply immersed and obsessed with completing her book, to the point of neglecting other aspects of her life. She is consumed by her work, exhibiting signs of intense focus and anxiety.

17   C

She stops for one thing; therefore, just is the correct word to replace only in this context.

18   E

This is a simile because of the comparison using the words "like" and "as."

19   A

The passage describes the writer's increasing anxiety, feeling like stage fright, and being terrified of making a mistake.

20   E

The author is more focused on describing the writer and her thoughts even more so than the process of writing.

21   B

The passage primarily discusses the writer's intense focus on completing her book, particularly in the context of writing historical fiction.

Questions 22-24

Honore de Balzac is a French novelist who is considered one of the founders of realism in European literature. He was known for his keen observation of detail and complex, morally ambiguous characters. He also imbued inanimate objects with character. Despite showing financial wisdom in his fiction, Balzac lost all his money in real life, and the same can be said of his relationships with women, who were drawn to him through his fiction but were disappointed by his real-life insensitivity.

22   C

Balzac was paradoxically successful in his fiction while struggling in real life, as seen in his financial situation and in his relationships with women who were attracted to the characters he created but were disappointed by his own personality.

23   A

It is used to illustrate how his imagination was shaped and how he discovered that life is a prison and only imagination can open its doors.

24 B

"multifaceted" in the context means "versatile," meaning having diverse aspects.

Questions 25-30

The excerpt is a narrative of the coming of the hound in the Baskerville family, as told by Dr. Mortimer. The hound, described as a "foul thing" and "great black beast," killed Hugo Baskerville and caused terror in three daredevil men who witnessed the event. The narrative implies that the hound has caused many sudden, bloody, and mysterious deaths in the family over the generations. The author of the narrative, Hugo Baskerville, instructs his sons Rodger and John to take caution and avoid crossing the moor during the dark hours. After Dr. Mortimer finishes reading the narrative, he looks to Sherlock Holmes, who is unimpressed and indifferent.

25 B

Sherlock Holmes is introduced when Dr. Mortimer, "stared across at Mr. Sherlock Holmes." When the writing says, "the latter," it means the last mentioned person, which is Sherlock Holmes.

26 D

Apathetic is another word for unmoved or unconcerned. Sherlock Holmes' actions depict someone who is unmoved by the story, "The latter yawned…fire."

27 B

This is a metaphor due to the comparison of eyes blazing. His eyes were not literally ablaze.

28 A

This excerpt is suspenseful and leaves the reader with a desire to understand what exactly is happening in the story.

29 B

"God's will" is the best word choice for "Providence" due to its positive nature unlike the other options listed. The "P" in "Providence" is capitalized, which also indicates this word is in lieu of a proper noun such as God.

30 D

For "dear life" is an idiom because it is a phrase meaning the person is trying to get away so that they may stay alive.

Questions 31-35

The theory being proposed here is that animals do not consciously make calculations, but instead their survival and success is determined by their genetic makeup, which leads them to make decisions that have a higher probability of leading to survival. These decisions, such as when to drink from a river, are considered gambles, as there is a risk involved. The genes are said to program the brain to make decisions that on average will result in a positive outcome.

31 E

To illustrate that every decision made by a survival machine (such as the gnu) is a gamble and that genes play a role in programming the brain to make decisions that are likely to pay off in terms of survival and propagation.

32   D

It is to make successful gambles according to their genetic makeup, which increases their chances of survival and ability to propagate their genes.

33   D

The tone of the passage is primarily informative. It presents information and facts about the importance of decision-making and its connection to survival.

34   D

Animals mainly make decisions by their genes programming their brains rather than conscious calculations.

35   A

The term "survival machine" is used to describe living organisms or life forms in general. It refers to the idea that animals are shaped by natural selection to be efficient and effective in surviving and reproducing in their respective environments.

Questions 36-40

This is a summary of William Shakespeare's monologue from "As You Like It," where the speaker reflects on the seven stages of life. The speaker views all people as players on the stage of life, with various exits and entrances as they progress through different phases of life. The seven stages include the infant, school-boy, lover, soldier, justice, old man, and the final stage of second childishness and oblivion.

36   B

"Stage" is used metaphorically to refer to life, and all the people in it are referred to as "players". The idea is that just as actors in a play different roles, people go through different stages in their lives, each with its own distinct characteristics and behaviors. The seven ages of man are described, starting from infancy, going through adolescence, young adulthood, middle age, old age, and finally, second childhood and oblivion. The idea is that life is a performance, and each person goes through different stages, playing different parts, until the final stage of death.

37   B

It means the beginning and end of a person's life, or the different roles and experiences they go through in life. The words suggest that people enter and exit different stages and roles, much like actors entering and exiting the stage in a play.

38   D

The word "stage" in this poem represents a metaphor. The "stage" represents life, and the "players" represent all human beings who play different roles, or "parts," throughout their lives.

39   C

"Even in the cannon's mouth" most nearly means (C) The soldier is ready to face all kinds of danger. The line "Seeking the bubble reputation/ Even in the cannon's mouth" means that the soldier is willing to face all kinds of danger to achieve fame and glory.

40   **A**

The poet uses the phrase "fair round belly" to emphasize (A) He is stout. The line "In fair round belly, with a good capon lined" describes the physical appearance of the character playing the role of a justice in the play of life. The phrase emphasizes that the character has a large, round belly, suggesting that he is well-fed and well-nourished, and perhaps a bit stout.

SECTION 3

1   **A**

Malleable means capable of being shaped or formed. Synonym of malleable is docile which means easy to manage or control.

2   **D**

To cajole means to coax or persuade with flattery. Synonym of cajole is entice which means to tempt or attract.

3   **C**

To relinquish means to give up possession or control. Synonym of relinquish is renounce which means to give up.

4   **A**

Temper refers to a person's disposition or manner. Synonym of temper is disposition which means a person's inherent qualities of character.

5   **B**

Trifling means unimportant or insignificant. Synonym of trifling is trivial which means of little or no value or importance.

6   **E**

Ignorant means uneducated or uninformed. Synonym of ignorant is unaware which means lacking knowledge or understanding.

7   **E**

An epoch is a particular period of time in history. Synonym of epoch is era which means a period of time marked by distinct character or events.

8   **D**

To convey means to transport or carry something. Synonym of convey is carry which means to transport something from one place to another.

9   **D**

To sequester means to isolate or set apart. Synonym of sequester is seclude which means to keep away from others or shut off from the world.

10   **E**

Compassionate means showing sympathy or pity. Synonym of compassionate is sympathetic which means showing mercy or forbearance.

11   **E**

To prowl means to move stealthily like you're looking for something to prey on.

12   **A**

Exotic means originating from a foreign country or unusual. Synonym of exotic is outlandish which means strange or unusual.

13   **C**

Ephemeral means lasting for a very short time. Synonym of ephemeral is fleeting which means passing quickly.

14   **C**

Hapless means unlucky. Synonym of hapless is unfortunate.

15   **D**

To adopt means to take as one's own. Synonym of adopt is choose which means to select or pick.

16   **A**

Kindred means related or belonging to the same family. Synonym of kindred is clan which means a group of people related by blood or descent.

17   **C**

To grovel means to act in a servile or abject manner. Synonym of grovel is abase which means to lower in rank or status.

18   **A**

singular means the same thing as unique, which means one of a kind, or having no equal.

19   **B**

blatant means openly and boldly defiant, which is a synonym of flagrant.

20 E

reflection means the act of considering or examining one's own thoughts and feelings, which is a synonym of introspection.

21 A

Metamorphosis means transformation or conversion. Synonym of metamorphosis is transformation.

22 D

Jocular means playful or jokingly, often used to describe someone's behavior or manner of speaking. Synonym of jocular is humorous.

23 C

A coterie refers to a small, exclusive group of people who associate with one another, often having similar interests and veiws. Synonym of coterie is a clique.

24 A

To genuflect is to bend the knees and bow in a servile manner as a sign of respect or worship, typically in a religious context. Synonym of genuflect is kowtow.

25 C

To reproach someone is to express disapproval or criticism towards them, often in a scolding manner. Synonym of reproach is reprimand.

26 A

Intricate means complicated or having many interrelated parts, often referring to a design or system. Synonym of intricate is complicated.

27 D

Timid means being shy, nervous, or lacking confidence, often in social situations. Synonym of timid is timorous.

28 E

Faux means not genuine or spurious. Synonym of faux is fake.

29 A

Theatrical means artificial, melodramatic or overly dramatic in a manner that is reminiscent of the theater. Synonym of theatrical is histrionic.

30 D

Ludicrous means ridiculous, nonsensical or absurd, often used to describe something that is humorously or severely unbelievable. Synonym of ludicrous is absurd.

31 D

Sprint refers to a fast run, usually in a short distance, usually for sport or competition. Gallop refers to a fast run of a horse, in a way that all four hooves leave the ground at different times. Both "man" and "horse" are runners, and "sprint" and "gallop" are the corresponding types of fast runs.

32 B

Cardiac refers to the heart. Cerebral refers to the brain. Both "cardiac" and "cerebral" are adjectives that modify body parts, and "heart" and "brain" are the corresponding body parts.

33 A

Rectify means to correct or set right. Amend means to make corrections to laws. Both "rectify" and "amend" refer to the process of making corrections, with "mistake" and "law" being the corresponding objects of correction.

34 B

Chemistry is a branch of natural science that deals with the composition, structure, properties, and reactions of matter. statistics is a branch of mathematics.

35 E

Both "stray" and "wander" suggest deviation from a path, a set direction, or a specific goal, while "digress" means "off the topic,"

36 C

Both "Suggestible" and "vulnerable" suggest weakness or susceptibility to external factors, while "influence" and "attack" refer to something that affects or has an impact on the subject.

37 D

Snakes are known for making a hissing sound. Similarly, owls are known for making a hooting sound. Roosters typically crow, cats meow, horses neigh, and frogs croak.

38 D

Both "worker" and "state" are groups of individuals, and "union" and "federation" refer to organizations or associations that represent or unite them.

39 A

Both "counselor" and "donor" give something, while "advice" and "contribution" denote what they give.

40 E

Both "void" and "nullify" mean to render something invalid or ineffective, while "check" while "annul" means to cancel the contract.

41 C

Both "incredulous" and "praise" express an attitude towards something, and "skeptic" and "critic" are the corresponding opposite attitudes.

42 D

Both "architect" and "playwright" are professions involved in making "blueprint" and "script" as the respective products of their work.

43 B

Both words are synonyms. "Conundrum" means "riddle" and "labyrinth" means "maze".

44 A

"Connoisseur" means "expert," someone who has a deep knowledge and appreciation of a particular subject, usually referring to art, wine, or cuisine. On the other hand, a "dilettante" is someone who dabbles in a specific subject without serious commitment or knowledge, often referring to someone who is an "amateur."

45   B

A clamp is a device used to grip or secure something firmly in place, while a dolly is a platform on wheels used to transport heavy objects. The relationship between the two words is that both are tools used to secure or move objects.

46   E

A prologue is the introductory part of a book or play, while an epilogue is a concluding part. The relationship between the two words is that prologue comes first, and the epilogue comes last as overture comes first, and finale is to coming last in operas.

47   A

Euphony refers to pleasing or harmonious sounds, while fragrant refers to pleasant or sweet odors. The relationship between the two words is that both describe sensory experiences that are pleasing to the senses.

48   D

Vacant refers to an empty or unoccupied space, while occupants refers to the people or entities occupying that space. The relationship is "abscence." Similarly, "impoverished" refers to being poor or destitute.

49   C

Mislead means to deceive or defraud someone. Similarly, cling means to stick.

50   A

An arena is a place where spectators gather to watch an event or performance. Similarly, a church is a place where a congregation assembles for religious services.

51   B

An armory is a building where weapons and ammunition are stored, while munitions refers to military supplies and weapons. The relationship between the two words is that both describe supplies used for military purposes. Similarly, a shed is a small building used for storage, while tools refer to implements used for various tasks.

52   C

A jaunt is a short trip or excursion, often for pleasure. In a similar manner, a skit is short play.

53   B

Albino refers to a genetic condition characterized by a lack of melanin in the skin, hair, and eyes, while pigment refers to a substance that gives color to living things. The relationship between the two words is that they describe the absence of coloring in living things. Similarly, drought refers to a absence of water.

54   E

The word "adroit" means "skillful in physical movement or action" and The word "articulate" means "able to express one's thoughts or feelings easily and clearly in speech or writing" and the word "speech" refers to the act of speaking. The relation between "articulate" and "speech" is similar to the relation between "adroit" and "motion".

55 — C

In this analogy, hospitable and gregarious are opposite adjectives meaning mild-mannered and sociable, respectively. On the other hand, belligerent and antisocial are opposite adjectives meaning hostile and unsociable, respectively. So, the comparison is being made between opposite adjectives.

56 — D

In this analogy, a diplomat is an tactful official who represents his or her country in other nations. Similarly, a gymnast is someone who has agility.

57 — B

A scoundrel is someone who behaves in a dishonest, immoral, or evil manner, and "virtue" refers to moral excellence or righteousness. The relationship between "scoundrel" and "virtue" is an "absence" relation. Similarly, a "glutton" is someone who does not have "moderation" in food or drink, often to the point of overeating.

58 — E

A monologue refers to a speech delivered by one person. Similarly, an aria is a song sung by a single person.

59 — A

Prudent means showing good judgment or wisdom, while rash means acting without proper thought or consideration. In a similar manner, discreet is the synonym for prudent, and reckless is the synonym for rash.

60 — C

"Forgery" is a deceptive imitation or replication of something, often with the intent to deceive or commit fraud. Similarly, "collusion" is a secretive, deceptive cooperation between individuals or parties, typically for an illegal or dishonest purpose.

SECTION 4

1 E

To solve for x, we can cross-multiply $4/12 = 4/x + 2$ which gives us $4(x+2) = 48$. Expanding the bracket gives us $4x + 8 = 48$. Substracting 8 from both sides gives $4x = 40$. Dividing both sides by 4 gives us $x = 10$. Therefore, the value of x is (E) 10.

2 C

To hold 6P liters of juice, we need 3 jars of 2-liter capacity.

Each jar can hold 2 liters of juice, so 3 jars can hold a total of 6 liters of juice, which is equal to 6P/P = 6. Therefore, we need 3 jars to hold 6P liters of juice.

So, the answer is (C) 3P.

3 B

If Peter bought a stereo for x dollars and sold it at 5% profit, then his selling price would be $(1 + 0.05)x = 1.05x$ dollars. Therefore, Peter's profit is the difference between the selling price and the buying price, which is $1.05x - x = 0.05x$ dollars. Therefore, the amount of Peter's profit is (B) $0.05x$.

4 E

Since the ratio of a to b to c to d to e is 5 to 4 to 3 to 2 to 1, we can write:

a:b:c:d:e = 5:4:3:2:1

We are given that a = 45, so we can substitute to get:

45:b:c:d:e = 5:4:3:2:1

To find c, we need to find the value that corresponds to the ratio a: c = 5:3 in the original ratio.

So the value of c in the original ratio is $3 \times 9 = 27$. Therefore, the answer is (E) 27.

5 C

Let a be the smallest integer, then the next three consecutive odd integers are a+2, a+4, and a+6. Their sum is given as $32 + a + 2 + a + 4 + a + 6$ or $4a + 12 = 32$, which simplifies to $4a = 20$ or $a = 5$. Therefore, the four consecutive odd integers are 5, 7, 9, and 11. The median of the set $\{a, b, c, d, 24\}$ is the middle number when the five integers are arranged in order. Therefore, the median is (C) 9.

6 D

To solve this problem, we need to simplify the expression $1 + (100$ percent of $1)$. Since 100 percent of any number is the number itself, we can rewrite the expression as $1 + 1 = 2$. Therefore, the value that is equal to 1 plus (100 percent of 1) is (D) 200 percent of 1.

7 D

If Team A was 12 points behind at halftime, and won the game by 5 points, then Team A scored 17 points more than Team B after halftime.

If Team B scored 21 points in the second half, then Team×must have scored $21 + 17 = 38$ points after halftime.

Therefore, the answer is (D) 38.

8 D

The area of a circle is given by the formula $A = \pi r^2$, where r is the radius. Therefore, the area of the larger circle is $\pi 1^2 = \pi$ and the area of the

Answers & Explanations 249

smaller circle is $\pi(\frac{1}{2})^2 = \frac{\pi}{4}$

The ratio of the area of the larger circle to the area of the smaller circle is:

$\pi \ / \ (\frac{\pi}{4}) = 4$

Therefore, the ratio of the area of the larger circle to the area of the smaller circle is (D) 4:1.

9   **E**

Jason is currently 6 years old (half of Steph's age). When Steph is 30, she will have aged 30 − 12 = 18 years. Since Jason is 18 years younger than Steph, he will be 6 + 18 = 24 years old when Steph is 30. Therefore, the answer is (E) 24.

10   **A**

Since A and B are different digits, their sum will be between 1 and 18.

In the units place, we have B + A = 2, so B + A must be 2, 12, or 22. However, since A and B are different digits, we can eliminate the possibility of B + A being 22.

So, we have B + A = 12. Since A and B are different digits, the only possibility is that B = 9 and A = 3.

Therefore, A represents the digit (A) 3.

11   **B**

The total number of long-sleeved dresses sold in June is 5,500, and the number of orange long-sleeved dresses sold is 4,000. Therefore, the total number of orange dresses sold is 10,000 − 7,600 = 2,400. Then, the total number of green short-sleeved dresses sold is 2,400 − 1,500 = 900. However, we should count the total number of green dresses sold, and it is 2,400 as we calculated. Therefore, the answer is (B) 2,400, not 900.

12   **D**

Let's use algebra to solve for the number. Let x be the number, then we can write the equation $2x - 7 = 123$. Adding 7 to both sides gives $2x = 130$. Dividing both sides by 2 gives us $x = 65$. Therefore, the number is (D) 65.

13   **C**

Let's use algebra to solve for the number. Let x be the number, then we can write the following equations:
− If x is odd, $2x = 34$
− If x is even, $x = 34$

The first equation is not possible, because $2x$ would have to be an even number, and 34 is even. Therefore, we can eliminate option I. The second equation is not possible, because 34 is not an even number. Therefore, we can eliminate option II. The third equation is possible, because 34 is even, and so it could have been printed if x was even. Therefore, the answer is (C) I and III only.

14   **E**

Let's use algebra to solve for the options.
− (A) $ab + 1$ = even + odd = odd
− (B) $a^2 + 1$ = even + 1 = odd
− (C) $a^2 + a^2$ = even + odd = odd
− (D) $a^2 b^2 + 1$ = even + 1 = odd
− (E) $a^2 + 3$ = odd + 3 = even

Therefore, the answer is (E) $b^2 + 3$.

15   **C**

To distinguish figures that have a path that can be traveled without lifting the pencil or retracing, you need to loof for specific points. There must be either 0 or 2 points where an odd number of line segments intersect. By counting the number of points where an odd number of line segments intersect, we can determine whether a polygon can be drawn with one stroke. Therefore the answer is (C).

16   D

The amount of money Johnny saves each day is given by the sequence 1, 2, 3, ..., 30. The sum of the first n terms of this sequence is given by the formula $n(n+1)/2$. Therefore, the sum of the first 30 terms is $30(30+1)/2 = 465$. Since each term represents 5 cents, the total amount of money Johnny saves is $23.25. Therefore, the answer is (D) $23.25.

17   D

To find the x-intercept of a line, we need to set $y=0$ and solve for x.
So, let's set $y=0$:
$3x + 2(0) = 12$
Simplifying the equation, we get:
$3x = 12$
Dividing both sides by 3, we get:
$x = 4$
Therefore, the x-intercept of the line $3x + 2y = 12$ is 4.
So, the correct answer is (D) 4.

18   D

We can solve this problem using the principle of inclusion-exclusion. If we add the number of people with checking accounts and the number of people with savings accounts, we count the people with both types of accounts twice, so we need to subtract the number of people with both types of accounts once to get the total.

Let C be the number of people with checking accounts, S be the number of people with savings accounts, and B be the number of people with both types of accounts. Then we have:

C + S − B = 1000

Substituting C = 600 and S = 600, we get:

600 + 600 − B = 1000

B = 1200 − 1000

B = 200

Therefore, (D) 200 people have both a checking account and a savings account.

19   B

The radius of the circle is 6 because the area of the triangle ACB is 18. To find the area of the shaded region, we need to subtract the area of the right triangle ACB from the area of the circle. This can be represented as $[(6 \times 6 \times \pi)/4] - 18$.
$(6 \times 6 \times \pi)/4 - 18$
$= (36\pi)/4 - 18$
$= 9\pi - 18$

Therefore, the area of the shaded region is (B) $9\pi - 18$.

20   D

We use the formula for the volume of a cylinder, which is $V = \pi r^2 h$. The original can has a base diameter of 8 inches, which means that its radius is 4 inches. Its volume is enough to serve four people, so we calculate it to be 160π. To find the new base diameter for a single-serving can with the same height of 10 inches, we set its volume to be 1/4 of the original can's volume.
new radius = $\sqrt{4}$ inches
new radius = 2 inches
New base diameter = 2 × new radius = 2 × 2 inches = (D) 4 inches

21   E

The formula for calculating the slope (m) between two points (x_1, y_1) and (x_2, y_2) is:

$m = (y_2 - y_1)/(x_2 - x_1)$

Given that the slope of the line passing through (1, 2) and (a, −4) is −3, we can set up the equation:

−3 = {(−4)−2}/ (a−1)

Now, let's solve for a:
−3 = −6 / (a−1)

Multiply both sides by $(a-1)$ to get rid of the fraction:

$-3(a-1) = -6$

Distribute the −3:

$-3a + 3 = -6$

Subtract 3 from both sides:

$-3a = -9$

Divide by −3:

$a = 3$

So, the value of a is 3. Therefore, the correct answer is (E) 3.

22   B

To find the range of the average speed, we need to divide the distance traveled by the time taken:

Minimum speed: 200 miles ÷ 4 hours = 50 miles per hour
Maximum speed: 200 miles ÷ (5/2) hours = 80 miles per hour
Therefore, the average speed must have been between (B) 50 and 80 miles per hour.

23   E

To solve this inequality, we can subtract 4 from both sides:

$4 - x < \frac{1}{2}$

$x < -\frac{7}{2}$

Multiplying both sides by −1 and reversing the inequality, we get:

$x > \frac{7}{2}$

Therefore, the only answer choice that could be x is $\frac{9}{2}$, which is greater than $\frac{7}{2}$. So the answer is (E) $\frac{9}{2}$.

24   D

The mass of the 5oz mouse in grams is:
5 oz × 28 g/oz = 140g

To not set off the trap, the mass of the cheese and the mouse must be less than 175g. Let's call the mass of the cheese "x" in grams. Then we can write the inequality:
140g + x < 175g
Subtracting 140g from both sides, we get:
x < 35g
Therefore, the largest mass of cheese the 5oz. mouse could carry and not set off the trap is (D) 34g.

25   A

Since the circle has the largest area-to-perimeter ratio of any shape, it will have the largest area. The square and the equilateral triangle have the same perimeter, but the equilateral triangle has the largest area-to-perimeter ratio of any polygon, so it will have the second largest area. Therefore, the correct order from largest to smallest area is:

Circle, Equilateral triangle, Square.

So the answer is (A).

The area of each shape is determined by its

own formula:
1. Circle: The area of a circle is given by $=2A$ $=\pi r^2$, where r is the radius.
2. Square: The area of a square is given by $=2A$ $=side^2$.
3. Equilateral Triangle: The area of an equilateral triangle is given by $=\dfrac{\sqrt{3}}{4}34 \times side^2$

Now, since they all have the same perimeter, let's denote the common perimeter as P.

1. Circle: For a circle with perimeter P, the radius (r) is given by $r=\dfrac{P}{2\pi}$.
2. Square: For a square with perimeter P, each side (s) is given by $s=\dfrac{P}{4}$.
3. Equilateral Triangle: For an equilateral triangle with perimeter P, each side (s) is given by $s=\dfrac{P}{3}$.

Now, let's compare their areas:

1. Circle: $\pi\left(\dfrac{P}{2\pi}\right)^2 = \dfrac{p^2}{4\pi}$
2. Square: $\left(\dfrac{P}{4}\right)^2 = \dfrac{p^2}{16}$
3. Equilateral Triangle: $\dfrac{\sqrt{3}}{4} \times \left(\dfrac{P}{3}\right)^2 = \dfrac{\sqrt{3}}{36}p^2$

Now, in decreasing order of area:
circle〉square〉triangle
So, the correct order is Circle, Square, Equilateral Triangle in decreasing order of area.

TEST ANSWERS

Practice 2

Section 1, 4: Quantitative (MATH) Answer

*Quantitative (Math) scores should be calculated based on the total of 50 questions from Section 1 and Section 4.

pp.79 – 88

TEST 2 SECTION 1 MATH 1

1. E	6. B	11. D	16. B	21. B
2. A	7. B	12. C	17. A	22. D
3. B	8. E	13. D	18. E	23. D
4. D	9. A	14. C	19. E	24. E
5. C	10. D	15. C	20. D	25. C

pp.112 – 122

TEST 2 SECTION 4 MATH 2

1. E	6. A	11. C	16. C	21. C
2. B	7. D	12. B	17. E	22. A
3. B	8. D	13. B	18. D	23. E
4. D	9. B	14. D	19. E	24. C
5. A	10. D	15. A	20. B	25. D

My Quantitative(Math) Score (Section 1 + Section 4)

Right	Wrong	Omitted	Raw Score ($=$ right $-\dfrac{\text{wrong}}{4}$)	Scaled Score	Percentile
					%

Please consult the Scaled Score & Percentile Chart on the back of this book for the calculation of your Scaled Score and Percentile.

Section 2: Reading Answer

pp.89 – 103

TEST 2 SECTION 2 READING

1. B	9. A	17. A	25. B	33. E
2. C	10. D	18. A	26. C	34. C
3. C	11. A	19. C	27. D	35. A
4. E	12. A	20. B	28. E	36. D
5. D	13. C	21. E	29. C	37. E
6. C	14. A	22. E	30. B	38. A
7. C	15. C	23. D	31. C	39. C
8. A	16. E	24. A	32. B	40. D

My Reading Score

Right	Wrong	Omitted	Raw Score ($= \text{right} - \dfrac{\text{wrong}}{4}$)	Scaled Score	Percentile
					%

Please consult the Scaled Score & Percentile Chart on the back of this book for the calculation of your Scaled Score and Percentile.

Section 3: Verbal Answer

pp.104 – 111

TEST 2 SECTION 3 VERBAL

1. C	13. B	25. D	37. E	49. E
2. A	14. E	26. A	38. C	50. C
3. E	15. D	27. C	39. D	51. B
4. A	16. A	28. A	40. B	52. E
5. B	17. E	29. E	41. D	53. E
6. D	18. C	30. C	42. D	54. D
7. B	19. E	31. E	43. A	55. C
8. A	20. E	32. C	44. C	56. D
9. D	21. B	33. B	45. C	57. A
10. D	22. A	34. C	46. A	58. C
11. B	23. A	35. C	47. D	59. B
12. E	24. D	36. A	48. C	60. B

My Reading Score

Right	Wrong	Omitted	Raw Score ($=$ right $- \dfrac{\text{wrong}}{4}$)	Scaled Score	Percentile
					%

Please consult the Scaled Score & Percentile Chart on the back of this book for the calculation of your Scaled Score and Percentile.

Practice Test 2

SECTION 1

1 E

We can solve this problem through multiplication. 14 × 3 × 6 × 1 = 252. Now we need to find a number that when multiplied by 9 gives us 252. By doing some mental math we can realize that 28 × 9 = 252. Therefore, the answer is (E) 28.

2 A

If Alexander is currently 9 squares behind Logan, and he moves forward by 5 and 6 squares, then he will move a total of 11 squares. Therefore, Alexander will be 2 squares ahead of Logan because 11 − 9 = 2.

So the answer is (A) 2 squares ahead of Logan.

3 B

We know that a dozen is equal to 12, so four dozen is equal to 48. The cost of 4 dozen marbles is $96, so we can divide 96 by 48 to find the cost per marble. 96 ÷ 48 = 2. Therefore, the answer is (B) $2.

4 D

The discount is the difference between the original price and the sale price. In this case, the discount is $1,500 − $960 = $540. Now we need to find what percentage of the original price is $540. We can do this by dividing $540 by $1,500 and then multiplying by 100 to get a percentage. ($540 ÷ $1,500) × 100 = 36.

Therefore, the answer is (D) 36%.

5 C

To find the interest earned after two years, we can use the simple interest formula:

Interest = Principal × Rate × Time

where I is the interest earned, P is the principal (the amount deposited), r is the interest rate per year (as a decimal), and t is the time in years.

In this case, we have:

P = $7,200
r = 0.04 (since the interest rate is 4% per year)
t = 2 (since the interest is earned for two years)

Substituting these values into the formula, we get:

I = $7,200 × 0.04 × 2 = $576

Therefore, the interest earned after two years is $576.

So, the correct answer is (C) $576.

6 B

To find the total time, we need to calculate the time taken for the outbound and return journeys separately.
For the outbound journey:

time = distance ÷ speed
time = 120 miles ÷ 60 mph
time = 2 hours

For the return journey:
time = distance ÷ speed
time = 120 miles ÷ 30 mph
time = 4 hours

The total time for the round trip is the sum of the

Answers & Explanations   257

outbound and return journey times:
total time = 2 hours + 4 hours
total time = 6 hours

Now we can calculate the average speed:
average speed = total distance ÷ total time
average speed = 240 miles ÷ 6 hours
average speed = 40 mph

Therefore, the average rate of speed for the entire trip is (B) 40 mph.

7   B

We can start by plugging in the value of B into the equation A × B = 2.8 to get A × 100 = 2.8. Dividing both sides by 100, we get A = 0.028.
The difference between 0.028 and 0.02 is 0.008.
The difference between 0.028 and 0.03 is 0.002.
So 0.028 is closer to 0.03.
Therefore, the answer is (B) 0.03.

8   E

Let's call the number of quarters q and the number of nickels n. We can set up two equations based on the information given: q + n = 10 (because there are 10 coins in total), and 0.25q + 0.05n = 1.1 (because the value of the coins is $1.10). We can solve the first equation for q to get q = 10 − n, and substitute this into the second equation to get 0.25(10 − n) + 0.05n = 1.1. Simplifying this expression, we get 2.5 − 0.2n = 1.1, which can be further simplified to −0.2n = −1.4. Dividing both sides by −0.2, we get n = 7. Therefore, the answer is (E) 7.

9   A

Let's call the height of the tree h. We can set up a proportion based on the similar triangles formed by the pole, its shadow, the tree, and its shadow: (3 / 6) = (h / 12). Cross-multiplying,

we get 6h = 36, so h = 6. Therefore, the answer is (A) 6 feet.

10   D

Let's call the total amount of money saved per week T. If four roommates each contribute $5 per week, then T = 4 × $5 = $20. If five roommates each contribute the same amount per week, then each person would pay T / 5 = $4 per week. Therefore, the answer is (D) $4.

11   D

Let's begin by expanding the left-hand side of the equation:
$(3+x) \times (5+y) = 1$
$15 + 3y + 5x + xy = 1$
$xy + 5x + 3y + 14 = 0$

We can rewrite this equation as:
$xy + 5x + 3y = -14$

Now we need to use the fact that x is greater than zero to determine the possible values of y. Since x is positive and the other terms on the left-hand side of the equation are non-negative, we know that xy must be negative in order for the left-hand side of the equation to equal −14.

Since x is positive, y must be negative in order for xy to be negative. Therefore, the answer is (D) negative.

12   C

We can start by looking at the value of the digit in the thousands place. In the number 7,531.317, the digit in the thousands place is 5. Therefore, we need to find the value of the digit 3 places to the left of the thousands place. This is the ten thousands place. The value of the digit in the ten thousands place is 7. Therefore, the value of the "3" in place x is 7 times the value of the "3" in place y. So if the value of the "3" in place y is 1 unit, then the value of the "3" in place x is 7 units. Therefore, the answer is (C) 100.

13   D

After moving 12 books from the second shelf to the first, the second shelf has $e+8-12=e-4$ books left. Then, after adding 7 new books to the second shelf, it has a total of $e-4+7=e+3$ books. Therefore, the answer is (D) $e+3$.

14   C

Ryan has one quarter (25 cents).
He also has at least one dime (10 cents).
He also has at least one nickel (5 cents).

Now, let's consider the remaining two coins. To maximize the amount, we'll assume they are both dimes:

Two dimes (2×10 cents).
Total = 25 (quarter) + 10 (dime) + 5 (nickel) + 2×10 (dimes) = 60 cents.
Therefore, the maximum amount of money Ryan could be holding is $0.60, which corresponds to option (C) in the given choices.

15   C

We know that the value of each quarter is 25 cents, the value of each dime is 10 cents, and the value of each nickel is 5 cents. Therefore, any combination of quarters, dimes, and nickels that adds up to a multiple of 5 cents is possible. In other words, any value of the form 5n (where n is a non-negative integer) is possible.
Checking each answer choice, we see that all of them are possible except for (C) 37.
Therefore, the answer is (C) 37.

16   B

When we multiply numbers written in scientific notation, we can multiply the coefficients (the numbers before the 10) and add the exponents of the 10. Using this rule, we get:
$(1.7 \times 10^{-5})(2.3 \times 10^7)$
$=(1.7 \times 2.3) \times (10)^{-5+7}$
$=3.91 \times 10^2$

Therefore, the answer is (B) 3.91×10^2.

17   A

To determine which points lie on the same line as $(-6, 23)$ and $(6, -10)$, we'll need to use the equation of a line in the form $y=mx+b$, where m is the slope and b is the y-intercept.

First, we calculate the slope of the line as the change in y over the change in x:

slope $= (y2-y1)/(x2-x1)$

Using the given points, this becomes:

slope $=(-10-23) / (6-(-6))=-33/12=$ $-11/4$

Next, we'll rearrange the formula to solve for b (the y-intercept):
$b=y-mx$

We can use any point on the line and the slope we just calculated to solve for b. Let's use the point $(-6, 23)$:

$b=23-(-11/4)\times(-6)=23-33/2=46/2-$ $33/2=13/2=6.5$

So the equation of the line is $y=-11/4x+6.5$

Now we'll substitute the x and y values for each of the provided points into this equation. If the equation holds true, the point is on the line:

(A) (−2,12): $12=-11/4\times(-2)+6.5 \rightarrow 12=5.5$ $+6.5 \rightarrow 12=12$. So, point (A) is on the line.

(B) (−1, 9): $9=-11/4\times(-1)+6.5 \rightarrow 9=2.75+$ $6.5 \rightarrow 9 \neq 9.25$. So, point (B) is not on the line.

(C) (0, −8): $-8=-11/4\times 0+6.5 \rightarrow -8 \neq 6.5$. So, point (C) is not on the line.

(D) (−3, 23): $23=-11/4\times(-3)+6.5 \rightarrow 23=$

8.25+6.5 → 23 ≠ 14.75. So, point (D) is not on the line.

(E) (5, 15): 15=−11/4×5+6.5 → 15 ≠ −8.25. So, point (E) is not on the line.

So, the only point among those given that also lies on the line is (A) (−2,12).

18   E

Let's start by using the formula for the perimeter of a rectangle:
Perimeter = 2×(length+width)
We know that the perimeter is 32 meters and the length is 12 meters, so we can solve for the width:
32=2×(12+width)
16=12+width
4=width

Now we can use the formula for the area of a rectangle:
Area = length×width
Area = 12×4
Area = 48
Rounding this value to the nearest square meter, we get:
Area ≈ 48 square meters

Therefore, the answer is (E) 48m^2

19   E

Let the original number be x. When we multiply it by 10 in step 2, we get $10x$.

In step 3, Jennie adds a constant value to the answer. Let's call this constant value C. So the answer after step 3 is:

$10x + C$

Now, Jennie can use algebra to solve for × in terms of the answer:

$10x + C = (10x - 10) \times 2$
$10x + C = 20x - 20$
$C + 20 = 10x$
$x = (C + 20) / 10$

So if Jennie divides the answer by 100 and multiplies by 10, she can find the original number.

For example, let's say the person chose the number 3. After step 2, we get 30. Let's say the constant C in step 3 is 50. Then the answer after step 3 is:
10 × 3+50=80
If Jennie divides this by 100 and multiplies by 10, she gets:
80 / 100 × 10=8
So the original number is 8.

Therefore, the answer is (E) She divides the answer by 100 and multiply by 10.

20   D

We can solve for x by cross-multiplying and simplifying:

$$\frac{5}{x} = \frac{2x}{10}$$

$5(10) = 2x^2$
$50 = 2x^2$
$x^2 = 25$
$x = \pm 5$

Both $x=5$ and $x=-5$ satisfy the equation, so the answer is (D) 5.

21   B

We know that 30% of the students are taking German, 60% are taking Spanish, and the rest are taking French, Latin, or Russian. Therefore, the percentage of students taking French is 100%−30%−60%=10%. Let's call the total number of students taking French, Latin, or Russian "x". We know that there are 3,500 students in total, so we can set up the equation: 0.3(3,500)+0.6(3,500)+x=3,500. Simplifying this equation, we get $x=350-148-50=152$. Therefore, the answer is (B) 152.

22 D

To find the median test score, we need to order the scores from least to greatest and find the middle value.

Arranging the test scores in order, we get:

74, 78, 83, 88, 90, 94, 94, 99, 100

Since there are nine test scores, the median will be the fifth value, which is 90. Therefore, the answer is (D) 90.

23 D

The average of a set of values is calculated by summing all the values and then dividing by the number of values. If we increase a single value, the total sum increases, and hence the average also increases.

Let's calculate by how much the average increases if we increase a single value by 1.5 in a set of 12 values.

The increase in the average would be the amount of the increase divided by the number of entries. In this case, it's 1.5 divided by 12.

1.5 / 12 = 0.125

So, the average increases by 0.125.

Hence, the correct answer is (D) 0.125.

24 E

We want to find the smallest value of n such that $(\frac{2}{5})^n$ is less than 10% or $\frac{1}{10}$.

We can rewrite 10% as a fraction: $0.1 = \frac{1}{10}$.

So, we want to find the smallest value of n such that $(\frac{2}{5})^n < \frac{1}{10}$.

We can simplify $(\frac{2}{5})^n$ as $(\frac{2}{5})$ multiplied by itself n times:

$(\frac{2}{5})^n = (\frac{2}{5}) \times (\frac{2}{5}) \times \cdots \times (\frac{2}{5})$

We can see that if we multiply $(\frac{2}{5})$ by itself enough times, it will eventually become less than $\frac{1}{10}$.

We can start by multiplying $(\frac{2}{5})$ by itself once to get:

$(\frac{2}{5})^1 = \frac{2}{5}$

Since $\frac{2}{5}$ is greater than $\frac{1}{10}$, we need to multiply $(\frac{2}{5})$ by itself again.

$(\frac{2}{5})^n = (\frac{2}{5}) \times (\frac{2}{5}) = \frac{4}{25}$

$\frac{4}{25}$ is still greater than $\frac{1}{10}$, so we need to multiply $(\frac{2}{5})$ by itself again.

$(\frac{2}{5})^n = (\frac{2}{5}) \times (\frac{2}{5}) \times (\frac{2}{5}) = \frac{8}{125}$

$\frac{8}{125}$ is less than $\frac{1}{10}$, so the smallest value of n that satisfies the inequality is 3. Therefore, the answer is (E) 3.

25 C

The left figure consists of four right-angled triangles put together, so it can be transformed into two squares of 4 units each. Similarly, the right figure can be thought of as consisting of three squares of 4 units each. Therefore, the left figure is lacking 4 units compared to the right figure.

Therefore, the answer is (C) 4.

SECTION 2

Questions 1-5

The passage describes the characteristics of humpback whales, including their physical features, peaceful behavior, and distinctive calls. The main focus of the passage is on humpback whale songs, which are a series of sounds that last 10–15 minutes and consist of several different themes. The songs are sung by male humpback whales for roughly six months out of the year and are believed to be used to attract females and ward off other male whales. Whale songs are typically sung 50–60 feet below the water's surface for 20–40 minutes at a time and have a sound frequency ranging from 20 Hz to 10,000 Hz. Research has found that humpback whales from different locations in the South Pacific Ocean are connected by a shared song.

1   **B**

The Humpback's Cantata is the most suitable name for this passage due to it combining both humpbacks as well as their song. Cantata is another word for musical arrangement.

2   **C**

The author's primary purpose in the passage is to specifically discuss humpback whale songs, as it is the main topic of the passage. The author provides detailed information on the length, composition, repetition, and frequency of humpback whale songs.

3   **C**

The author's description of the humpback whale is attributed to completed research, as it is indicated that there is research on the humpback whale song and its connection between whales throughout the South Pacific Ocean.

4   **E**

As used in line 11, "encroaching" most nearly means "intruding," as in the context of the passage, it refers to male whales intruding into the territory of other male whales, possibly to mate with the females.

5   **D**

The passage mentions that researchers believe male humpback whales sing as both a way to attract females and to ward off encroaching male whales.

Questions 6-10

Daisy, the protagonist's cousin, is feeling turbulent emotions and is cynical about everything. She tells Nick about her feelings when her daughter was born and hopes she'll be a fool. Daisy thinks the world is terrible and claims to have seen and done everything, showing her sophistication. However, the protagonist feels that her words are insincere and that she is trying to manipulate him.

6   **C**

In the passage, Daisy responds to Nick's questions about her daughter by saying, "We don't know each other very well, Nick," and expressing that they are not close despite being cousins. This indicates that she does not feel comfortable discussing personal matters with Nick.

| 7 | C |

Daisy's words and behavior in the passage reveal that she thinks the world views girls as foolish, which is a negative and demeaning view.

| 8 | A |

The word "sedative" in the context of the passage means calming, as Nick intended to calm Daisy with his questions about her daughter.

| 9 | A |

The word "scorn" in the context of the passage means contempt, which Daisy shows through her defiant attitude toward the world's view of girls.

| 10 | D |

Nick waited to respond to Daisy because he felt she was trying to manipulate or trick him with her insincere comments, and he wanted to observe her further.

| 11 | A |

In the passage, Daisy mentions that Tom was "God knows where" when she woke up after giving birth to their daughter. She also mentions crying when she found out the baby was a girl and hoping that the girl will be a "fool" because, in her opinion, it's the best thing a girl can be in the world. These statements imply that Daisy was disappointed that Tom was not present for his daughter's birth and had mixed feelings about having a daughter.

| 12 | A |

The sentence "I hope she'll be a fool—that's the best thing a girl can be in this world, a beautiful little fool." exemplifies (A) irony. Irony is a literary device where there is a contrast between what is expected and what actually happens or is said. In this case, Daisy expresses a hope for daughter to be a "fool," which is typically not considered a positive trait, and yet, it is described as the best thing for a girl in the world. This creates a sense of irony.

| 13 | C |

The metaphorical expression suggests a sense of exclusivity and privilege associated with Daisy and Tom's relationship, emphasizing their elevated status as part of a "distinguished secret society." This choice best aligns with the implied notion of elite membership and privileged status.

Questions 14-18

This book is a guide for writing special feature articles for newspapers and popular magazines. It is based on the author's 12 years of experience teaching university students. The author believes that the methods outlined in the book can help others achieve success in writing special articles. The book includes a systematic classification of different types of articles and suggestions for titles, beginnings, and other elements. The author's methods are based on an analysis of current practices in writing special feature stories and popular magazine articles. The book includes examples from representative newspapers and magazines, as well as a collection of articles for analysis. The focus is on popularizing knowledge for the general reader, to help them keep up with advances in various fields. The goal is to show aspiring writers how to present information accurately and attractively.

14   A

The best title for this selection is "How to Write Special Feature Articles." This is the most appropriate title as the main purpose of the book is to guide individuals in writing special feature articles, as stated in the first sentence "This book is the result of twelve years' experience in teaching university students to write special feature articles for newspapers and popular magazines."

15   C

The word "endeavor" means "effort." This definition aligns with the context in which the word is used in the passage. The author states "it is important for the average person to know of the progress that is being made in every field of human endeavor, in order that he may, if possible, apply the results to his own affairs." Here, "endeavor" refers to efforts made in various fields of study or work.

16   E

The author's tone can best be described as informative. The purpose of the book is to provide guidance and suggestions for writing special feature articles, and the author presents information and examples in a straightforward manner to achieve this goal.

17   A

The selection can be found in a preface. The text appears to be an introduction to a book and provides an overview of the book's content and purpose.

18   A

According to the passage, the main difference between this book and other books on short-story writing is that it discusses in detail the writing of special feature articles. The author notes that while many books have been published on short-story writing, this is the first to address the specific topic of writing special feature articles. The author goes on to explain the systematic approach and analysis used in the book to help aspiring writers in this area.

Questions 19-26

The poem contrasts those who easily "soar" through life with those who work hard or "plod" their way to success. The latter group, who face challenges and obstacles, are considered the true heroes as they are able to conquer difficulties and overcome adversity. The poem emphasizes the importance of hard work and perseverance and implies that success is not just about ease and glamour.

19   C

The tone of the poem is inspiring, as it encourages the reader to embrace difficulties and challenges and to strive for their goals with determination and courage. The poem celebrates the bravery of those who take the hard road and shows that true success can only be achieved through hard work and perseverance.

20   B

The poem emphasizes the value of hard work and perseverance in life. It argues that those who "plod their rugged way, unhelped, to God" are the true heroes, not those who "soar" or take shortcuts. The idea is that it is the effort and struggle of those who walk the hard path that makes them heroic, not the ease of flight.

| 21 | E |

The poem defines heroes as those who work hard and persevere in life, not those who take shortcuts or soar above others. This is made clear in lines 1–4, where the poem says that those who "plod their rugged way, unhelped, to God" are the heroes, not those who "higher fare, and, flying, fan the upper air."

| 22 | E |

The poem implies that those who soar or take shortcuts in life miss out on the valuable experience of hard work and struggle. This is seen in lines 5–8, where the poem says that those who soar "miss all the toil that hugs the sod" and do not experience the difficulties that come with walking the hard path.

| 23 | D |

The author is using the phrase "the toil that hugs the sod" to represent the difficulties and challenges of slavery.

| 24 | A |

To plod means to walk slowly, heavily, and deliberately. Similarly, to trudge means to walk heavily.

| 25 | B |

"they who higher fare" is the opposite of "those whose feet have pressed the path unshod." It means people who have easy lives.

| 26 | C |

"boulders" means the difficulties and hardships of slavery.

Questions 27-31

The story takes place in September 1664, when the rumor of the return of the plague in Holland spread among the people. This information was obtained from letters from merchants and others abroad and was passed on by word of mouth. The government had accurate information about the plague but kept it confidential, so the rumor eventually died down. However, in December of the same year, two men, believed to be French, died of the plague in Long Acre. The family tried to hide this, but the information was discovered by the Secretaries of State. Two physicians and a surgeon were then sent to examine the bodies and confirm that the men had died of the plague.

| 27 | D |

The government found out about the plague outbreak in Long Acre through the inquiries of the Secretaries of State after the rumor had gotten some vent in the discourse of the neighborhood.

| 28 | E |

The main topic of the passage is the outbreak of the plague and the initial rumors and reports about it in 1664.

| 29 | C |

The role of the two physicians and a surgeon was to determine the truth about the plague by going to the house of the two dead men, making inspection, and giving their opinions publicly that they died of the plague.

30   B

The source of information about the outbreak of plague in 1664 in Holland was from the letters of merchants and others who corresponded abroad, and from them was handed about by word of mouth only. There were no such things as printed newspapers in those days to spread rumors and reports of things.

31   C

It is mentioned in the passage that "This they did; and finding evident tokens of the sickness upon both the bodies that were dead, they gave their opinions publicly that they died of the plague."

Questions 32-36

English spelling mastery is a challenging task requiring memorization of 1–3 thousand irregularly spelled words and understanding of homonyms, pronounced alike but spelled differently. The dictionary contains over 200,000 words, but it is only sometimes possible to refer to the dictionary for spelling. It would be beneficial to find a key for spelling infrequently used words.

32   B

The passage discusses the serious undertaking of mastering English spelling, emphasizing the challenges and proposing strategies, such as memorization, classification, and association.

33   E

The word "drudgery" in line 4 is used to describe the task of memorizing words, which is a tedious and difficult process.

34   C

The passage suggests that because we cannot predict which words we might need, we should be prepared to write any of them without prior notice or hesitation. This aligns with the meaning of "at the drop of a hat," which indicates an immediate and spontaneous response.

35   A

The passage states that it would be of immense advantage to find a key to spelling these numerous but infrequently used words. Therefore, the author should discuss a method or strategy for remembering these words.

36   D

The tone of the author in the passage is instructional or educational. The author is presenting information about the mastery of English spelling and the difficulty of memorizing words in a straightforward and instructional manner.

Questions 37-40

The writer attended a theatrical performance of "Henry VIII" and was impressed by the scenery, costumes, and acting, particularly Kean as Cardinal Wolsey and Mrs. Kean as Queen Catherine. The play raised the writer's minds and made them feel as if they were in a dream-like state. They describe a scene in which Queen Catherine sees two angel forms and the audience burst into applause. The writer states that they have never enjoyed anything as much and felt inclined to cry at a fictional event, only before the death of Little Paul in work by Dickens.

37 — E

The author describes Mrs. Kean as a "worthy successor to Mrs. Siddons as Queen Catherine." This implies that the author sees her as a talented actress worthy of comparison to the great Mrs. Siddons.

38 — A

The "petty cares" referred to in the passage are the small, everyday worries that the author feels are lifted from their mind by the beauty and artistry of the play.

39 — C

The author expresses great admiration for the play, the actors, and the production, describing the experience as "the greatest theatrical treat I ever had or ever expected to have" and "a delicious reverie, or the most beautiful poetry." This tone can be described as laudatory, or full of praise.

40 — D

The author writes about the great impact that the play "Henry VIII" had on them, stating that they have never enjoyed anything as much and describing the evening as "the greatest theatrical treat I ever had or ever expected to have." A title that captures this sentiment could be "A Great Play of My Life."

SECTION 3

1 — C

Disquiet means to make someone feel uneasy or anxious. Therefore, the most fitting option is (C) unsettle as it aligns with the concept of causing disturbance or unease.

2 — A

To splice means to join two or more things together, usually by intertwining or overlapping them. Synonym of splice is (A) join.

3 — E

To be bewildered means to be confused or puzzled. Synonym of BEWILDERED is (E) perplexed.

4 — A

Jumble refers to a mixture or confused collection of things that are difficult to separate or sort out. Synonym of JUMBLE is (A) mixture.

5 — B

Bizarre often means something unusual or strange, and (B) peculiar is a synonym that captures that sense of oddity or distinctiveness.

6 — D

To retort means to make a sharp or witty reply in response to a comment or question. Synonym of RETORT is (D) snappy answer.

Answers & Explanations

7. B

Shimmer means a subdued, tremulous light or gleam. Synonym of Shimmer is (B) gleam.

8. A

A nudge is a gentle push or touch, often used to get someone's attention or to encourage them to take action. It is not a forceful action but rather a subtle urging, so (A) push is the correct answer.

9. D

Muffle means to wrap or cover something to reduce its noise or sound. Synonym of MUFFLE is (D) wrap.

10. D

To repudiate something means to reject or disown it, and Synonym of REPUDIATE is (D) relinquish.

11. B

A facsimile is a copy or reproduction of something. It is especially used to refer to copies of documents, books, or artworks that attempt to be as similar as possible to the original. Synonym of FACSIMILE is (B) replica.

12. E

Adverse means harmful or unfavorable, often in a serious or significant way. (E) hostile is the best answer because it suggests a level of active opposition or aggression, which is often associated with adverse conditions or situations.

13. B

An affront is an offense or an action that causes outrage or offense, making (B) insult the most appropriate choice among the options.

14. E

Gaunt means thin and bony, often due to illness, malnourishment, or suffering. (E) emaciated is the best answer because it suggests a tired or worn appearance, which is often associated with someone who is gaunt.

15. D

Indigenous refers to something or someone that is native or original to a particular region or area. Synonym of INDIGENOUS is (D) native.

16. A

Scanty means very small or insufficient in quantity or amount. Synonym of SCANTY is (A) meager.

17. E

Fastidious refers to someone who is very attentive to detail and cleanliness. Synonym of FASTIDIOUS is (E) meticulous.

18. C

Tentative means unsettled, uncertain, hesitant, or not fully developed. Synonym of TENTATIVE is (C) uncertain.

19. **E**

Segregate means to separate or isolate a particular group of people or things from the rest, often based on race, ethnicity, or some other characteristic. Synonym of SEGREGATE is (E) isolate.

20. **E**

Amenable means willing to comply or cooperate. Synonym of AMENABLE is (E) compliant.

21. **B**

Therapeutic refers to something that is used to treat or heal a condition. Synonym of THERAPEUTIC is (B) healing.

22. **A**

Decimate means to destroy or kill a large proportion of something or someone. Synonym of DECIMATE is (A) annihilate.

23. **A**

Rescind means to revoke or cancel. Among the given options, (A) nullify is the most appropriate word.

24. **D**

Portal refers to an entrance, a gate or a doorway. Synonym of PORTAL is (D) gate.

25. **D**

A token is a symbol or representation of something else. It can be a physical object, gesture, or action that is used to represent something else or convey a message. Synonym of TOKEN is (D) symbol.

26. **A**

To substantiate means to provide evidence or proof to support a claim or argument. It involves showing that something is true or valid by providing supporting evidence. Synonym of SUBSTANTIATE is (A) prove.

27. **C**

Adroit means skillful and adept in performing tasks or activities, particularly those that require dexterity and coordination. Synonym of ADROIT is (C) nimble.

28. **A**

To ponder means to think deeply and carefully about something. It implies a process of contemplation and reflection, often with the goal of gaining insight or understanding. Synonym of PONDER is (A) meditate.

29. **E**

Zeal refers to intense enthusiasm or passion for a particular cause or pursuit. It implies a strong and active commitment to something, often with a sense of fervor or urgency. Synonym of ZEAL is (E) ardor.

30. **C**

The word "acquiesce" means to accept, comply, or agree to something reluctantly or without protest. Therefore, (C) concede is the answer.

31	E

A caricature is an exaggerated representation of a person or thing, typically in a drawing or a portrait. Similarly, hyperbole is an expression of a statement.

32	C

A yard is a unit of measurement for distance. Similarly, a pint is a measure of volume.

33	B

A school is a group of fish swimming together, while pride is a group of lions.

34	C

A scalpel is a surgical tool used by a surgeon, while a cleaver is a tool used by a butcher to chop meat. Both tools are used by professionals in their respective fields.

35	C

Towering refers to height, while hulking refers to size.

36	A

The sole is the bottom part of the foot, while the palm is the bottom part of the hand. Both are the flat inner surfaces of their respective body parts.

37	E

Mutton is meat obtained from a mature sheep. Similarly, veal is meat obtained from a young calf.

38	C

An obituary is a written article about someone who has recently died. Similarly, an elegy is a type of poem that is written to lament the loss of someone.

39	D

Anthem is a specific type song. Similarly, still life is a specific type of painting.

40	B

A scroll is a type of writing material made of parchment, which is an animal skin that has been specially prepared for writing. Similarly, a book is typically made of paper.

41	D

To raise something up, you might use a crane. Similarly, to dig or move earth, you would use a shovel to excavate.

42	D

A bear's baby is called a cub, and a kangaroo's baby is called a joey.

43	A

Geriatrics is the medical specialty that deals with the care of elderly people, and pediatrics is the medical specialty that deals with the care of children.

44 C

A newspaper informs, a drama cautions, a script is written by a playwright, and a fiction book is perused, but a novel is specifically written to entertain the reader.

45 C

recede and retreat are synonyms, meaning to move back or withdraw. depict is to portray, has a similar relationship to retreat and recede, as both depict and portray are synonyms that mean to represent something visually or in words.

46 A

A symphony is a musical composition made up of movements, and a book is a written work made up of chapters.

47 D

A quill is a spiky feature of a porcupine that it uses for defense. Similarly, a skunk has a unique and strong odor that it uses for defense.

48 C

A racquet is a specialized tool used to hit a ball in tennis, and similarly, a club is a specialized tool used to hit a ball in golf.

49 E

An engine is a device used to produce power, and in the context of an automobile, it is the part that powers the car. Similarly, a locomotive is part of a train that powers the train.

50 C

A trickle is a slow, small flow, while gush implies a rapid and abundant flow. Similarly, a flicker is a brief, wavering light, and blaze suggests a steady, strong presence of light.

51 B

Beneficial means helpful, and dubious means skeptical.

52 E

In a choir, there are many singers who come together to sing as a group. Similarly, in a faculty, there are many teachers.

53 E

A daydream is a pleasant and mild fantasy, while a hallucination is an intense and often unpleasant experience. Similarly, a cave is a small dwelling, and a cavern is a huge one.

54 D

A limousine is a luxurious and expensive car, while a jalopy is an old and dilapidated car. Similarly, a mansion is a large and luxurious house, while a hovel is a small and poor-quality dwelling.

55 C

In a joust, two knights use lances to compete against each other. Similarly, in a debate, two or more individuals use speech to argue and present their opinions.

56 D

A misdemeanor is a less serious crime, while a felony is a more serious crime. Similarly, filching is a less serious form of theft, while embezzling is a more serious form of theft.

57 A

Timeless means something that is always relevant or not affected by the passage of time, while interminable is the antonym of transient.

58 C

Jog is a slow and steady pace, while sprint is a fast and explosive burst of speed. Stare is a much more powerful form of looking than a glimpse.

59 B

The relationship between a cobbler and an awl is that an awl is a tool commonly used by cobblers to punch holes in leather or other materials, and scissors are a tool commonly used by tailors to cut fabric.

60 B

A tune is a simple, single melody, while a symphony is a complex, multi-movement musical composition. Sleep is much simpler than a coma.

SECTION 4

1 E

To find out how much larger is 28 than 20, we need to subtract 20 from 28.
$28 - 20 = 8$
Therefore, the answer is (E) 8.

2 B

If a and b are positive numbers and c is a negative number, then $ac - b$ must be:
(A) positive if $ac > b$
(B) negative if $ac < b$
(C) zero if $ac = b$

So, the answer is (B) negative.

3 B

To find out which of the following numbers is divisible by 3, we need to calculate the sum of their digits and check if it is divisible by 3.

(A) 125, sum of digits $= 1 + 2 + 5 = 8$, not divisible by 3
(B) 324, sum of digits $= 3 + 2 + 4 = 9$, divisible by 3
(C) 301, sum of digits $= 3 + 0 + 1 = 4$, not divisible by 3
(D) 407, sum of digits $= 4 + 0 + 7 = 11$, not divisible by 3
(E) 908, sum of digits $= 9 + 0 + 8 = 17$, not divisible by 3

Therefore, the answer is (B) 324.

4 D

To find out what number is 13 one-third of, we need to multiply 13 by 3.
$13 \times 3 = 39$
Therefore, the answer is (D) 39.

5 A

If a building has 3/7 of its floors below ground, then the ratio of the number of floors below ground to the number of floors above ground is:

Below ground: 3
Above ground: 7−3=4

So, the answer is (A) 3:4.

6 A

To find out how many feet of snow will fall in 9 hours if snow is falling at the rate of one foot every three hours, we need to multiply the rate of snowfall by the number of intervals of three hours in 9 hours.

1 foot / 3 hours = 1/3 feet per hour
9 hours / 3 hours = 3 intervals
1/3 feet per hour x 3 intervals = 1 foot

Therefore, the answer is (A) 3'.

7 D

The cost of a phone call lasting exactly m minutes is calculated by adding the cost of the first 2 minutes (x cents) to the cost of the remaining ($m-2$) minutes (y cents per minute).

cos$t = x + (m-2) \times y$

Therefore, the answer is (D) $x + y(m-2)$.

8 D

The numbers in figure 1 are multiples of 3. To find out what **10 equals, we need to multiply 10 by 3:

**10 = 10 × 3 = 30

Therefore, the answer is (D) 30.

9 B

(**3) = 9, so to get 27, we need to multiply (**3) by 3:
(**3) x 3 = 9 x 3 = 27

You can see the chart with the information (**1) = 3.

(**3)(**1) = 9 * 3 = 27

Therefore, the answer is (B) (**3)(**1).

10 D

If there are x chairs in each row, then there are $12x$ chairs in total. If there are 8 empty chairs, then the number of people seated is $12x-8$.

We need to find a number that satisfies this equation and is also a positive integer.

The answer choices give us a shortcut to find the correct answer by testing each choice:

(A) If there are 50 people seated, then there are $12x-8=50$ people in total. Solving for x, we get $x=58/12$, which is not a positive integer.
(B) If there are 54 people seated, then there are $12x-8=54$ people in total. Solving for x, we get $x=62/12$, which is not a positive integer.
(C) If there are 68 people seated, then there are $12x-8=68$ people in total. Solving for x, we get $x=76/12$, which is not a positive integer.
(D) If there are 100 people seated, then there are $12x-8=100$ people in total. Solving for x, we get $x=108/12=9$, which is a positive integer. Therefore, the answer is (D) 100.
(E) If there are 106 people seated, then there are $12x-8=106$ people in total. Solving for x, we get $x=114/12$, which is not a positive integer.

Therefore, the correct answer is (D) 100.

Answers & Explanations

11   C

To find out what percent of the regular menu price Alex ended up paying for his meal, we need to calculate the total discount as a combination of 30% off and 20% off. To calculate the final price, we need to subtract the total discount from the regular price, and divide the result by the regular price.

Total discount = 30% + 20% − (30% × 20%) = 44%

Final price = 100% − 44% = 56%

Therefore, the answer is (C) 56%.

12   B

The total number of pieces of candy is 8 + 14 = 22. To find out how many pieces of candy Adam should give Colleen, we need to find half of the total number of pieces of candy:

22 ÷ 2 = 11

Each of them should have 11 pieces of candy, and currently, Colleen has 8 pieces of candy. Therefore, Adam should give Colleen:

11 − 8 = 3

pieces of candy.

So the answer is (B) 3.

13   B

Let x be the number of sides of the polygon. Then, the perimeter is equal to the product of the number of sides and the average length, or $6x$. Therefore, we can set up the equation $6x = 72$, which simplifies to $x = 12$. So, the answer is (B) 12.

14   D

Let x be the smallest number in the set of 25 consecutive whole numbers. Then, the largest number is $x + 24$. The average of the set is given by the sum of the numbers divided by the number of numbers, or $(25x + 300)/25 = x + 12$. Therefore, we can set up the equation $x + 12 = 57$, which simplifies to $x = 45$. So, the largest number is $45 + 24 = 69$. The largest number is $69 - 45 = 24$ greater than the smallest number. Therefore, the answer is (D) 24.

15   A

To multiply two fractions, we multiply their numerators and denominators separately.

So $\frac{1}{4}$ of $\frac{2}{3}$ can be found as:

$$\frac{1}{4} \times \frac{2}{3} = \frac{2}{12} = \frac{1}{6}$$

Therefore, $\frac{1}{4}$ of $\frac{2}{3}$ is equal to (A) $\frac{1}{6}$.

16   C

To find Austin's average speed, we need to divide the total distance he travels by the time it takes him to complete the 80-mile trip. According to the problem, the time it takes him to complete the trip is between 2.5 and 4 hours. Therefore, the range of his average speed in miles per hour is:

80 miles ÷ 4 hours = 20 miles per hour (the slowest average speed)
80 miles ÷ 2.5 hours = 32 miles per hour (the fastest average speed)

Therefore, his average speed must be between 20 and 32 miles per hour.

So, the correct answer is (C) 20 and 32.

17   E

The answer is (E) 19,750 (1 x .25) since this simply multiplies 19,750 by 0.25, which is not the same as multiplying by 1.25. Therefore, the answer is (E) 19,750 (1 x .25)

18 D

Let's call the length of the original square cardboard x. Then, each side of the base of the box is $x-2$, since we cut out 2 inches from each side. The perimeter of the base is then $4(x-2)=24$, which simplifies to $x-2=6$, or $x=8$.

Therefore, the original square piece of cardboard has an area of $x^2 = 64$ square inches.
Therefore, the answer is (D) 64.

19 E

The overlapping region of two triangles can have the same number of sides as a triangle if the two triangles share a side and the other sides overlap.

It is not possible for the overlapping region to have fewer sides than a triangle because it must have at least three sides to be a polygon.

It is also not possible for the overlapping region to have more sides than a triangle because it is formed by the intersection of two triangles, which each have three sides. The overlapping region can only have fewer or the same number of sides as a triangle.

Therefore, the answer is (E) II and III only.

20 B

To find the smallest value among the given options, we need to plug in the largest possible value for y and compare the results. Since $y > 12$, the largest possible value for y is 13.

- (A) $\dfrac{(y+4)}{y} = \dfrac{17}{13}$
- (B) $\dfrac{2}{(y+2)} = \dfrac{2}{15}$
- (C) $y^2 = 169$
- (D) $2\sqrt{y} = 2\sqrt{13}$
- (E) $y\sqrt{49} = 13\sqrt{49}$

Therefore, the smallest value is (B), which is $\dfrac{2}{15}$.

21 C

1 foot = 12 inches

So, 3 feet = 3 × 12 = 36 inches

The length given was 3 feet or 36 inches, but it should have been 3 inches. Therefore, it is 12 times too long.

So the answer is (C) 12.

22 A

To determine which expression is the least when $x > 2$, we can substitute a value greater than 2 into each expression and compare the results.

Let's evaluate each expression for $x = 3$:

(A) $\dfrac{x}{(x+2)} = \dfrac{3}{(3+2)} = \dfrac{3}{5} = 0.6$
(B) $x - 2 = 3 - 2 = 1$
(C) $x + 2 = 3 + 2 = 5$
(D) $2x - 1 = 2(3) - 1 = 6 - 1 = 5$
(E) $\dfrac{(x+2)}{x} = \dfrac{(3+2)}{3} = \dfrac{5}{3} \approx 1.67$

Comparing the results, we can see that expression (A) $\dfrac{x}{(x+2)}$ is the least value among the given expressions when $x > 2$.

23 E

If Cara started 5 meters below sea level and climbed up 12 meters, then she is 7 meters above sea level. Therefore, the answer is (E) 7 meters above sea level.

24 C

Let x be the number of sides of the polygon. Then, the perimeter is equal to the product of the number of sides and the average length, or $11x$. Therefore, we can set up the equation $11x = 154$, which simplifies to $x = 14$. So, the answer is (C) 14.

25 D

The copier prints 700 sheets every 12 minutes, which is equivalent to printing 350 sheets every 6 minutes (by dividing both numbers by 2). So, to print 12,000 sheets, the copier would need:

12,000 sheets ÷ 350 sheets per 6 minutes = 34.28 (rounded to two decimal places) sets of 350 sheets

Each set takes 6 minutes to print, so:

34 sets x 6 minutes per set = 204 minutes

So, it would take the copier between 3 and 3.5 hours (since 204 minutes is between 180 and 210 minutes, which is equivalent to 3–3.5 hours). Therefore, the answer is (D) Between 3 and 3.5 hours.

TEST ANSWERS

Practice 3

Section 1, 4: Quantitative (MATH) Answer

*Quantitative (Math) scores should be calculated based on the total of 50 questions from Section 1 and Section 4.

pp.131 – 140

TEST 3 SECTION 1 MATH 1

1. C	6. C	11. C	16. A	21. E
2. D	7. E	12. D	17. A	22. C
3. E	8. E	13. B	18. C	23. B
4. E	9. B	14. D	19. E	24. C
5. B	10. E	15. E	20. B	25. C

pp.166 – 175

TEST 3 SECTION 4 MATH 2

1. C	6. B	11. D	16. E	21. D
2. A	7. C	12. D	17. A	22. D
3. D	8. B	13. D	18. A	23. B
4. E	9. A	14. E	19. D	24. A
5. E	10. E	15. B	20. B	25. D

My Quantitative(Math) Score (Section 1 + Section 4)

Right	Wrong	Omitted	Raw Score ($= right - \frac{wrong}{4}$)	Scaled Score	Percentile
					%

Please consult the Scaled Score & Percentile Chart on the back of this book for the calculation of your Scaled Score and Percentile.

Section 2: Reading Answer

pp.141 — 157

TEST 3 SECTION 2 READING

1. D	9. A	17. C	25. B	33. C
2. D	10. B	18. A	26. E	34. B
3. C	11. D	19. B	27. A	35. B
4. E	12. B	20. D	28. D	36. A
5. A	13. C	21. C	29. B	37. D
6. B	14. A	22. D	30. A	38. C
7. A	15. B	23. A	31. C	39. B
8. B	16. E	24. A	32. D	40. A

My Reading Score

Right	Wrong	Omitted	Raw Score $(= \text{right} - \frac{\text{wrong}}{4})$	Scaled Score	Percentile
					%

Please consult the Scaled Score & Percentile Chart on the back of this book for the calculation of your Scaled Score and Percentile.

Section 3: Verbal Answer

pp.158 – 165

TEST 3 SECTION 3 VERBAL

1. E	13. D	25. C	37. C	49. E
2. D	14. E	26. A	38. C	50. A
3. C	15. E	27. C	39. E	51. B
4. B	16. E	28. B	40. A	52. D
5. C	17. C	29. B	41. E	53. C
6. A	18. C	30. A	42. E	54. D
7. B	19. D	31. C	43. B	55. C
8. C	20. A	32. E	44. C	56. C
9. B	21. A	33. C	45. A	57. C
10. A	22. D	34. C	46. A	58. D
11. A	23. E	35. A	47. D	59. E
12. E	24. E	36. C	48. E	60. C

My Reading Score

Right	Wrong	Omitted	Raw Score $(= \text{right} - \dfrac{\text{wrong}}{4})$	Scaled Score	Percentile
					%

Please consult the Scaled Score & Percentile Chart on the back of this book for the calculation of your Scaled Score and Percentile.

Practice Test 3

SECTION 1

1   C

Translating 3 units to the left means subtracting 3 from the x-coordinate, giving us $(5-3, -2) = (2, -2)$. Reflecting over the y-axis negates the x-coordinate, resulting in $(-2, -2)$, which matches option (C).

2   D

To find the remainder when 47 is divided by 8, we divide 47 by 8 using long division:

```
    5
 8)47
   40
   ――
    7
```

Therefore, 47 divided by 8 is 5 with a remainder of 7. Therefore, the answer is (D) 7.

3   E

The tens digit of a number is the digit in the second place from the right. In 12,497, the digit in the tens place is 9. Therefore, the answer is (E) 9.

4   E

Find the values of $7(a+b)$, if $a = 2b - 6$ and $4a + 2b = 16$.
To solve for a and b, we can use the second equation to eliminate b:
$4a + 2b = 16$
$2b = 16 - 4a$
$b = 8 - 2a$
Substituting this value of b into the first equation, we get:
$a = 2(8 - 2a) - 6$
$a = 10 - 4a$
$5a = 10$
$a = 2$
Using this value of a, we can find the value of b:
$b = 8 - 2a = 8 - 2(2) = 4$
Finally, we can substitute these values of a and b into $7(a+b)$:
$7(a+b) = 7(2+4) = 7(6) = 42$
Therefore, the answer is (E) 42.

5   B

Since N is the midpoint of MP, we have MN = NP = 12. Also, since O is the midpoint of NP, we have $OP = NP/2 = 12/2 = 6$. Therefore, the answer is (B) 6.

6   C

To find the percentage, we need to divide 27 by 3 and multiply by 100:
$(27/3) \times 100 = 900\%$
Therefore, the answer is (C) 900%.

7   E

To find the new selling price, we can use the formula:
new price = old price + (percent increase/100) × old price
Substituting the values given in the question, we get:

new price = 1200 + (25/100) × 1200 = 1200 + 300 = 1500

Therefore, the answer is (E) $1,500.

8   E

If the ratio of men to women to children is 4:3:2, then we can divide the total number of people (243) into 9 equal parts (4+3+2). Each part represents the same number of people. Therefore, each part is equal to 243/9 = 27.

Since there are 4 parts representing men, there are 4 × 27 = 108 men in the room.

Similarly, there are 3 × 27 = 81 women and 2 × 27 = 54 children in the room.

Therefore, the number of adults (men + women) is 108 + 81 = 189.

Therefore, the answer is (E) 189.

9   B

We can solve this problem by setting up a proportion:

1 inch on map = 90 yards in reality

Let x be the number of inches on the map that represents a 480-yard-long distance. Then we can write:

$x/1 = 480/90$

Simplifying the right-hand side gives:

$x/1 = 16/3$

Multiplying both sides by 3 gives:

$x = 16/3$

So, the answer is approximately 5.3 inches, which is option (B).

10   E

David's rate is 1/3 of the garden per hour, and Richard's rate is 1/2 of the garden per hour. Working together, their combined rate is (1/3 + 1/2) = 5/6 of the garden per hour.

Let's use the formula:

time = work / rate

where time is measured in hours, work is measured in units of the task being performed (in this case, weeding the garden), and rate is measured in units of work per unit of time (in this case, fraction of the garden per hour).

We want to find the time it takes for them to complete the task, so let's set work equal to 1 (the whole garden). Then we have:

time = work / rate = 1 / (5/6) = 6/5 hours = 1 hour and 12 minutes

So the answer is (E) 72 min.

11   C

Let x be the temperature on the seventh day. Then, we can use the formula for the average:

(6 days × 30 degrees + 1 day × x degrees) / 7 days = 31 degrees

Simplifying this equation, we get:

$180 + x = 217$

$x = 37$

Therefore, the answer is (C) 37 degrees.

12   D

25% of $200 is equal to

To find 25% of $200, we can multiply 200 by 0.25:

25% of $200 = 0.25 × $200 = $50

Therefore, the answer is (D) 100% of $50.

13   B

To minimize the number of buses, we should try to put as many staff as possible on each bus without exceeding the maximum limit of 8. Let's start by putting 8 staff on the first bus, then 7 on the second, and so on, until we cannot put any more staff on a bus without exceeding the limit.

First bus: 8 staff
Second bus: 7 staff

Third bus: 6 staff
Fourth bus: 5 staff
Fifth bus: 2 staff
Total: 8+7+6+5+2=28

Therefore, we need 5 buses, and the answer is (B).

14   D

We have:

$(2+2)/(3+4) = ∀/42$

Simplifying the left-hand side gives:

$4/7 = ∀/42$

Cross-multiplying gives:

$∀ = 42 × (4/7) = 24$

Therefore, the answer is (D) 24.

15   E

Find a shape that cannot be made by folding a paper in half, and it should not be symmetrical. Therefore, the answer is (E).

16   A

An octagon has 8 sides of equal length. To find the length of each side, we can divide the perimeter by 8:
192 inches / 8 = 24 inches
To convert inches to feet, we divide by 12:
24 inches / 12 = 2 feet
Therefore, the length of each side of the table is 2 feet. The answer is (A) 2.

17   A

We are told that the independent school association provided financial aid to 79,000 students, which is 82.7% of their total enrollment. Let's set up an equation to represent this:

(Number of students receiving financial aid) / (Total enrollment) = 82.7% = 0.827
Let's denote the total enrollment as "T". Then we have:
79,000 / T = 0.827
Now, we can solve for T:
T = 79,000 / 0.827 ≈ 95,473
So, the total enrollment is approximately 95,473 students.
Therefore, the total enrollment is between between 50,000 and 100,000. The answer is (A).

18   C

To find Joseph's average time for each lap of the race, we need to divide the total time by the number of laps:
12 minutes and 15 seconds = 12 × 60 seconds + 15 seconds = 735 seconds
Average time for each lap = total time / number of laps = 735 seconds / 30 laps = 24.5 seconds
Therefore, the answer is (C) 24.5.

19   E

3 to get the weight of the jet, which is 18 tons. To find the weight of 8 identical planes, we multiply 18 by 8, which is:
18 × 8 = 144
Therefore, the weight of 8 identical planes can be found by multiplying 6 by (E) 24.

20   B

Ramon traveled the first 10 km of the distance at a speed of 10 km/hour, which took him 1 hour. Let's denote his walking speed as x km/hour. The remaining distance he covered by walking at a speed of x km/hour, and this took him 2 hours (since the total time of 3 hours was already spent).

Using the formula distance = speed × time, we have:

10 km + (20 km − 10 km) = x km/hour × 2 hours
Simplifying this equation, we get:
20 km = 2x km/hour × 2 hours
20 km = 4x km
x = 5 km/hour
Therefore, Ramon's walking speed is 5 km/hour, and the answer is (B).

21   E

Let x be the number of years since 2011. Then, the population of Town A in year x is 9,600 and the population of Town B in year x is 8,600 + 100x. We want to find the value of x when the populations are equal:
9,600 = 8,600 + 100x
Subtracting 8,600 from both sides, we get:
1,000 = 100x
Dividing both sides by 100, we get:
x = 10
Therefore, the populations will be equal in 2011 + 10 years = 2021. The answer is (E) 2021.

22   C

Using the formula A★B = (A × B) − (A + B), we get:
2★7 = (2 × 7) − (2 + 7) = 14 − 9 = 5
Therefore, the answer is (C) 5.

23   B

Using the formula A★B = (A × B) − (A + B), we can set up the equation:
Z × 5 − (Z + 5) = 27
Simplifying this equation, we get:
4Z − 5 = 27
Adding 5 to both sides, we get:
4Z = 32
Dividing both sides by 4, we get:
Z = 8
Therefore, the answer is (B) 8.

24   C

The mode is the most frequent value in a set of data. In this case, the mode is 82, as it appears three times, while all other values appear only once or twice. Therefore, the answer is (C) 82.

25   C

To find the solution of the system of equations, we need to find the values of x and y that satisfy both equations simultaneously.

We can start by setting y1 equal to y2:

5/2x − 3 = (−1/2)x + 2

Simplifying this equation, we get:

6x/2 = 5

3x = 5

x = 5/3

Now, we can substitute this value of x into either of the original equations to find y:

y1 = 5/2(5/3) − 3

y1 = 25/6 − 18/6

y1 = 7/6

Therefore, the answer is (C) ($\frac{5}{3}$, $\frac{7}{6}$).

SECTION 2

Questions 1-6

The article is discussing the concept of "magnetism" as it applies to successful pianists. The author explores why some pianists with weaker technical skills can still draw larger crowds and applause, despite their shortcomings. The author references the views of Charles Frohman, a keen theatrical producer, who attributed the success of actors to "vitality," which he sees as a weaker synonym for magnetism. The author then cites the definition of magnetism by Professor John D. Quackenbos, who defines it as "earnestness and sincerity, coupled with insight, sympathy, patience, and tact." However, the author notes that this definition is too narrow and does not account for the phenomenon of a pianist with "volcanic vitality" overwhelming an audience.

1 D

The author describes magnetism as "an unusual, powerful, and exciting quality which attracts people." This fits (D), "It is unusual, powerful, and the exciting quality which attracts people."

2 D

The primary focus of the passage is the definition of magnetism and its characteristics. (D), "the meaning of magnetism and its characteristics," best describes this focus.

3 C

The author mentions Rubinstein as an example of a pianist who often makes mistakes but still draws large crowds. The author uses this example to elaborate on the meaning of magnetism. (C), "to elaborate on the meaning of magnetism," best fits this purpose.

4 E

According to the passage, John D. Quackenbos was a physician and a philosopher but not a lexicographer. (D), "He was a lexicographer," is not true.

5 A

The word "blunder" means to make a gross mistake. (A), "to make a gross mistake," best fits this definition.

6 B

The author mentions that pianists with magnetism, such as Rubinstein, are able to draw larger audiences and arouse more applause. (B), "draws larger audiences and arouses more applause," accurately reflects this point.

Questions 7-11

The Harlem Renaissance in the 1920s was a period of significant growth and celebration of African American culture. It showcased black dance, music, comedy, and theater to the country and the world, giving people a chance to appreciate the talents of black artists. The Harlem Renaissance also represented a cultural and social movement in which black pride was beginning to influence changes in African Americans' self-perception and, eventually, how all Americans viewed black Americans. The migration of African Americans to northern urban areas, mainly for economic opportunities, contributed to the explosion of black culture, especially in New York City, which was already a mecca for artists of all cultures.

7   A

The passage primarily discusses the significance of the Harlem Renaissance to African Americans, as evidenced by the line, "the Harlem Renaissance was more than just a greater exposure to black dance, music, comedy, or theater, even though the chance for all people to appreciate the talents of black artists were indeed worthwhile in their own right." and "the cultural and social movements of the time in which black pride was beginning to cause significant changes in the way African Americans thought about themselves and, eventually, how all Americans thought of black Americans."

8   B

The information in the passage states that the Harlem Renaissance was more than just a limited cultural movement among black people, as evidenced by the line "the Harlem Renaissance was more than just a greater exposure to black dance, music, comedy, or theater."

9   A

The information in the passage answers the question of how the Harlem Renaissance changed the thought of black culture, as evidenced by the line "many factors led to black culture's explosion, especially in New York City…And during this time, the cultural and social movements of the time in which black pride was beginning to cause significant changes in the way African Americans thought about themselves and, eventually, how all Americans thought of black Americans."

10   B

The word "mecca" means a place where many people who are interested in a culture go there, as used in the line "New York City had been a mecca for artists of every culture for a long time as it is today."

11   D

The author's tone can be described as objective, as the author neutrally presents the information without personal opinions or biases.

Questions 12-19

This passage is a conversation between Juliet and Romeo in Shakespeare's play, Romeo and Juliet. Juliet is expressing her desire for Romeo to reject his family name of Montague and instead be only known as her love. Romeo agrees to be "re-baptized" and take on a new name just for her. However, when Juliet asks him who he is, he reveals that his name is hateful to himself because it is an enemy to her. Despite this, Juliet recognizes his voice and asks if he is Romeo, a Montague. Romeo responds by saying that he is neither, if either name is not pleasing to her.

12   B

The main idea of Juliet's first two speeches is that a name is not as important as the thing or person it names. This is demonstrated when she says, "What's in a name? That which we call a rose / By any other name would smell as sweet." She is suggesting that the name of a person or object does not change its essence.

13   C

The main problem that Juliet expresses is that she cannot love Romeo because he is a Montague. This is evident when she says, "'Tis but thy name that is my enemy. / Thou art thyself, though not a Montague. / What's

Montague? It is nor hand, nor foot, / Nor arm, nor face, nor any other part / Belonging to a man." The Montagues and Capulets are two families that are feuding, and Juliet feels that this is preventing her from being able to love Romeo.

14   A

In the context of the passage, the word "doff" means to remove. This is evident when Juliet says, "Romeo, doff thy name; / And for that name, which is no part of thee, / Take all myself." She is asking Romeo to remove his name, which is associated with the Montagues and preventing them from being together.

15   B

Juliet offers to give herself to Romeo if he swears his love for her. This is demonstrated when she says, "Romeo, doff thy name; / And for that name, which is no part of thee, / Take all myself." She is essentially saying that she will be his if he renounces his association with the Montagues.

16   E

The action in this scene takes place at night. This is evident when Juliet says, "What man art thou that, thus bescreeen'd in night, / So stumblest on my counsel?" She is addressing someone who is hidden in the night, suggesting that it is nighttime.

17   C

Readers can infer from the passage that Romeo and Juliet have not known each other for long. This is evident from their conversation, as Juliet says, "My ears have yet not drunk a hundred words / Of that tongue's utterance, yet I know the sound." She is suggesting that she is just beginning to get to know him, and therefore they have not known each other for very long.

18   A

In the passage, Romeo says that he is willing to change his name (doff his name) because he loves Juliet. He says "Call me but love, and I'll be new baptiz'd; Henceforth I never will be Romeo." This shows that Romeo values his love for Juliet more than his name and that he is willing to change his identity for her.

19   B

When Juliet believes she is alone and expresses her thoughts about Romeo and the significance of names, her mood is contemplative and romantic. She reflects on the idea that a name is just a label and doesn't define the true essence of a person.

Questions 20-24

The author describes a lack of family meals and proper dining during their childhood and early boyhood. Meals were obtained irregularly and without any formal setting. The author also mentions being required to work at the "big house" during meal times, where they learned about freedom and the war from white people's conversations. One memorable moment for the author was seeing two of their young mistresses eating ginger cakes, symbolizing their ambition for freedom.

20   D

The author's description of their experiences on the plantation and being required to perform duties such as fanning the flies from the table for the white people supports the conclusion that the author was a slave.

| 21 | C |

The author's use of first-person narrative and personal recollection of their experiences suggest that the passage is part of an autobiography.

| 22 | D |

The passage mentions that the author's greatest ambition, once he was freed, was to get to the point where he could secure and eat ginger cakes in the way he saw some ladies doing.

| 23 | A |

The author's descriptions of their experiences as a slave and their ultimate desire for freedom are consistent with the theme of "Up from Slavery."

| 24 | A |

The author's description of the ginger cakes as the "most tempting and desirable things" they had ever seen and their resolution to secure and eat them if they ever got free suggests that the ginger cakes symbolize freedom.

Questions 25-28

The poem portrays an aged knight reflecting on his past. Wearing worn armor and weathered by time, he holds a sword and shield, each telling stories of battles and triumphs. The knight reminisces about his youth in bright armor, chasing dreams in the morning light. The poem captures the essence of a seasoned warrior contemplating the passage of time and the memories etched in his weapons.

| 25 | B |

The central theme revolves around the aged knight reflecting on his youth as he looks at his sword and shield.

| 26 | E |

The scars on the shield are likely from past victories in battles, representing the triumphs and challenges faced by the knight.

| 27 | A |

In the context of the poem, "tethered" means connected or restrained, reflecting the knight's connection to time and the limitations it imposes.

| 28 | D |

The tone of the poem is somber and reflective, as the knight contemplates his past and the effects of time on his armor and weapons.

Questions 29-32

The passage talks about how impressive it is that New York City works well even though it has complicated systems. The city has intricate ways of getting water, communicating, and doing everyday things, and it manages to handle many challenges. The passage highlights how New York City can adapt and keep going, facing problems like supply issues, traffic, and environmental threats.

| 29 | B |

The passage mentions that a love message from a young man in Manhattan to his girl in Brooklyn gets blown through a pneumatic tube.

| 30 | A |

In the passage, "ganglia" refers to a complex network of connections in the underground infrastructure of New York City.

| 31 | C |

The passage primarily focuses on the challenges and potential crises that New York City faces, highlighting its improbable functioning.

| 32 | D |

The passage mentions that New York City should have perished of hunger when food lines failed for a few days.

Questions 33-37

The speaker and the person he is talking to are discussing different types of personal struggles and failures in life. The speaker says that it may be a type of failure where a person becomes unhappy and hates others, but the person he is talking to disagrees, saying that hate doesn't last long for them. The speaker then talks about a "special kind of fall" that he thinks the person is headed for, where a person falls without hitting bottom and it is caused by giving up on finding something that their environment couldn't provide.

| 33 | C |

The tone of Mr. Antolini in this passage can be described as earnest and concerned. He engages in a sincere and thoughtful conversation with the protagonist, expressing a genuine interest in the protagonist's well-being and future.

| 34 | B |

In the given context, "environment" most likely refers to the social, cultural, and personal surroundings or circumstances in which individuals find themselves. It encompasses the external factors that influence and shape a person's experiences, beliefs, and opportunities. Mr. Antolini suggests that some individuals may give up searching for something meaningful in their lives because they feel that their current environment cannot provide what they are looking for or what they believe they need.

| 35 | B |

The main idea revolves around Mr. Antolini's perspective on a specific type of fall, which is designed for men seeking something their own environment couldn't provide.

| 36 | A |

The protagonist admits that after a while, if he didn't see the people he hated, he sort of missed them.

| 37 | D |

Throughout the passage, the speaker seems to have a high regard for Mr. Antolini and his opinions. He listens attentively to Mr. Antolini's speech and seems to trust his words.

Questions 38-40

Cynthia Moss studied elephants in Amboseli, Kenya, in 1972, observing their undisturbed behavior. Unlike threatened counterparts, these elephants adapted to environmental changes, forming smaller groups in droughts and larger herds in abundance. Moss challenged the idea of a fixed social structure, highlighting the elephants' dynamic nature. She concluded that while elephants prefer large groups, they exhibit resilience by adapting to challenges with flexibility.

38 C

The passage mentions that Moss chose Amboseli because the elephants there were among the least harassed, providing a peaceful setting for observation.

39 B

In the context of the passage, "congregate" means to gather, reflecting the tendency of elephants to form large groups.

40 A

Moss concludes that elephants prefer to congregate in large groups but may split up when forced by a lack of food.

SECTION 3

1 E

Delegate means a person chosen or elected to act as a representative. Among the given options, (E) representative is the best fit as a delegate can be defined as a representative who is authorized to act on behalf of others.

2 D

Supreme means the highest in rank, authority, or quality. Among the given options, (D) paramount is the closest in meaning to supreme.

3 C

Audacious means showing a willingness to take surprisingly bold risks, showing an impudent lack of respect, or showing an original and fearless approach. Among the given options, (C) daring is the best fit as it means to be adventurous or willing to take risks.

4 B

Futile means incapable of producing any useful result, pointless or unproductive. Among the given options, (B) useless is the closest in meaning to futile.

5 C

Prevalent is used to describe something that is widespread or commonly found. Synonym of prevalent is (C) common.

6   **A**

A chide is used to describe the act of scolding or reprimanding someone for their behavior or actions. Synonym of chide is (A) rebuke.

7   **B**

This word is used to describe something that is illegal or not authorized by law. For example, an illicit drug is one that is not legally available for use. Synonym of illegitimate is (B) illicit.

8   **C**

Authentic is used to describe something that is real or true, often in contrast to something that is fake or counterfeit. Synonym of authentic is genuine.

9   **B**

Meantime is used to describe the period of time between two events or actions. For example, if someone is waiting for a job offer, they might take an interim job in the meantime.

10   **A**

Brandish is often used to describe the act of waving something, such as a weapon, in a threatening or aggressive manner. Synonym of brandish is (A) wield.

11   **A**

Terse is used to describe speech or writing that is brief and brusque, often to the point of being rude or unfriendly. For example, a terse email might simply say "not interested" instead of offering an explanation.

12   **E**

Steadfast means firm, unwavering, or resolute in purpose or loyalty. The (E) unswerving emphasizes the quality of not deviating or changing, aligning well with the meaning of steadfast.

13   **D**

Valiant is used to describe someone who is brave or gallant in the face of danger or adversity. For example, a valiant firefighter might risk their life to save others from a burning building.

14   **E**

Humility means the quality of being modest or unassuming, often in contrast to someone who is arrogant or boastful. Synonym of humility is (E) humbleness.

15   **E**

Motif is often used in the context of art or literature to refer to a recurring element or idea that is used to convey a particular message or theme. Synonym of motif is (E) theme.

16   **E**

Preposterous is used to describe something that is ridiculous or contrary to reason. For example, the idea that the earth is flat is preposterous, since it has been proven through scientific evidence that the earth is in fact round.

17   **C**

Haughty is used to describe someone who has an arrogant or superior attitude towards others.

For example, a haughty person might act as if they are better than others and look down on them.

18   C

Hurl is often used to describe the act of throwing something with great force, such as a ball or a rock. Synonym of hurl is (C) fling.

19   D

Frail is used to describe something that is weak and delicate, often due to illness or old age. Synonym of frail is (D) feeble

20   A

Lavish is often used to describe someone who gives or spends generously, often to excess. Synonym of lavish is (A) profuse.

21   A

Placate is used to describe the act of making someone less angry or hostile by soothing or calming them. Synonym of placate is (A) appease.

22   D

Penance is often used in a religious context to describe an act of self-punishment or sacrifice in order to show remorse or to make amends for one's wrongdoing. Synonym of penance is (D) atonement.

23   E

Lethargic is used to describe a feeling of sluggishness or lack of energy. For example, a person might feel lethargic if they have not slept well. Synonym of lethargic is (E) languid.

24   E

Clandestine is used to describe something that is kept secret or done in a way that is hidden from others. For example, a clandestine meeting might be held in a private location to avoid detection by others who might disapprove. Synonym of clandestine is (E) surreptitious

25   C

Perpetuate is used to describe the act of maintaining or continuing something, often in an ongoing or unchanging way. For example, a person might perpetuate a tradition by passing it down to their children or by continuing to celebrate it each year.

26   A

Retrospect is often used to describe the act of looking back on past events or memories. Synonym of retrospect is (A) reminisce.

27   C

Reimburse is used to describe the act of repaying or compensating someone for expenses or losses incurred. For example, a person might be reimbursed for travel expenses incurred during a business trip.

28   B

Impart is used to describe the act of conveying or communicating information or knowledge to someone else. For example, a teacher might impart knowledge to their students through lectures or discussions.

29   B

Sojourn is used to describe a temporary stay or brief travel to a place that is not one's usual or permanent residence. For example, a person might take a sojourn to a foreign country in order to experience a different culture or way of life.

30   A

Momentum is often used to describe the force or energy that drives something forward or causes it to continue moving. For example, a person might say that a political movement has gained momentum if it has gained widespread support and is continuing to grow.

31   C

"Pungent" is used to describe a strong, often unpleasant odor, while "poignant" is used to describe a strong, often emotionally moving experience or feeling. For example, a poignant moment might be one that evokes strong feelings of sadness or nostalgia.

32   E

Just as an armada is composed of multiple ships, a regiment is composed of multiple soldiers. The analogy highlights the relationship between the collective and its individual components within each pair.

33   C

"Boring" is used to describe something that is dull or uninteresting, while "bland" is used to describe food or drink that lacks flavor. For example, a bland meal might be one that is lacking in spices or seasoning.

34   C

An "artery" is a blood vessel that carries blood away from the heart, while an "aqueduct" carries water. Both words are used to describe a type of tube or conduit

35   A

A "necklace" is a piece of jewelry that is worn around the neck, while a "clasp" is a device that is used to fasten or secure the necklace. Similarly, a "latch" is a device that is used to fasten or secure a door.

36   C

"Trivial" is used to describe something that is unimportant or insignificant, while "trifling" is used to describe something that is small or of little consequence. Similarly, "unwilling" is used to describe someone who is reluctant.

37   C

"Innate" and "acquired" are antonyms. Similarly, "knotty" and "facile" are antonyms, too.

38   C

"Grape" is an ingredient to make "wine," and "pulp" is a matter to make "paper."

39   E

A "dermatologist" is a medical professional who specializes in the treatment of skin conditions, while "skin" is the largest organ of the body. Similarly, a "mechanic" is a person who repairs cars, engines or other machines.

40   A

"Headstrong" and "stubborn" are used to describe someone who is unwilling to change their mind or behavior, similarly, "sly" and "wily" are synonyms.

41   E

"S(la)t" is changed into "s(al)t" as "c(al)m" is changed into "c(la)m"

42   E

A "mongrel" is a dog that is of mixed breed and has no purebred heritage, while a "pedigree" is a record of an animal's purebred heritage. Similarly, a "hybrid" is a plant or animal that is the result of crossbreeding, while a "purebred" is an animal that is the result of many generations of selective breeding.

43   B

"Famine" and "food" are used to describe a lack of food and the substance that is necessary for sustaining life, respectively. Similarly, a "drought" is a period of time during which there is little or no rainfall, while "rain" is the precipitation that falls from the sky.

44   C

"Ladder" and "rung" are used to describe a type of climbing tool and a step or crosspiece that is used to climb it, respectively. Similarly, a "staircase" is a type of structure that is used for ascending or descending a building, while a "step" is one of the individual parts that make up the staircase.

45   A

A "tonic" is a substance that is believed to have a positive effect on health or well-being, while "invigorate" is to give energy or vitality to something. Similarly, a "sedative" is a substance that is used to calm or soothe, while "soothe" is the state of being relaxed or free from stress or anxiety.

46   A

"Island" and "ocean" are used to describe a landmass surrounded by water and the body of water that surrounds it, respectively. Similarly, an "oasis" is a fertile area in a desert where water is available, while "sand" is the dry, granular material that makes up most of the desert landscape.

47   D

A "talon" is a sharp, hooked claw that is used by birds of prey, such as falcons, to catch and kill their prey. Similarly, a "claw" is a sharp, curved appendage that is used by many animals, including tigers, to grab and hold onto their prey.

48   E

A "stanza" is a group of lines in a poem that are separated by a blank line, while a "line" is a single row of words in a poem or other written work. Similarly, a "paragraph" is a group of sentences that are related to a single topic or idea.

49   E

A "book" often contains a "preface" that introduces the reader to the author or the subject matter of the book. Similarly, a "constitution" often contains a "preamble" that introduces the reader to the principles and values that the document embodies.

50	A

A "medley" is a mixture or combination of different things, often in music or art. Similarly, a "mosaic" is a type of art that uses small, colored tiles or pieces of glass to create a larger image or design.

51	B

"Knack" and "skill" are synonyms. Similarly, "query" means "question."

52	D

"Meritorious" means deserving of praise or reward, while "despicable" means deserving of blame or condemnation.

53	C

A "buck" is a male deer, while a "doe" is a female deer. Similarly, a "ram" is a male sheep, while an "ewe" is a female sheep.

54	D

A "budget" is a plan for how to allocate money, while a "schedule" is a plan for how to allocate time.

55	C

A "meal" can be characterized as "sumptuous" if it is very rich or elaborate. Similarly, an "evening gown" can be as "ostentatious" if it is flashy or showy.

56	C

Telepathy is the supposed ability to communicate with others thorugh mind, while telekinesis deals with the control of movement using the power of the mind.

57	C

"Apogee" is the point in an object's orbit that is farthest from the center of the body it is orbiting, while a "crest" is the highest point of a wave. Both words are used to describe a high point or peak of something.

58	D

"Funny" is used to describe something that is amusing or comical, while "hilarious" is used to describe something that is extremely funny. Similarly, "torrid" is an intense degree of "warm."

59	E

An "owl" is often used as a symbol of wisdom or knowledge. Similarly, "ant" is often used as a symbol of diligence.

60	C

A "tapestry" is a type of decorative textile that is often hung on a wall. Similarly, "carpet" is a type of decorative textile that is often on a floor.

SECTION 4

1   **C**

To find 25% of 32, we can multiply 32 by 0.25:
25% of $32 = 0.25 \times 32 = 8$
Therefore, the answer is (C) 8.

2   **A**

To find the product of 0.03 and 21/5, we can multiply the two numbers:
$0.03 \times 21/5 = 0.03 \times 4.2 = 0.126$
Therefore, the answer is (A) 0.126.

3   **D**

To find 20% more than 80, we can multiply 80 by 1.2:
20% more than $80 = 80 \times 1.2 = 96$
Therefore, the answer is (D) 96.

4   **E**

If $y = 4x - 8$, then $y - 4 = (4x - 8) - 4 = 4x - 12$. Therefore, the value of $y - 4$ in terms of x is (E) $4x - 12$.

5   **E**

Let's assume that there are a total of 100 dancers in the class. If 20% of them are male, then 80% of them are female. We can find the total age of the male dancers by multiplying the average age by the number of male dancers, which is 20:
Total age of male dancers $= 35 \times 20 = 700$
We can find the total age of the female dancers by multiplying the average age by the number of female dancers, which is 80:
Total age of female dancers $= 25 \times 80 = 2000$
The total age of all the dancers is the sum of the total age of the male dancers and the total age of the female dancers:
Total age of all dancers $= 700 + 2000 = 2700$
The average age of all the dancers is the total age divided by the total number of dancers:
Average age of all dancers $= 2700/100 = 27$
Therefore, the answer is (E) 27.

6   **B**

The exterior angle at B is equal to the sum of the two interior angles at A and C. Therefore:
$112° = 49° + C$
Solving for C, we get:
$C = 112° - 49° = 63°$
So the interior angle at C measures 63°, which is answer (B).

7   **C**

Let's assume that there are $3x$ white marbles and x red marbles in the bag. According to the problem, the total number of marbles is 72:
$3x + x = 72$
Simplifying the equation:
$4x = 72$
$x = 18$
Therefore, there are 18 red marbles in the bag. The answer is (C) 18.

8   **B**

If Deborah paints x houses per day, then in one day she will paint x houses. In y days, she will paint y times x houses, which is equal to xy. Therefore, the answer is (B) xy.

9   **A**

If the original price of the couch is $2,000 and it is reduced by 20%, then the new price is 80% of the original price:
New price after first reduction $= 0.8 \times \$2,000 =$

Answers & Explanations

$1,600

If the new price of the couch is reduced by 10%, then the final price is 90% of the new price:
Final price = 0.9 × $1,600 = $1,440
Therefore, the answer is (A) $1,440.

10   E

The answer is (E) None of the above. All of the given statements are true.

11   D

Keith travels at a rate of 90/1.5 = 60 miles per hour. If he travels for 5 more hours at the same rate, he will travel a total distance of:
Distance = rate × time = 60 × 5 = 300 miles
Therefore, the answer is (D) 300 miles.

12   D

Let's call the regular price of the dress "x". The sale price would then be "$x - 20$", since it's $20 off the regular price. With a 50% discount off the sale price, Sandra paid $(1/2)(x - 20)$. Therefore, we can set up the equation $(1/2)(x - 20) = 35$ and solve for x :
$(1/2)(x - 20) = 35$
$x - 20 = 70$
$x = 90$
So the regular price of the dress was $90. Therefore, the answer is (D) $90.

13   D

To find the range of the average speed, we need to consider the extremes of the time taken and the distance covered. The minimum average speed is when the cab driver takes the longest time (2 hours) to cover the shortest distance (90 miles), and the maximum average speed is when the cab driver takes the shortest time (1.5 hours) to cover the longest distance (90 miles).

Minimum average speed = 90 miles ÷ 2 hours = 45 miles per hour
Maximum average speed = 90 miles ÷ 1.5 hours = 60 miles per hour

Therefore, the average speed must have been between 45 and 60 miles per hour, and the answer is (D) 45 and 60.

14   E

Let's call the rate at which pipe A fills the aquarium "a" (in units of aquarium per minute) and the rate at which pipe B fills the aquarium "b". We know that:
a = 1/6 (since it takes 6 minutes to fill the aquarium with pipe A alone)
b = 1/4 (since it takes 2 minutes less than pipe A to fill the aquarium)
We want to find the rate at which both pipes together fill the aquarium. This rate is simply the sum of the rates of pipes A and B:
a + b = 1/6 + 1/4 = 5/12
So together, pipes A and B can fill 5/12 of the aquarium in one minute. Therefore, it will take 1 / (5/12) = 2.4 minutes to fill the aquarium with both pipes together. Answer: (E) 2.4 min

15   B

To find the answer, we can multiply 9.97 by 0.29 (which is the same as finding 29% of 9.97):

9.97 × 0.29 = 2.8903

Rounding to the nearest cent, we get:

2.89

So the answer is (B) $2.89.

16 — E

This is an analogy of a picture that has been rotated twice clockwise. If you find something that is the same among the options, the answer is (E).

17 — A

If each friend pays $180 and there are 5 friends, the total cost of the hotel suite is 5 × $180 = $900.

If one friend cancels, the remaining four friends will split the cost of the hotel suite, which is $900 / 4 = $225 per person.

So each person would spend $225 − $180 = $45 more on the hotel room.
Therefore, the answer is (A) $45.

18 — A

The annual interest earned by Ann is: 0.06 × $14,600 = $876.

Since the question is asking for the interest earned in the last six months, we need to divide this by 2: $876/2 = $438.

Therefore, the answer is (A) $438.

19 — D

After a 20% increase, the population in 2000 would be:
100 × 1.20 = 120

After a 30% increase from that population, the population in 2010 would be:
120 × 1.30 = 156

The percent increase from 100 to 156 is:
(156 − 100)/100 × 100% = 56%

Therefore, the answer is (D) 56%.

20 — B

There are 9 digits in the number, but we can see that not all digits are unique. To count the number of distinct digits, we can simply list the digits that appear and count how many there are.

1, 2, 3, 4, 5, 6, 7, 9

There are 8 distinct digits in the number.

Therefore, the answer is (B) 8.

21 — D

Carrie biked for 48 miles uphill at 8 miles per hour for 6 hours and for 32 miles downhill at 16 miles per hour for 2 hours, so the total time it took for her to bike the entire 80 miles is 6 + 2 = 8 hours. To find the average speed, we divide the total distance by the total time:
average speed = total distance / total time = 80 miles / 8 hours = 10 miles per hour

Therefore, the answer is (D) 10.

22 — D

The sides of the right triangle are given as 5, 12, and 13. We can see that the sides are in the ratio of 5:12:13, which means that the triangle is a multiple of a Pythagorean triple. In fact, it is a 5−12−13 right triangle, with the hypotenuse being the side of length 13. The area of this triangle is:
(area) = (1/2) × (base) × (height) = (1/2) × 5 × 12 = 30 square units.

Therefore, the answer is (D) 30.

23 — B

The lateral surface area of a right circular cone is given by the formula:
$S = \pi r \sqrt{r^2 + h^2}$

where r is the radius of the base and h is the altitude. Plugging in the values given, we have:
S = $\pi(2)(2\sqrt{10})$
S = $4\pi\sqrt{10}$
The lateral surface area of the cone is $4\pi\sqrt{10}$.
Therefore, the answer is (B) $4\pi\sqrt{10}$.

24   A

To find 39 x 594, we can add another 594 to the product of 38 x 594. Therefore, the correct answer is 22,572+594, which is equal to 23,166.

So, the answer is (A) 22,572+594.

25   D

If we add two additional black circles to the board so that each column and row has exactly 2 black circles, the board will look like this:

●	6	●	14
3	7	11	●
●	●	12	16
1	●	9	13

11 and 13 would be replaced with black circles. The sum of the numbers still showing is:
6+14+3+7+12+16+1+9=68
Therefore, the answer is (D) 68.

TEST ANSWERS

Practice 4

Section 1, 4: Quantitative (MATH) Answer

*Quantitative (Math) scores should be calculated based on the total of 50 questions from Section 1 and Section 4.

pp.183 – 192

TEST 4 SECTION 1 MATH 1

1. A	6. B	11. A	16. A	21. E
2. B	7. C	12. B	17. A	22. B
3. D	8. D	13. A	18. B	23. D
4. B	9. B	14. E	19. B	24. B
5. B	10. D	15. E	20. D	25. C

pp.215 – 225

TEST 4 SECTION 4 MATH 2

1. C	6. B	11. A	16. D	21. E
2. B	7. E	12. D	17. D	22. B
3. A	8. C	13. E	18. B	23. E
4. A	9. B	14. C	19. B	24. E
5. C	10. E	15. B	20. B	25. C

My Quantitative(Math) Score (Section 1 + Section 4)

Right	Wrong	Omitted	Raw Score ($= \text{right} - \frac{\text{wrong}}{4}$)	Scaled Score	Percentile
					%

Please consult the Scaled Score & Percentile Chart on the back of this book for the calculation of your Scaled Score and Percentile.

Section 2: Reading Answer

pp.193-206

TEST 4 SECTION 2 READING

1. C	9. D	17. A	25. B	33. C
2. C	10. A	18. B	26. D	34. E
3. E	11. C	19. D	27. C	35. B
4. A	12. B	20. D	28. C	36. E
5. E	13. A	21. B	29. D	37. E
6. C	14. E	22. D	30. E	38. D
7. B	15. A	23. C	31. D	39. C
8. C	16. C	24. E	32. E	40. B

My Reading Score

Right	Wrong	Omitted	Raw Score (= right − $\frac{wrong}{4}$)	Scaled Score	Percentile
					%

Please consult the Scaled Score & Percentile Chart on the back of this book for the calculation of your Scaled Score and Percentile.

Section 3: Verbal Answer

TEST 4 SECTION 3 VERBAL

1. A	13. B	25. B	37. D	49. E
2. E	14. E	26. E	38. B	50. A
3. B	15. A	27. C	39. C	51. B
4. D	16. E	28. A	40. D	52. C
5. B	17. B	29. C	41. C	53. D
6. B	18. E	30. E	42. D	54. E
7. A	19. E	31. B	43. D	55. B
8. A	20. C	32. A	44. A	56. C
9. D	21. C	33. C	45. C	57. A
10. A	22. E	34. B	46. D	58. D
11. D	23. A	35. C	47. C	59. C
12. B	24. E	36. C	48. B	60. A

My Reading Score

Right	Wrong	Omitted	Raw Score $(= \text{right} - \dfrac{\text{wrong}}{4})$	Scaled Score	Percentile
					%

Please consult the Scaled Score & Percentile Chart on the back of this book for the calculation of your Scaled Score and Percentile.

Practice Test 4

SECTION 1

1   **A**

To find the missing number in the sequence, we need to identify the pattern or rule followed by the given numbers.

Looking at the sequence, we can see that each number is obtained by adding 6 to the previous number.

So, if we add 6 to 28, we get 34. If we add 6 to 34, we get 40. If we add 6 to 40, we get 46.

Therefore, the missing number should be obtained by subtracting 6 from 28.

Missing number $= 28 - 6 = 22$

Therefore the answer is (A) 22.

2   **B**

To quickly estimate the value of 102.29 x (270.58 − 193.79), we can use the following approximation:

270.58 − 193.79 is approximately equal to 270 − 194 = 76
102.29 is approximately equal to 100
Substituting these approximations into the expression, we get:

102.29 x (270.58 − 193.79) ≈ 100 x 76 = 7600

The closest answer choice to this result is (B) 8,000. Therefore, the answer closest to 102.29 x (270.58 − 193.79) is (B) 8,000.

3   **D**

We can use the given information to find the value of y, and then use both x and y to find $x^2 + y^2$.

If $x + y = 9$ and $x = 8$, then we can substitute $x = 8$ into the first equation and solve for y:
$8 + y = 9$
$y = 1$
Now we have $x = 8$ and $y = 1$, so we can find $x^2 + y^2$:
$x^2 + y^2 = 8^2 + 1^2 = 64 + 1 = 65$
Therefore, $x^2 + y^2$ has a value of 65.

4   **B**

If x represents the height of a rectangle, and the base is 5 less than the height, then the base of the rectangle can be expressed as $x - 5$.

The perimeter of a rectangle is the sum of the lengths of all four sides. For a rectangle with height x and base $x - 5$, the perimeter P can be expressed as:

$P = 2x + 2(x - 5)$

Simplifying the expression, we get:

$P = 2x + 2x - 10$

$P = 4x - 10$

Therefore, the expression that represents the perimeter of this rectangle is (B) $4h - 10$.

5   **B**

The digit 2 in the number 358.727 is located in the hundredths place, which means it represents 2 hundredths.

Therefore, the answer is (B) 2 hundredths.

6   **B**

To find the missing digits in the problem $2 \times \square 3$, we can look at the potential products given:

(A) 406
(B) 546
(C) 716
(D) 1,366
(E) 1,816

We know that the product has to be divisible by 2 since the first digit is 2. Let's narrow it down:
(B) 546 is divisible by 2 ($2 \times 3 = 6$).
(D) 1,366 is also divisible by 2 ($2 \times 6 = 12$).
Now, we need to check if the product is divisible by 3 because of the $\square 3$ in the problem. Adding the digits in the potential products, we get:
(B) $5 + 4 + 6 = 15$ (divisible by 3).
(D) $1 + 3 + 6 + 6 = 16$ (not divisible by 3).
Therefore, the only option that satisfies both conditions is (B) 546.

7   **C**

We know that the patio is 12 yards long and 24 feet wide. Since a yard equals 3 feet, we can convert the width to yards by dividing by 3:

24 feet ÷ 3 feet/yard = 8 yards.

Now we know that the patio is 12 yards by 8 yards. To find the patio's perimeter, we can add the four sides:

P = 2(12 yards) + 2(8 yards).

Simplifying the expression, we get

P = 24 yards + 16 yards

P = 40 yards.

Therefore, we need 40 yards of fencing to enclose the patio. The answer is (C) 40 yd.

8   **D**

If the average time for each leg of a three-leg bus journey took Carl four hours and twenty minutes, we can first convert this time to minutes to make it easier to work with:

4 hours and 20 minutes = (4×60) minutes + 20 minutes = 240 + 20 = 260 minutes

Now, we can find the total time for the entire journey by multiplying the average time by the number of legs:

Total time = 260 minutes/leg × 3 legs = 780 minutes

To convert this back to hours and minutes, we can divide by 60 to get the number of hours and then take the remainder as the number of minutes:

780 minutes ÷ 60 minutes/hour = 13 hours with a remainder of 0 minutes

Therefore, it took Carl 13 hours to complete the journey. The answer is (D) 13 hours.

9   **B**

Since each person contributed the same amount toward a gift and $80 was collected, we can find the possible amount each person gave by dividing $80 by various numbers:

(A) $80 ÷ 0.5 = $160
(B) $80 ÷ 3 = $26.67
(C) $80 ÷ 5 = $16
(D) $80 ÷ 20 = $4
(E) $80 ÷ 40 = $2

(B) $26.67 is not a whole number. Therefore the answer is (B).

10   **D**

We can use the formula for finding a percentage of a number to solve this problem. If 28 is 25 percent of a number, we can write:

$0.25x = 28$

where x is the unknown number we're trying to find. To solve for x, we can divide both sides of the equation by 0.25:

Answers & Explanations

$x = 28 \div 0.25$

$x = 112$

Therefore, 28 is 25 percent of 112. The answer is (D) 112.

11　　　　　　　　　　　　　　　　　　A

Since W is between 0.9 and 1, we know that W^2 is greater than $\frac{1}{W}$, since squaring a number between 0.9 and 1 will result in a larger value. Therefore, we can eliminate option (B).

To determine which is greater between W^2 and $\frac{1}{W}$, we can compare their values when W is at its minimum and maximum values.

When W is 0.9:

$W^2 = 0.81$

$\frac{1}{W} = \frac{1}{0.9} = 1.11...$

When W is 1:

$W^2 = 1$

$\frac{1}{W} = \frac{1}{1} = 1$

Therefore, we can see that $\frac{1}{W}$ is greater than W^2 when W is between 0.9 and 1. The answer is (A) $\frac{1}{W}$.

12　　　　　　　　　　　　　　　　　　B

There are 9 square feet in 1 square yard, so there are:

9 × 873 = 7857 square feet in 873 square yards

To find the cost per square foot, we can divide the total cost by the total area:

$23,571 ÷ 7857 = $3

Therefore, the cost per square foot is $3. The answer is (B).

13　　　　　　　　　　　　　　　　　　A

Let's subtract the initial $30.00 from the total fare of $60.00 to find out how much is left for the additional miles:

$60.00 − $30.00 = $30.00

We know that $7.50 is charged for each additional 1/2 mile. Therefore, we can find out how many additional half miles the passenger can ride for $30.00:

$30.00 ÷ $7.50 = 4

So, the passenger can ride an additional 4 half miles. Since 1 mile is equal to 2 half miles, this means the passenger can ride 2 miles:

Initial mile ($\frac{1}{2}$ mile) + additional miles (2 miles) = 2.5 miles.

Therefore, the answer is (A) 2.5 miles.

14　　　　　　　　　　　　　　　　　　E

We can use the point-slope form of the equation of a line to find the equation of the line passing through the given points. The point-slope form of the equation of a line passing through the point $(x1, y1)$ with slope m is:

$y - y1 = m(x - x1)$

Let's use (−3, 5) as our $(x1, y1)$ point. We can find the slope, m, using the formula:

$m = (y2 - y1)/(x2 - x1)$

Using the coordinates of the other point (2, 1), we get:

$m = (1 - 5)/(2 - (-3)) = -\frac{4}{5}$

Now we can plug in the values we found to get the equation of the line:

$y - 5 = -\frac{4}{5}(x - (-3))$

Simplifying and rearranging, we get:

$$y - 5 = -\frac{4}{5}x - \frac{12}{5}$$

$$y = -\frac{4}{5}x - \frac{12}{5} + \frac{25}{5}$$

$$y = -\frac{4}{5}x + \frac{13}{5}$$

Therefore, the equation of the line passing through the points (−3, 5) and (2, 1) is $y = -\frac{4}{5}x + \frac{13}{5}$. The answer is (E).

15   E

To find the number of packages Tony needs to buy, we can divide the total number of balloons required by the number of balloons in each package, which is 3.

Since Tony needs 25 balloons for his 25 grandchildren, we have:

25 balloons ÷ 3 balloons per package ≈ 8.33

Tony cannot buy a fractional number of packages, so he needs to round up to the nearest whole number. Therefore, he needs to buy 9 packages of balloons.

So the answer is (E) 9.

16   A

We can use the inclusion–exclusion principle to find the number of bakers who have both a spatula and a whisk.

The total number of bakers who have either a spatula or a whisk is given by the sum of the number of bakers who have a spatula, the number of bakers who have a whisk, minus the number of bakers who have both:

Total = Spatula + Whisk − Both

We know that there are 530 bakers in total, 253 have a spatula, and 351 have a whisk. Substituting these values, we have:

530 = 253 + 351 − Both

Simplifying, we get:

Both = 253 + 351 − 530 = 74

Therefore, 74 bakers have both a spatula and a whisk, and the answer is (A) 74.

17   A

We can compare the expressions by simplifying them and finding a common denominator.

(A) $2n + 2$ can be written as $2(n + 1)$.
(B) $n + 2$ can be written as $1(n + 2)$.
(C) $n - 2$ can be written as $1(n - 2)$.
(D) $n/(n + 2)$ can be written as $n/n(1 + 2/n)$, which simplifies to $1/(1 + 2/n)$.
(E) $(n + 3)/n$ can be written as $1 + 3/n$.

We can see that (A) $2(n + 1)$ is greater than (B) $1(n + 2)$ and (C) $1(n - 2)$ since n is greater than 2.

For (D) $1/(1 + 2/n)$, as n gets larger, the denominator gets closer to 1, so the value of the expression gets closer to 1/1, or 1.

For (E) $1 + 3/n$, as n gets larger, the denominator gets smaller, so the value of the expression gets closer to 1 + 0, or 1.

Therefore, the greatest expression is (A) $2n + 2$.

18   B

To find how many times the number of units sold in 2015 was compared to 2011, we can divide the number of units sold in 2015 by the number of units sold in 2011:

2,000,000 / 50,000 = 40

Therefore, the number of units sold in 2015 was 40 times the number sold in 2011. The answer is (B) 40.

19 B

To determine which of the given options 7.07 is closest to, we can compare the distances between 7.07 and each option.

Distance between 7.07 and 7 = 0.07
Distance between 7.07 and 7.1 = 0.03
Distance between 7.07 and 7.7 = 0.63
Distance between 7.07 and 8 = 0.93
Distance between 7.07 and 71 = 63.93

Therefore, the closest option to 7.07 is (B) 7.1.

20 D

There are 1.25 millionaires for every 1,000 people in City A. We can use this ratio to find the number of millionaires in the city:

1.25 millionaires / 1,000 people = x millionaires / 9 million people

Cross-multiplying, we get:

1.25 millionaires x 9 million people = 1,000 people x (x millionaires)

11.25 millionaires = 1,000x

Dividing both sides by 1,000, we get:

$x = 11.25$

Therefore, there are 11,250 millionaires in City A. The answer is (D).

21 E

The number of plants in each row will be $7+x$. Therefore, the total number of plants in the garden will be:

(r rows) x ($7+x$ plants per row) = $r(7+x)$

So the answer is (E) $7r + rx$.

22 B

Since triangle ABD is isosceles, we have BD = AD.
Also, since D is the midpoint of AC, we have AD = DC.

Therefore, BD = AD = DC.
Now, in triangle ABC, we have AB = AC = 3 (since it is isosceles), and we know that D is the midpoint of AC. Therefore, AD = DC = 3

Using the Pythagorean theorem, we can find BC as follows:
$1 : \sqrt{3} : 2 = 3 : x : 6$
$1 : \sqrt{3} = 3 : x$
$x = 3\sqrt{3}$

Therefore, the answer is (B) $3\sqrt{3}$

23 D

The equation should represent Michelle's current amount of money (x) minus the extra $34 she needs to have to be able to afford the jacket equals the price of the jacket, which is $73. Therefore the answer is (D) $x + 34 = 73$.

24 B

The slope of the second line must also be $-\frac{4}{3}$ since the two lines are parallel. Using the slope-intercept form of a line, $y = mx + b$, where m is the slope and b is the y-intercept, we can check which sets of points satisfy the equation:

For (3, 6) and (−3, 10):
The slope of the line passing through these two points is $(10-6)/(-3-3) = -\frac{4}{3}$, which is the same as the slope of the first line. Therefore, these points cannot lie on the second line.

For (7, 5) and (4, 9):
The slope of the line passing through these two points is $(9-5)/(4-7) = -\frac{4}{3}$, which is the same as the slope of the first line. Therefore, these points could lie on the second line.

For (3, 6) and (−6, −10):
The slope of the line passing through these two points is $(-10-6)/(-6-3) = \frac{16}{9}$, which is not the same as the slope of the first line. Therefore, these points cannot lie on the second line.

For (−5, 5) and (2, −9):
The slope of the line passing through these two points is $(-9-5)/(2-(-5)) = -\frac{14}{7} = -2$, which is not the same as the slope of the first line. Therefore, these points cannot lie on the second line.

For (10, 4) and (3, 7):
The slope of the line passing through these two points is $(7-4)/(3-10) = -\frac{7}{3}$, which is the same as the slope of the first line. Therefore, these points could lie on the second line.

Therefore, the only set of points that could lie on the second line with slope $-\frac{4}{3}$, is (7, 5) and (4, 9).

The answer is (B) (7, 5) and (4, 9)

25 C

If Jessie is the 12th tallest, then there are 11 people taller than her. Similarly, if Jessie is the 12th shortest, then there are 11 people shorter than her. Therefore, there are at least 23 people in the class (11 people taller than her + Jessie + 11 people shorter than her). Since it is given that everyone in the class is of a different height, there cannot be more than 23 people in the class.

Therefore, the answer is (C) 23.

SECTION 2

Questions 1-5

The passage is about Dr. Sophie Anderson's journey to become a doctor despite her initial reluctance to follow in her father's footsteps. She expressed that her father's fame made her training harder in some ways, but he never pressured her to study medicine, warning her of its difficulty instead. Anderson initially desired to teach classics, but after college, she enrolled in the College of Physicians and Surgeons in New York and eventually graduated from medical school in 1974.

1 C

The passage suggests that Sophie Anderson's medical training was made more difficult because (C) she was inevitably compared to her father. The passage mentions that her father, Derrick Anderson, was a famous surgeon which made her training harder in some ways, as everyone knew who he was. This suggests that she was inevitably compared to her father.

2 C

The passage is primarily concerned with Sophie Anderson's (C) route to becoming a doctor. The passage is mainly focused on the route Sophie Anderson took to become a doctor. It provides information about her reluctance to study medicine, her yearning to teach classics, and how she eventually ended up studying medicine at the College of Physicians and Surgeons in New York.

3 E

The type of passage is (E) biography. The passage provides information about the life of

Sophie Anderson, from her childhood to her becoming a doctor. It provides details about her aspirations and her father's influence on her.

4 A

The word "tortuous" is used in the sentence, "She came by a necessarily tortuous route because the last thing she had wanted as a youth was to follow in her father's footsteps and take medicine." This means that the route she took was not straightforward, but rather it was complicated and indirect.

5 E

The attitude of Dr. Sophie Anderson, as portrayed in the provided passage, appears to be one of reluctance and initial disinterest in pursuing a medical career.

Questions 6-9

The passage discusses the concept of heroism and its significance in the real world. It suggests that heroes are necessary to redeem a fallen world and that they are created to fit our dreams. Heroism needs an initial instability to thrive, as it feeds on the energy released when consensus dissipates and expectations fail. The distinction between a hero and a fraud can only be made in retrospect when the quest is complete. Ambiguity disappears, but it is too late, and the hero's life as a hero is finished. The passage ends by stating that when this order is threatened, a new hero slowly begins to emerge, and nostalgia replaces the dangerous uncertainty of action.

6 C

The passage explores the dynamic between heroes and society and how society creates heroes to fit their dreams and alter their lives.

7 B

The passage states that heroism needs initial instability, and heroes always rise from uncertainty. It also suggests that when the hero stands adored at society's center, the hero's life as a hero is effectively finished, and a new hero begins slowly to emerge. This implies a cyclical nature to the emergence of heroes in society.

8 C

The passage suggests that a hero initially may not be distinguishable from a villain and that heroism requires an initial instability and a willingness to suffer for a cause. There is no mention of a hero spurring their admirers to become actual heroes themselves.

9 D

The passage implies that chance and societal needs influence who becomes a hero. (D) Chance determines who will be regarded as a hero or a villain aligns more closely with the passage's emphasis on unpredictability and societal roles in hero creation.

Questions 10-15

The passage discusses Ralph Waldo Emerson, an influential American thinker and essayist known for his personal integrity, broad intellectual interests, and humanitarian sympathy. At the age of 20, he became a supporter of the abolitionist cause and believed that slavery was a moral wrong. Over time, his antipathy towards slavery expanded to encompass the whole region that practiced it. The author expresses concern that Emerson's preoccupation with the issue of slavery may have interfered with his achievements as a pure philosopher.

| 10 | A |

The passage discusses Emerson's response to slavery, his beliefs, and how they developed over time.

| 11 | C |

The passage mentions humanitarian sympathy, personal integrity, persistent curiosity, and broad intellectual interests as traits that Emerson was renowned for, but does not mention "faithful fidelity."

| 12 | B |

The phrase "peculiar institution" is used as a euphemism for slavery in the South.

| 13 | A |

The passage mentions that Southerners defended slavery with ingenious sophistry.

| 14 | E |

The tone shifts from an initial admiration of Emerson to a more critical perspective on the South's defense of slavery.

| 15 | A |

In the context of the passage, "vested" means fixed and absolute, referring to the interest that Southerners had in the institution of slavery, which naturally prejudiced them in its favor.

Questions 16-20

The author's mother taught them the value of picking up even small amounts of money and the importance of honest labor. Although the author initially did not understand the lessons, they have come to appreciate them with age. As a result, the author picks up any amount of money found and will correct any errors made in financial transactions. These lessons have become guiding principles that allow the author to interact with others more easily.

| 16 | C |

Imparting a lesson is the overall theme of this passage. The last sentence of the first paragraph is an example of the theme, ("That lesson… me.").

| 17 | A |

This is a simile due to the comparison using "like."

| 18 | B |

In the context of the passage, "chalked" means attributed or credited. When the author says, "I chalked it up to her having grown up in the Great Depression," he/she means that he/she attributed or credited his/her mother's advice to her experiences during the Great Depression.

| 19 | D |

Nostalgia is the overall tone due to her remembering her past due to her sentimental remembrance of her parents and their wise words.

| 20 | D |

Due to the Great Depression, the penny carried power even though it is not worth much today. In that time, it was cherished and therefore carried influence or power.

Questions 21-25

The poem uses a rose-tree as a metaphor for people who are envious of others' talents and abilities. The tree cannot change its nature or bear different flowers, just as envious people cannot change who they are. The poem suggests that everyone has unique talents and abilities that they should focus on and develop instead of being envious of others.

21   **B**

The passage mentions, "Or wished to change its natural bent, It all in vain would fret."

22   **D**

The passage states, "It ne'er had seen its own red rose."

23   **C**

Personification is a literary device in which non-human objects or animals are given human characteristics. In this case, the tree is described as if it has feelings and desires.

24   **E**

Mignionet is a type of fragrant flower, often used in perfumes and soaps.

25   **B**

The line attributes human-like qualities of fretting to the rose-tree, which is a form of personification.

26   **D**

In this context, "bear" means to produce or bring forth.

27   **C**

In the second stanza, the poet adopts a tone of contemplation and reflection. The tone suggests a gentle and thoughtful exploration of the idea that individuals, like the rose-tree, have their own unique qualities and beauty that they may not fully recognize.

Questions 28-33

Project Mercury was the United States' first manned spaceflight initiative from 1958 to 1963, with the aim of sending a man into Earth orbit and returning him safely. NASA took over the US Air Force and conducted 20 unmanned flights, followed by six successful astronaut trips, with the crew known as the "Mercury Seven." The Soviet Union launched astronaut Yuri Gagarin into space aboard Vostok 1 in 1961, and the US followed with Alan Shepard's suborbital journey. The US achieved its orbital aim on February 20, 1962, when John Glenn completed three circles of the Earth. The Manned Space Flight Network was used to direct the flight from the ground, with backup controls on board. The spacecraft had retrorockets to launch it into orbit, an ablative heat shield for atmospheric reentry, and a parachute for water landing, where the astronaut was rescued by US Navy helicopters.

28   **C**

In the context of the sentence, "moniker" refers to the nickname that each of the Mercury spacecraft pilots gave to their spacecraft.

| 29 | D |

The passage describes the Space Race between the United States and the Soviet Union, with a focus on Project Mercury and its importance in the race.

| 30 | E |

"Employing" in this context means "using." The sentence is describing the various test flights that were carried out during the development of Project Mercury, some of which involved animals.

| 31 | D |

According to the passage, the Manned Space Flight Network was a system of tracking and communications stations used to direct the flight from the ground.

| 32 | E |

The passage is expository because its primary purpose is to provide factual information and explanations about Project Mercury, the nation's first manned spaceflight initiative.

| 33 | C |

According to the passage, NASA's establishment is because of (C)competition between the United States and the Soviet Union. The launching of the Soviet satellite Sputnik 1 in 1957 prompted the establishment of NASA in response to the shock and to accelerate existing U.S. space exploration efforts.

Questions 34-40

The Pony Express was a mail service that delivered messages and mail on horseback from St. Joseph, Missouri to Sacramento, California in about ten days, reducing the travel time between the Atlantic and Pacific coasts. It operated for 19 months and was vital for connecting California to the rest of the United States. Riders had to be young, skinny, and expert horse riders willing to risk their lives daily. The development of the Pony Express is a mix of fact and legend, with many young men applying for jobs despite the dangers and challenges along the delivery route. Despite the legendary full-tilt gallop, riders had to average only 10 miles an hour and usually arrived on time.

| 34 | E |

The passage states that the Pony Express was vital for tying the new state of California to the rest of the United States and reduced the time for messages to travel between the Atlantic and Pacific coasts to about ten days.

| 35 | B |

The passage describes the riders as having to be "rugged and lightweight" and "willing to risk death daily."

| 36 | E |

The passage states that the Pony Express reduced the time for messages to travel between the Atlantic and Pacific coasts, indicating that people waiting for news from home lived west of the Rocky Mountains.

37	E

The passage states that during its 19 months of operation, the Pony Express reduced the time for messages to travel between the Atlantic and Pacific coasts to about ten days.

38	D

"Looms" means to appear as a large or threatening shape or to be imminent, so "appears" is the closest in meaning.

39	C

The tone of the passage is described as illuminative because it seeks to shed light on the history and operations of the Pony Express.

40	B

The advertisement states that the riders must be "willing to risk death daily," indicating that the job was hazardous.

SECTION 3

1	A

The word "inquire" is often used to ask for information or to investigate something. For example, you might inquire about the price of a product, or a detective might inquire about a suspect's alibi. The correct answer is (A) ask, which means to seek information by questioning.

2	E

The word "murky" is often used to describe something that is unclear or hard to understand. For example, a murky legal issue might be one that is open to interpretation or difficult to resolve. The correct answer is (E) gloomy, which means dark, dim, or obscure.

3	B

The word "implicate" is often used to describe a situation where someone is involved in a crime or wrongdoing. For example, if a witness testifies that they saw someone near the scene of a crime, that person might be implicated in the crime. The correct answer is (B) involve, which means to connect or associate oneself with something or someone.

4	D

The word "infallible" is often used to describe something that is incapable of making mistakes. For example, some people might believe that certain religious texts are infallible, meaning that they are completely without error. The correct answer is (D) unerring, which means always accurate or correct.

5. B

The word "merely" is often used to indicate that something is only or simply what it appears to be, without any additional significance or importance. For example, you might say that a movie is merely entertaining, meaning that it doesn't have any deeper or more profound meaning. The correct answer is (B) slightly, which means to a small extent or barely.

6. B

The word "hideous" is often used to describe something that is extremely ugly or repulsive. For example, a hideous painting might be one that is so unattractive that you don't want to look at it. The correct answer is (B) unsightly, which means unpleasant to look at or unattractive.

7. A

The word "temporal" is often used to describe something that is related to time or the physical world, as opposed to the spiritual or eternal realm. For example, temporal power might refer to the influence or authority that someone holds in this life, rather than in the afterlife. The correct answer is (A) earthly, which means relating to the physical world or material things.

8. A

The word "implausible" is often used to describe something that is unlikely or difficult to believe. For example, if someone tells you a story that seems too far-fetched to be true, you might say that it's implausible. The correct answer is (A) dubious, which means doubtful or uncertain.

9. D

The word "polish" can have a few different meanings, but it is often used to refer to the act of making something smooth, shiny, or refined. For example, you might polish a piece of furniture to make it look new again, or you might polish your public speaking skills to make them more effective. The correct answer is (D) burnish, which means to make shiny or smooth by rubbing or polishing.

10. A

The word "trickery" is often used to describe the use of deception or cunning to achieve a goal. For example, a magician might use trickery to create the illusion of magic, or a con artist might use trickery to cheat someone out of their money. The correct answer is (A) deception, which means the act of deceiving someone.

11. D

The word "mundane" is often used to describe something that is ordinary or commonplace, and lacks excitement or interest. For example, a mundane task might be something like washing dishes or doing laundry, which is necessary but not particularly enjoyable. The correct answer is (D) ordinary, which means commonplace or unremarkable.

12. B

"Affix" means to attach or fasten something to another. In this context, (B) attach is a synonym because it also means to connect or join one thing to another.

13   B

The word "decree" is often used to describe an official order or proclamation issued by a person in authority, such as a judge, a king, or a president. For example, a judge might decree a verdict in a court case, or a president might decree a state of emergency in response to a crisis. The correct answer is (B) mandate, which means an official order or command.

14   E

The word "auspicious" is often used to describe something that is promising or favorable, and bodes well for the future. For example, an auspicious start to a new project might mean that things are off to a good start and are likely to continue going well. The correct answer is (E) favorable, which means advantageous or conducive to success.

15   A

The word "self-reliant" is often used to describe someone who is independent and able to take care of themselves without relying on others for help. For example, a self-reliant person might be someone who is able to fix things around the house or manage their own finances. The correct answer is (A) autonomous, which means independent or self-governing.

16   E

The word "gratitude" is often used to describe the feeling of being thankful or appreciative for something that has been done for you. For example, you might feel gratitude towards a friend who helped you out during a difficult time. The correct answer is (E) thankfulness, which means feeling or showing appreciation for something that has been done for you.

17   B

"Bourgeois" refers to the middle class, typically characterized by individuals or families with moderate wealth, social status, and conventional values. The correct answer is (B) middle class.

18   E

The word "brazen" is often used to describe someone who is bold or shameless, and doesn't care about what others think of them. For example, a brazen thief might be someone who steals things in broad daylight without trying to hide their actions. The correct answer is (E) unabashed, which means not ashamed or embarrassed.

19   E

The word "elusive" is often used to describe something that is difficult to pin down or grasp, and seems to always be just out of reach. For example, an elusive idea might be one that you've been trying to understand for a long time, but just can't seem to fully grasp. The correct answer is (E) ambiguous, which means unclear or open to more than one interpretation.

20   C

The word "signature" is often used to describe a distinctive mark, symbol, or style that is associated with a particular person, product, or company. For example, a designer might have a signature style that is recognizable in all of their work. The correct answer is (C) trademark, which means a distinctive symbol or sign that represents a company or product.

21   C

The word "uncharted" is often used to describe something that is unknown or unexplored, and hasn't been mapped or documented yet. For example, an uncharted region might be one that hasn't been explored by humans yet. The correct answer is (C) unknown, which means not explored or not yet discovered.

22   E

The word "prejudice" is often used to describe a negative or unfair attitude towards a particular group of people or idea, based on preconceived notions or stereotypes. For example, someone might have prejudice against a particular race or religion without ever having met someone from that group. The correct answer is (E) egregious, which means extremely bad or offensive.

23   A

Baleful means threatening or harmful. Among the given options, (A) threatening is a synonym that conveys a similar meaning of something harmful or menacing.

24   E

Relapse refers to a setback or regression, typically in relation to someone's health or recovery from a condition or illness. It signifies a return to a previous undesirable state or condition after a period of improvement or recovery. The synonym for "relapse" is (E) deterioration.

25   B

The word "swivel" is often used to describe something that rotates or pivots around a central point. For example, a swivel chair might be one that you can turn around in to face different directions. The correct answer is (B) rotate, which means to turn around a central point or axis.

26   E

Both "ruse" and "stratagem" involve clever, sometimes deceptive, tactics to achieve goals. They share the concept of strategic planning and craftiness in approaching situations.

27   C

The word "quixotic" is often used to describe something that is impractical or unrealistic, often due to idealistic or romantic ideas. For example, a quixotic dream might be one that involves a lot of fantasy or wishful thinking. The correct answer is (C) idealistic, which means having high or unrealistic ideals or goals.

28   A

The word "revulsion" is often used to describe a strong feeling of disgust or repulsion towards something. For example, you might feel revulsion towards a particular food that you find very unappetizing. The correct answer is (A) disgust, which means a feeling of strong disapproval or nausea.

29 — C

The word "infamy" is often used to describe a state of being well-known for something negative or shameful. For example, a historical figure might be remembered for their infamy as a cruel or unjust ruler. The correct answer is (C) notoriety, which means being well-known for something negative or infamous.

30 — E

"Meticulous" refers to being extremely careful, precise, and thorough in one's work or attention to detail. It suggests a high level of accuracy, thoroughness, and a strong focus on the small details. Similarly, "fastidious" means being excessively attentive to details and having a strong desire for accuracy and precision. The correct answer is (E) fastidious.

31 — B

The relationship between head and hammer is that head is the part of the tool that strikes and causes the hammer to work. Similarly, a bit is a working part of a drill.

32 — A

Terrestrial means relating to the earth, while celestial means relating to the sky or the heavens. This is a direct relationship between the words.

33 — C

A needle is a tool used for sewing, while a loom is a tool used for weaving. Both are tools used in textile work.

34 — B

An aviary is a large cage for birds. The relationship between bee and apiary is that bee live in an apiary. Similarly, birds can be found in aviaries.

35 — C

A trucker is someone who drives a truck, and the cab is the compartment of the truck where the driver sits and operates the vehicle from. Similarly, a pilot is someone who operates an aircraft, and the cockpit is the area in the aircraft where the pilot sits and controls the plane from.

36 — C

The relationship between "pedestrian" and "sidewalk" is that a pedestrian typically walks on a sidewalk. Similarly, the relationship between "caravan" and "route" is that a caravan typically travels on a route.

37 — D

A snail is known for its slow movement and sluggishness. Similarly, a cat is known for its agility and quick movements.

38 — B

A coat is an article of clothing that provides warmth, and warmth is a quality that is provided by the coat. Similarly, a fan is an electrical appliance that provides a breeze, and a breeze is a quality that is provided by the fan.

39 — C

When we feel hungry, we eat to satisfy the feeling of hunger. Similarly, when we have an itch, we scratch to relieve the sensation.

40 — D

Ton is to weight as millennium is to time. A ton is a unit of weight, just as a millennium is a unit of time.

41 — C

A curtain offers privacy by physically obstructing views into a space, while a lantern provides illumination by emitting light.

42 — D

Gasp is a sound that can be made when someone is surprised. Among the options given, "blush" is the closest in meaning to "gasp" in that they are both physical reactions to an emotional state

43 — D

A biography is a written account of someone's life, and life is the subject matter of the biography. Similarly, a memoir is a written account of someone's personal experiences, and experience is the subject matter of the memoir.

44 — A

Pastry is a broad category of baked goods, and eclair is a specific type of pastry that falls within that category. Therefore, "eclair" is a type of "pastry." Similarly, (A) diamond is a specific type of gemstone.

45 — C

A hermit is someone who lives in seclusion, similar to how someone who is reclusive may avoid social interaction. Similarly, an extrovert is a person who is outgoing and social, and sociable is an adjective that describes this trait. Therefore, the answer is (C).

46 — D

A mogul is someone who has a lot of power or influence, similar to how a sage is someone who is very wise. Among the options given, wisdom is the closest in meaning to power in that they both refer to a type of influence or control.

47 — C

Thirst is a feeling of needing to drink, while quench means to satisfy that feeling by drinking something. Among the options given, uprising is the closest in meaning to quell in that they both refer to a situation in which something needs to be stopped or suppressed.

48 — B

Weld means to join two pieces of metal together by melting them and then allowing them to cool and solidify. Among the options given, glue is the closest in meaning to weld in that they both refer to joining two materials together.

49 — E

Singed means to burn something slightly, while charred means to burn something completely. The answer is (E) obvious is to conspicuous.

50 A

Anthology refers to a collection of literary works or other types of creative works. Among the options given, thesaurus is the closest in meaning to anthology in that they both refer to a collection of related things.

51 B

Wince means to make a facial expression of pain or discomfort. Similarly, (B) salute is a gesture of respect, particularly in a military context. Therefore, respect is the cause or motivation for a salute.

52 C

Bow is a device used for shooting arrows, while arrow is a projectile that is shot from a bow. Among the options given, slingshot is the closest in meaning to stone in that they both refer to a type of projectile that is shot from a device.

53 D

Municipal pertains to matters related to a city or local government, while maritime is associated with the sea or seafaring activities.

54 E

Euphemism is a type of circumlocution using indirect words or expressions to avoid using a harsh, offensive, or unpleasant word. Similarly, a pun is a type of wordplay involving using a word or phrase with multiple meanings or sounds.

55 B

In a submarine, a porthole is a small, typically round window that allows individuals inside the submarine to view the outside underwater environment. Among the options given, (B) camera is to aperture is the closest in that they both refer to an opening through which light enters to form an image.

56 C

Reprehensible means deserving of blame or criticism, while blame refers to responsibility for something negative. Similarly, (C) laudable means deserving of praise or commendation, and praise refers to expressing approval or admiration for something or someone.

57 A

Contentment shifts to complacency, where self-satisfaction may become negative and oblivious to risks. Similarly, obedience transforms into subservience, signifying a more passive and unquestioning submission to authority.

58 D

Indistinct means not clear or easily distinguishable, while discern means to perceive or understand something. Among the options given, abstruse is the closest in meaning to discern in that they both refer to something that is difficult to understand or perceive.

59 C

Skulk means to move around stealthily or with a sense of guilt or shame, while move refers to any kind of physical motion. Similarly, (C) lurk means to wait or remain hidden, often with the intention of surprising or attacking someone or something.

60 A

"Bustle" means to move around quickly and energetically, while "hurried" refers to the speed or pace of that movement. Among the options given, "fidget" is the closest in meaning to "restless" in that they both refer to a sense of nervous or agitated movement.

SECTION 4

1 C

$$-\left(\frac{1}{16}\right)^{-\frac{1}{2}} =$$

To do this, we can first deal with the negative exponent by taking the reciprocal of the base:

$$-\left(\frac{1}{\sqrt{16}}\right)$$

Now, simplify the square root:

$$-\left(\frac{1}{4}\right)$$

So, $-\left(\frac{1}{16}\right)^{-\frac{1}{2}}$ simplifies to $-\frac{1}{4}$.

2 B

If N is an odd number, then we can write it as N = 2k + 1, where k is some integer.

(A) N + 2 = (2k + 1) + 2 = 2k + 3 = 2(k + 1) + 1, which is an odd number.
(B) N + 3 = (2k + 1) + 3 = 2k + 4 = 2(k + 2), which is an even number.
(C) (3 × N) + 2 = 3(2k + 1) + 2 = 6k + 5 = 2(3k + 2) + 1, which is an odd number.
(D) (2 × N) + 3 = 2(2k + 1) + 3 = 4k + 5 = 2(2k + 2) + 1, which is an odd number.
(E) (2 × N) + 1 = 2(2k + 1) + 1 = 4k + 3 = 2(2k + 1) + 1, which is an odd number.

Therefore, the answer is (B) N + 3 is an even number.

3 A

We can start by converting the length of the cloth strip from feet to inches, since the length of each strip is given in inches.

$\frac{13}{4}$ feet = $\left(\frac{13}{4}\right)$ × 12 inches = 39 inches

Answers & Explanations **319**

Now, we can divide the total length of the cloth strip by the length of each individual strip:

39 inches / 13 inches = 3

Therefore, the cloth strip can be cut into 3 strips each 13 inches long.

The answer is (A) 3.

4   A

To find the average weight of all 8 children, we need to find the total weight of all the children and divide by 8.

The total weight of the 5 boys is 5 × 120 = 600 pounds.
The total weight of the 3 girls is 3 × 100 = 300 pounds.
The total weight of all 8 children is 600 + 300 = 900 pounds.

So, the average weight of all 8 children is 900/8 = 112.5 pounds.

Therefore, the answer is (A) 112.5.

5   C

To find the greatest remainder, we need to find the number that has the highest ones place value when divided by 10.
11 ÷ 10 = 1 R1
22 ÷ 10 = 2 R2
35 ÷ 10 = 3 R5
44 ÷ 10 = 4 R4
53 ÷ 10 = 5 R3
Therefore, the number with the greatest remainder is (C) 35.

6   B

The largest number of passengers that can be accommodated in a single shuttle is 8.
Therefore, at least 3 shuttles are needed to transport all 23 passengers.

To minimize the number of shuttles, we want to group the passengers so that each shuttle has as many passengers as possible without exceeding 8.

Starting with the largest number of passengers possible, we can fit 4 shuttles with 8, 7, 6, and 2 passengers respectively. Therefore, the answer is (B) 4.

7   E

If half of the weight of the given ship is 302 tons, then the weight of the whole given ship is 2*302 = 604 tons.

The weight of four ships of the exact same weight as the given ship would be 4 times the weight of the given ship, which is 4*604 = 2416 tons.

Therefore, to determine the weight of four ships of the exact same weight as the given ship, we need to multiply 302 by 8 (not 1/2, 1.5, 4, or 6). So the answer is (E) eight.

8   C

Let's start by setting up an equation to solve for the total number of questions on the exam:

$48 = 0.6x$

where x is the total number of questions on the exam.

To solve for x, we can divide both sides by 0.6:

$x = 80$

So there were 80 questions on the exam.

To find out how many questions Lisa got wrong, we can subtract the number she got right from the total number of questions:

80 − 48 = 32

Therefore, Lisa got 32 questions wrong.

The answer is (C) 32.

9   B

The perimeter of the field is 936 feet. Since each fence segment is 12 yards long, or 36 feet, the number of segments needed is equal to the perimeter of the field divided by the length of each segment:

number of segments = perimeter/length of segment = 936/36 = 26

Therefore, the answer is (B) 26.

10   E

If the answer to the problem is 48 when the last step is to divide by 2, then the original number that was divided by 2 must be 48 times 2, which is 96.

Dividing 96 by 4 gives:
96/4 = 24

Therefore, if the last step had been dividing 4 instead of dividing by 2, the answer would have been (E) 24.

11   A

$|4x| - 2 = -6$

First, isolate the absolute value expression by adding 2 to both sides:

$-|4x| = -4$

Divide both sides by -1 to get rid of the negative sign:

$|4x| = 4$

Since the absolute value of a number is always positive, we can write:

$4x = 4$ or $4x = -4$

Solving for x in each equation:

$4x = 4$
$x = 1$
$4x = -4$
$x = -1$

Therefore, the solution is $x = 1$ or $x = -1$.

Answer: $x = 1$ or $x = -1$.

12   D

The units digit of the sum is 0, which means that A + 9 = 10, so A = 1. Then we have:

  121
+ 6B9
―――――
  B10

To add the units digit of 1 and 9, the digit B must be 8, since 1 + 9 = 10 and the units digit of the sum must be 0. Therefore, B represents the digit 8. The answer is (D) 8.

13   E

The average of x, $2x$, and y is $(x + 2x + y)/3 = (3x + y)/3 = x + y/3$. We are given that this average is $2x$, so we can set up the equation:
$x + y/3 = 2x$
Subtracting x from both sides, we get:
$y/3 = x$
Multiplying both sides by 3, we get:
$y = 3x$
So the answer is (E) $3x$.

14   C

$13.2 \times 10^0 = 13.2 \times 1 = 13.2$. Therefore, the answer is (C) 13.2.

15   B

The formula for the maximum number of different lines that can be drawn through n points on a circle is $(n(n-3))/2$.

In this case, $n = 5$, so we have:

Answers & Explanations   321

(5(5−3))/2 = (5(2))/2 = 10

Therefore, the greatest number of different lines that can be drawn is 10, which is the answer (B).

16　　　　　　　　　　　　　　　　　D

The prime factorization of 38 is 2×19, so a = 19. The prime factorization of 10 is 2×5, so b = 5. Therefore, a + b = 19 + 5 = 24. The answer is (D) 24.

17　　　　　　　　　　　　　　　　　D

(5 + a)/3 = 25/3

Multiplying both sides by 3, we get:
5 + a = 25
Subtracting 5 from both sides, we get:
a = 20
Therefore, the answer is (D) 20.

18　　　　　　　　　　　　　　　　　B

Let's call the number of men and women on the bus before the first stop "x". After 4 men get off the bus, there will be "$x-4$" men left on the bus. We also know that the number of women on the bus is still "x".

Now, we are told that the number of women on the bus is twice the number of men:

$x = 2(x-4)$

Simplifying and solving for x, we get:

$x = 8$

So there were 8 men and 8 women on the bus before the first stop, and no one got on at the first stop. Therefore, there are still 8 women on the bus.

Answer: (B) 8

19　　　　　　　　　　　　　　　　　B

The oldest child calls home once every 18 days, the middle child once every 6 days, and the youngest child once every 2 days. We need to find the least common multiple of 18, 6, and 2, which is 18. Thus, all three children will call home on the same day after 18 days. Therefore, the answer is (B) 18.

20　　　　　　　　　　　　　　　　　B

The decimal number is 7.12122122212222122222... and it consists of only 1's and 2's to the right of the decimal point.

Starting from the left, the first 1 is followed by one 2, which means the first two digits are 12. The second 1 is followed by two 2's, so the next three digits are 122. The third 1 is followed by three 2's, so the next four digits are 1222. And so on, the pattern continues.

Now, we want to find the total number of 2's between the 98th and 101st 1 in this decimal number.

To do that, we need to find the position of the 98th 1 and the position of the 101st 1. We can do this by counting the number of 2's between the 1's.

Starting from the left, the first 1 is followed by one 2, and the second 1 is followed by two 2's. This means there are three 2's between the first and second 1. The third 1 is followed by three 2's, so there are six 2's between the second and third 1.

Using this pattern, we can see that the nth 1 is followed by n 2's. So the 98th 1 is followed by 98 2's, and the 101st 1 is followed by 101 2's.

To find the total number of 2's between the 98th and 101st 1, we need to subtract the number of 2's between the first 1 and the 98th 1 from the number of 2's between the first 1 and the 101st 1.

From our previous counting, we know that there

are $1+2+3+\ldots+97$ 2's between the first and 98th 1. This is an arithmetic sequence with a first term of 1, a common difference of 1, and 97 terms. We can use the formula for the sum of an arithmetic sequence to find the sum of these 97 terms:

$(97/2)(1+97) = 4753$

Similarly, there are $1+2+3+\ldots+100$ 2's between the first and 101st 1. This is an arithmetic sequence with a first term of 1, a common difference of 1, and 100 terms. We can use the formula for the sum of an arithmetic sequence to find the sum of these 100 terms:

$(100/2)(1+100) = 5050$

Therefore, the total number of 2's between the 98th and 101st 1 is:

$5050 - 4753 = 297$

So the answer is (B) 297.

21   E

Let's assume David's initial weight is 100 units.

After increasing his weight by 10 percent, his weight becomes 110 units.

Then, after decreasing his new weight by 25 percent, his weight becomes 82.5 units.

Therefore, his final weight is 82.5 percent of his initial weight.

So, the answer is (E) 82.5%.

22   B

Let the total number of books in the library be x. Then we have:

30% of x are on Music: $0.3x$
30% of x are on Psychology: $0.3x$
25% of x are on Communications: $0.25x$
10% of x are on Autobiography: $0.1x$
75 books are on Biology: 75
The total percentage of books accounted for is:

$0.3x + 0.3x + 0.25x + 0.1x + 75 = x$

Simplifying this equation, we get:

$0.95x + 75 = x$

$0.05x = 75$

$x = 1,500$

Therefore, the library has a total of $0.3(1,500) = 450$ Psychology books. Answer: (B) 450.

23   E

When we draw one line, the plane is divided into two parts. When we draw the second line, it intersects the first line at one point, and the plane is divided into four parts. Drawing the third line, we can see that it intersects the other two lines at three distinct points, dividing the plane into 7 parts. Therefore, the answer is (E) 7.

24   E

Now, let's analyze the expressions:
I. $(a+1) \times b$
   $= (2k+1+1) \times (2m+1)$
   $= (2k+2) \times (2m+1)$
   $= 4km + 2k + 2m + 1$
II. $(a+1) + b$
   $= (2k+1+1) + (2m+1)$
   $= 2k + 2 + 2m + 1$
   $= 2k + 2m + 3$
III. $(a+1) - b$
   $= (2k+1+1) - (2m+1)$
   $= 2k + 2 - 2m - 1$
   $= 2k - 2m + 1$

Now, let's look at their parity:
I. $4km + 2k + 2m + 1 =$ odd + even + even + 1 = odd
II. $2k + 2m + 3 =$ even + even + odd = odd
III. $2k - 2m + 1 =$ even − even + 1 = odd

So, both I and III must be odd. Therefore, the correct answer is (E) II and III.

Answers & Explanations

25 C

Since the center of the semicircle is at (3,0), the radius is 3 units. Therefore, the equation of the semicircle is:

$(x-3)^2 + y^2 = 3^2$

Since the semicircle is symmetric about the y-axis, the y-coordinates of any two points on the semicircle whose y-coordinates are equal must be 0. Therefore, we are looking for two x-coordinates of two points on the semicircle such that the y-coordinates of the two points are equal to 0.

Substituting y=0 into the equation above, we get:

$(x-3)^2 + 0^2 = 3^2$
$(x-3)^2 = 9$
$x-3 = \pm 3$
$x = 3 \pm 3$

Therefore, the possible x-coordinates of two points on this semicircle whose y-coordinates are equal are 0 and 6.

Among the given answer choices, the only pair of numbers that includes 0 and 6 is (C) 2 and 4. Therefore, the answer is (C) 2 and 4.

Scaled Score & Percentile Chart (Upper Level)

Scaled Score Chart

Raw Score	Reading	Verbal	Quantitative
60	—	800	—
55	—	800	—
50	—	779	800
45	—	752	782
40	800	725	755
35	722	698	725
30	692	671	698
25	662	644	668
20	632	617	641
15	602	590	614
10	572	563	584
5	542	533	557
0	512	506	530
−5 and lower	500	500	500

Scaled Score(Median 50th)

Grade	Reading	Verbal	Quantitative
Grade 8	647	660	676
Grade 9	653	667	699
Grade 10	659	670	705
Grade 11	647	656	704

Percentile Chart

Raw Score	Reading	Verbal	Quantitative
60	99	—	—
55	99	—	—
50	98	99	—
45	94	96	—
40	87	87	99
35	77	75	94
30	63	61	78
25	47	45	57
20	31	30	36
15	18	18	20
10	8	9	8
5	3	3	3
0	1	1	1
−5 and lower	1	1	1
−10 and lower	1	1	1